Build Your Own Boat

BUILD YOUR ——OWN BOAT——

Completing a Bare Hull

IAN NICOLSON

Sheridan House
New York

Seafarer Books
London

© Ian Nicolson, 1982, 1996

First published by Allen & Unwin, 1982
First published in paperback, 1996

Sheridan House, 145 Palisade St, Dobbs Ferry, NY 10522
Seafarer Books, 10 Malden Road, London NW5 3HR

British Library Cataloguing in Publication Data

Nicholson, Ian
  Build your own boat.
1. Boat-building
I. Title
623.8'202   VM351
ISBN 085036 458 2

Cover designed by Louis Mackay
Printed in Finland by WSOY

Contents

Figures

TO MY SON RICHARD

In thanks for helping with all the jobs which go into creating a boat, including:

Scheming, drawing, planning and tracing; ordering material, parts, paint and fastenings; buying wood and lugging it home; measuring and marking (and double checking); planing and sawing; cutting and fitting; nailing and bolting; fibreglassing and getting covered in resin and hiding messed up overalls from my wife; putting in sole bearers and floor-boards; fitting lining and cushions; heaving in engine and tanks; piping and wiring; working in impossibly small spaces upside down in poor light; fixing hinges, bolts, locks, stanchions, pulpits, chain-plates, handles, toe-rails, grab-rails, life-rails and one thousand two hundred and seventy-four bits and pieces; splicing and sail-making; mast-making and rigging; staggering from the mast store to the shore with a great big heavy mast; securing the bottle to the bow of the boat and reminding my wife of the time honoured words 'God bless this ship and all who sail in her'; dodging the splintered glass and flying froth; launching and trials; sailing and motoring; navigating, cooking and bringing up at moorings at the end of a long day and realising that there is nothing quite like building your own boat and sailing in her.

1 *So much can depend on* =*one cleat*=

Squall after squall rushed across the Clyde and we were glad to have a deep reef in the mainsail of our 28 footer. We had up the No. 2 genoa and kept wondering if we should reef it too. Not that we were worried about the boat. We had bought the bare hull from Weatherly Yachts, and completed her ourselves and knew that the gear was tough, reliable and well secured.

As we punched to windward the spray lashed aft, the sheets were hard and thin under the strain, the crew perched on the weather-side-deck and snuggled deeper into their oilskin hoods. Conversation was terse; no one wanted to open his mouth to let in a mixture of salt spray and rain.

We were racing, but it was the sort of event where winning can be a matter of plugging on grimly, hoping lesser boats will drop out through breakages. As we came up to the weather mark the wind shrieked louder in the rigging, the boat heeled further, bigger lashings of spray hurtled off the ugly waves. To windward of us a trimaran in another race scudded in towards the buoy, slicing through the wave tops. She looked over-canvassed. She was. Her mast went over.

Whenever a mast topples, there is at first a stunned silence on board the stricken boat and on the surrounding craft. Then experienced people hurl themselves into a flurry of activity to sort out the mess. On the trimaran the crew sat frozen for brief seconds, then rushed forward to haul the sails aboard, gather up the rigging, lash down the broken spar, and look around for a tow. We looked round too. Not long before there had been all sorts of boats, competitors and cruisers, a fishing boat and a ferry, all getting in our way when we wanted to tack. Now the sea was almost deserted, apart from a motor-boat plodding past, her crew snug in the wheelhouse. Spray on the windows must have made them opaque, because she chugged away unconcerned. It was lonely then. The wind seemed to get more vicious, the waves broke in awkward shapes, reminding us that the tide was up-wind. Someone murmured that we did not have long, the lee shore was close.

We got out fenders, but that was no more than a gesture; in this sea it would have been high folly to try and get alongside. One of our crew went up to our foredeck, taking a coiled warp with him. In the cockpit we prepared another warp. 'We'll reach past them to windward,' I said, 'and let them know what we plan to do.' Then we agreed that we would reach past to leeward of the tri, catch her warp, and tow her to harbour. It sounded easy, but in those waves . . .

As we came in to shout instructions I found myself bearing away, more and more. The tri had no grip on the water and was slithering to leeward at a tremendous rate. It was obvious the conventional pick-up from the lee side would be dangerous, perhaps impossible, so we changed the arrangements to a windward pick-up. In a few seconds we had foamed past the other boat, yelled out the plan and made two breathless tacks. It would all have been easy (well fairly easy) under power, but we had built our boat in a hurry and launched her for a summer's sailing without wasting time putting in an engine.

As we came in to grab the end of the towing line we had one person forward in the pulpit, one grasping the lee shrouds, and my youngest son hanging onto the aft pulpit, so that wherever the rope fell someone would be close enough to grab it. I tried to concentrate on the steering and ignore the closing distance to the lee shore. The seas made it impossible to steer straight, and dangerous to get too close to the trimaran. We approached in a series of half-controlled lurches, one second going too close, the next too far off. We all wished there had been time to tuck another reef or change to a smaller headsail.

On the tri the motion was horrible. Her crew could not stand on deck, and throwing the line from a sitting position was not likely to be successful. As we drew abeam, one of her crew took a gamble, stood up, and a second later the rope was a black zigzag against the dark sky. For a brief moment it looked like a perfect throw, then the wind caught the front of the coil and it started to drop . . . too soon.

My son leaned out until I was sure he would topple over the pulpit, while our boat lurched and rolled. At full arms stretch he just got the end of the coil. He wrenched it in, thrust it under the pulpit rails, and snatched it round the aft mooring cleat. Just in time. The rope twanged tight and brought us up with a start, as the tow began with a shuddering thud.

Towing under sail with a cross sea and a light trimaran astern is full of surprises. After the initial frights we settled down to enjoy the fun. Each time the tow-rope came taut the tri raced up to us, and had to be steered clear of our counter. We thought of lengthening the rope but decided that that would increase the jolting load when the strain was taken up.

I looked astern at the lee shore receding. The tri might have held off on her anchor, or the crew might have got a jury rig up in the time, or the tide might have taken her clear. I doubted if any of these miracles would have happened.

Every so often one of us would look at the cleat. If the under-deck pad had not been a big one, if the bolts had not been tightened properly, if the cleat had been too small, by now we would have had a jagged hole in the deck, and the tri a lot of holes torn in her three hulls.

It's at times like this that everything which boatbuilding involves is worthwhile. The cold fingers and the cramped back, the hours of work in awkward corners, the bashed knuckles and torn overalls, even the setbacks are all fully rewarded. The purpose of this book is to increase the enjoyment and to reduce the problems.

=2 Building time=

There can be no direct answer to the question, 'How long does it take to build or complete a boat?' There are so many factors, only half of which are strictly boat-building matters, which affect the issue.

For instance the most important influence on building time is the determination of the person in charge of the project. A thruster who sets a firm finishing date and concentrates on the job all day, all week, with no pauses, will achieve miracles of swift work. Another person, keen enough but not totally dedicated, will take half as long again. And someone with a variety of other interests may take four times as long.

There are certain broad principles which can be laid down:

1 Few amateurs can complete a boat over 35 feet (10 metres) long with engine(s) and full equipment in one winter. However, the same job can be done (sometimes with a scramble) if work is started in mid-summer, for launching the following spring.
2 A boat over 45 feet (13.7 metres) takes an amateur quite eighteen months and he must push hard, as well as having as least two people to help for more than a third of the time.
3 A boat over 55 feet (16.8 metres) takes any amateur a long time, usually well over two years, not least because many parts are so heavy and unwieldy.
4 Boats below 35 feet do not necessarily take progressively less time as the size is scaled down. This is partly because small boats are cramped, so access inside and on deck is bad. Another reason is that the bilge pump of a 22 footer (6.5 metres) may take just as long to fit as a boat twice that length. This applies to many other items of equipment.

Speed of building goes up dramatically as power tools are brought in. To carry this principle to its conclusion there will be three electric drills for each person working on the boat, so that when doing jobs like fitting a row of screws one machine has the shank size drill in it, one has the thread size drill in the chuck, and one has the counter-sink in it. Of course, it is possible to go one better than this and have a single drill with one of those special twist bits which drill and counter-sink the hole correctly all in one swift plunge. This sums up the importance of mechanisation. If there is a large and small circular saw, a band saw and a jig-saw, a planer and a sander, the work will go forward fast. For each machine not available there will be extra delays.

Another factor is the amount of work sub-contracted. One builder likes to make everything including his own mast, boom, goose-neck, cross-trees, his own tanks and cleats, his own toe-rails and hand-rails. Another buys all these things in, he gets his bookshelves from chandlers or from an industrial joiner, he not only buys his sails from a sail-maker but he pays to have the sail-maker bend them on and carry out sailing trials. Another amateur likes to do all the joinery but sub-contracts work which he thinks is boring like painting. Some professionals carry on in a similar way. If templates are available for parts like cabin-soles, berths, galley fronts, perhaps for windows and for the lining pieces too, this must save a quarter or even half the time it takes to make and fit these components.

After the determination and enthusiasm of the building team the most important influence on completion time must be the complexity of the boat. This depends on the use the boat is to have. If she is a skinned-out racing machine she will take less time to build than a trimly finished cruiser with ample lockers, and lots of furniture, electric equipment and gadgetry. If the designer is skilled at making the building quick and simple this can easily make a 20 per cent difference to the building time. Craft designed by men who never handle tools can be tediously complex and expensive in materials, time and the builder's temper.

Virtually all boats take longer to build than the original estimate, whether

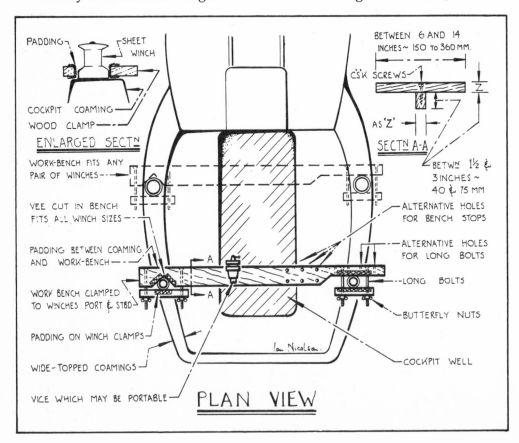

4

they are amateur or professionally finished. This is true even if the boat is one of a series professionally built.

It is risky to quote actual hours worked on a particular boat without providing a detailed specification, because while one boat is easy to complete, another may be complex, over-decorated, crawling with electronics and packed with inaccessible lockers. The first may be finished in perfect conditions with a full-length working platform at deck level, a skilled and experienced team, all the parts and fastenings, paint and stopping materials readily to hand, all in the right size containers, with all the necessary tools, brushes, power points, lights, and a plentiful supply of tea or coffee. In short, the working conditions may be encouraging.

However, it may be useful to look at some actual working times, each in their context. A series of simple 28 foot (8.5 metres) sloops were completed in ninety hours each by a shipwright and two skilled young helpers. Everything was templated, and it was not till twenty-five identical craft had been made that the building time was reduced to this sharp limit. Also 'finish' was not of the finest, there were no instruments aboard, and work such as launching and stepping the mast was not included in this time. Above all the team was totally dedicated, practised and clever at reducing the hours for each part of the job.

Fig. 1   On-board work-bench

Much time is wasted if a boatbuilder has to climb down the side of the boat, walk to a work-bench, do a job, then go all the way back on board. A simple type of work-bench can be rigged up in the cockpit, clamped to sheet winches or cleats. The bench shown here has a Vee cut on the port side which will fit all sizes of winch. On the starboard side there is a clamp made from two long bolts and a bar of hardwood which can be moved athwartships by shifting the bolts to alternative holes. This means that the starboard clamp will fit different widths of cockpit, or different winch positions in the same cockpit. The bench is shown dotted fitted onto the forward winches.

To make the bench strong a glued and screwed stiffener extends under the major length of the bench, but this stiffener is tapered away at each end well inside the cockpit coamings. So that chisels are not blunted, and saws do not jag when cutting right through wood, the screws holding the stiffener are deeply countersunk.

Padding made from strips of carpet are secured to the bench where it lies on top of the coamings. More padding is nailed at the clamps so that the winches are not scratched. Copper nails should be used through the carpet as these are soft and less likely to cause damage if one accidentally protrudes. Much more important, though, the nails should be deeply punched in so that their heads nestle well below the surface of the padding.

Though an engineer's vice is shown, a woodworker's type may be preferred. Whichever vice is fitted it may need raising on wood chocks, or the bench itself may need raising above the coaming level.

The same bench can also be used with one end clamped to a mast and the other to a deck-mounted winch, or with modifications, down in the saloon. Just how it is fitted in the cabin depends on the structure and furnishings. The bench might be pinned down to wood blocks set on the settees, using large G-clamps, or it might be temporarily bolted in an engine compartment.

This type of bench is adaptable. It can be used afloat for rigging, engine repairs are made easier with it and if the bench cannot be secured across the cockpit it may be fitted on a strong pulpit or pushpit. During construction it may not be convenient to have the cockpit obstructed, so one end may be clamped to a sheet winch and the other end extended outboard over some broad staging alongside the boat, at deck level.

However it is fitted and used, this bench pays for itself in a short time simply by saving the fatigue of climbing up and down the ship's ladder a dozen dozen times.

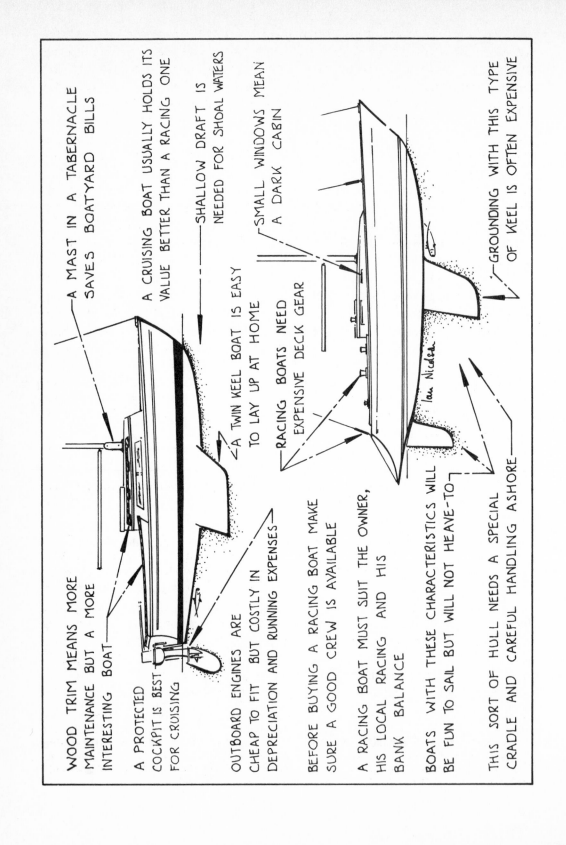

A MAST IN A TABERNACLE
SAVES BOATYARD BILLS

A CRUISING BOAT USUALLY HOLDS ITS
VALUE BETTER THAN A RACING ONE

SHALLOW DRAFT IS
NEEDED FOR SHOAL WATERS

SMALL WINDOWS MEAN
A DARK CABIN

A TWIN KEEL BOAT IS EASY
TO LAY UP AT HOME

RACING BOATS NEED
EXPENSIVE DECK GEAR

GROUNDING WITH THIS TYPE
OF KEEL IS OFTEN EXPENSIVE

WOOD TRIM MEANS MORE
MAINTENANCE BUT A MORE
INTERESTING BOAT

A PROTECTED
COCKPIT IS BEST
FOR CRUISING

OUTBOARD ENGINES ARE
CHEAP TO FIT BUT COSTLY IN
DEPRECIATION AND RUNNING EXPENSES

BEFORE BUYING A RACING BOAT MAKE
SURE A GOOD CREW IS AVAILABLE

A RACING BOAT MUST SUIT THE OWNER,
HIS LOCAL RACING AND HIS
BANK BALANCE

BOATS WITH THESE CHARACTERISTICS WILL
BE FUN TO SAIL BUT WILL NOT HEAVE-TO

THIS SORT OF HULL NEEDS A SPECIAL
CRADLE AND CAREFUL HANDLING ASHORE

Ian Nicolson

A boat 3 feet (1 metre) longer built in a yard with better facilities but markedly less enthusiasm in the work force took 200 hours to complete, but the interior furnishings were more complex. However, they were all templated, the builders knew exactly what they were doing as this time was achieved after dozens of the class were built, and the whole process was 'productionised'.

In both the above cases the people on the job never needed to look at the plans because they had built numerous identical boats. Most of the parts were pre-finished, so that they just needed popping into place. No varnishing or painting was done inside the boat, and finishing times would not include the antifouling or launching and rigging. Also this was factory work and the hulls were not cleaned out after completion, sometimes rows of screw heads would not be lined up, in short there was a certain coarseness about the work.

Amateurs vary a lot in working speed, in time available, in their ability to translate plans into parts, so examples are given with diffidence. I've completed a 30 footer (9.1 metres) in seven weeks working full time, with full-time help by a shipwright for the first three weeks. This completion time was for a simple boat with no engine, but it included every job up to and including launching and trials. In contrast I took four years over a 40 footer (12.2 metres) working in the evenings and at weekends, sometimes with help, often alone. In this case I made everything including the mast. This confirmed the well-known dictum that no amateur should ever undertake a building project which is likely to take more than twenty months, because it is hard to keep up the momentum. For the non-professional it is almost always a mistake to start a boatbuilding project which keeps him ashore more than one and a half summers because enthusiasm wilts, the job gets slower and slower and it becomes increasingly hard to maintain good standards. If a job looks like taking more than fifteen months an amateur should either go for a smaller boat or plan enough help to give an estimated finishing time of fifteen months. In practice this will almost certainly stretch to eighteen months or more.

Few builders, amateur or professional, work out a schedule, but it is a good idea, partly to keep up morale and to ensure equipment is ordered and delivered in ample time, partly to avoid extra expenses due to rising costs of materials and additional hiring fees for tools and the building shed. A detailed building programme starting with the delivery of the hull, and completing each major step is well worth having even though it takes time to work out and is seldom closely followed. It warns if the job is falling behind schedule and gives excuses to celebrate as major milestones such as the installation of the engine(s) or the fitting of all the bulkheads are completed.

For an amateur it is often better to get the boat launched quickly even if she is

---

Fig. 2   Choosing a hull shell

Before deciding which hull shell to buy, a list of all the qualities it must have is made. These two yachts are fairly extreme versions of cruising and racing styles. It is a good idea to talk to owners who sail in the same area the new yacht will use. A few days spent looking over local moorings will show which types and classes are popular for racing and cruising.

not completely finished, unless the owner gets more enjoyment from the building from time afloat. If a boat is bought in mid-winter it is possible to get her afloat in the following spring provided that only essential work is done. The forward cabin, maybe the whole of the chart-table area, perhaps even much of the galley furniture can be omitted till the boat is hauled up for her second winter. The deck gear need not be fully complete, a portable basin will do in the toilet compartment, the settee back-rests can be forgotten till the second building stage. Above all the engine of a sailing boat can be left out for a season or two. Anyone who has never sailed without an engine will be astonished at the extra fun and excitement, the new thrill of achievement found by manoeuvring and getting from port to port entirely by sail. It's an entirely different sport from contemporary cruising and in so many ways much better – often cheaper too.

This partial completion technique works wonders when trying to cut down completion times. I bought a 28 foot (8.5 metre) cruiser on 20 July and launched on 25 August the same year. Work on the boat was done only in the evenings and at weekends. Admittedly, I was lucky to have my three keen children, aged sixteen, thirteen and eleven to help and the boat was a Weatherly 'Ruffian', designed by Billy Brown, so that I had the advantage of a well-thought-out boat with ample moulded-in furniture. Above all the yard was helpful and the determination of the team on the job to get afloat before the summer died was ruthless. We worked on the principle that many things considered essential to life afloat bordered on luxuries. Instead of a bilge pump we had two buckets, instead of a galley we had sandwiches and thermos flasks, supplemented by rushed visits ashore to hotels. We left the fore-hatch and ventilators off, the toilet was a bucket, there was no pulpit at bow or stern, and where the engine now is there was a vast hole which made the finest oilskin locker anyone has ever enjoyed. We only had a third of the summer, but the sailing was fabulous because it was stolen time.

=3 *The delivery of a new hull*=

Before a bare hull is delivered there are lots of jobs for the team who are to complete her. The site has to be cleared so that when the boat is in position there is ample working space. Half the boat's width of beam all round the hull is about the minimum working space, but a little less might be acceptable. The first full size fibreglass yacht built in Europe was laid down so that her bow and stern almost touched the walls of the building shed. Anyone wanting to walk past the bow had to climb over all sorts of struts and props, which was so inconvenient that it is still talked about all these years later.

Branches overhanging the approach to the completion site may need cutting back, 'phone or electric cables may need shifting, bridges may need strengthening, gate-posts taken out, to let the lorry bringing the hull reach the site. If a crane is to be brought in to lift the hull off the lorry, the length, width and height of the crane should be checked before it arrives. Some mobile cranes are remarkably bulky and may need more space than the lorry with its precious load.

The terms on which a crane is hired need studying. Sometimes the hirer, not the crane owner, pays for accidents caused by and to a crane from the moment it leaves the depot. So the right insurance is needed not only for the boat but also for the crane. Insurance is a specialised business, and a broker who can deal smoothly with life insurance, or motor car, or house risks may know little about the special clauses and problems which boats require. A boat broker or surveyor is often the best person to get the precise insurance needed; he will almost certainly advise that the boat should be covered by a 'Building' policy, rather than a normal boat or yacht annual insurance policy. A building policy can be designed to cover just the building months, and extended if there are delays in completion. It covers movement of the boat by road, provided that this is specially mentioned by the insurer, also unloading, launching, trials and where necessary retrials. It may well be cheaper than an ordinary 'In-commission and Laid-up' policy because the value of the boat is small at first but grows as it nears completion. Even if the lorry owner has a comprehensive insurance, the owner should cover the boat from the moment it is lifted onto the lorry at the moulder's premises. Third party cover is an important part of the policy.

The chocks onto which the hull is lowered when it comes off the lorry have to be lined up at the correct slope. This inclination is measured on the plans, and must result in the hull resting with its water-line exactly level. As the boat nears completion its weight increases up to the final displacement. The final and the bare hull weight are needed before the correct size and power of crane can be ordered; the designer is the usual person to supply these figures if they are not on the plan or specification.

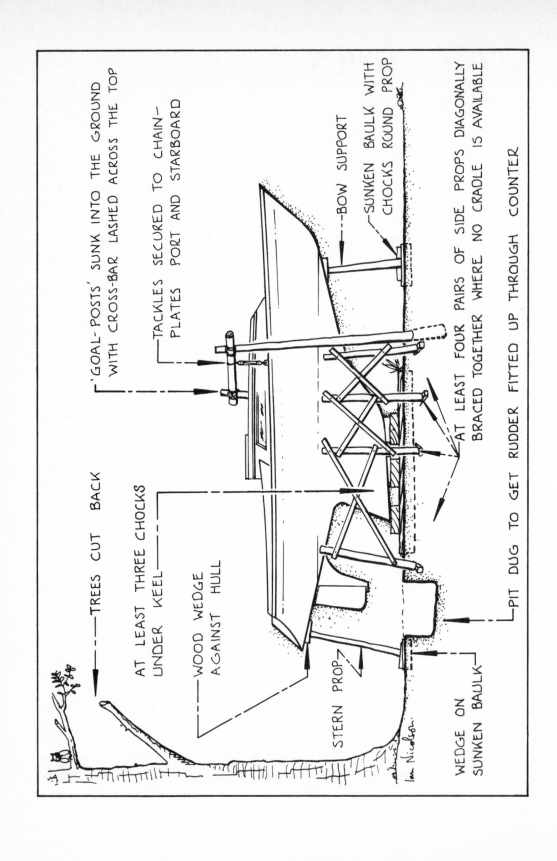

TREES CUT BACK

'GOAL-POSTS' SUNK INTO THE GROUND WITH CROSS-BAR LASHED ACROSS THE TOP

TACKLES SECURED TO CHAIN-PLATES PORT AND STARBOARD

BOW SUPPORT

SUNKEN BAULK WITH CHOCKS ROUND PROP

AT LEAST THREE CHOCKS UNDER KEEL

WOOD WEDGE AGAINST HULL

AT LEAST FOUR PAIRS OF SIDE PROPS DIAGONALLY BRACED TOGETHER WHERE NO CRADLE IS AVAILABLE

PIT DUG TO GET RUDDER FITTED UP THROUGH COUNTER

STERN PROP

WEDGE ON SUNKEN BAULK

Ian Nicolson

When setting up the keel support chocks the final weight has to be borne in mind. If the ground is soft rafts are needed under each chock. Old railway sleepers or baulks of wood about 8×3 inches (200×75 mm) in section spaced 12 inches (300 mm) apart and extending to the full beam of the boat should be adequate, provided there is a second set of sleepers or similar supports laid at right angles to the lowest layer, to spread the weight fully and evenly.

Keel chocks are usually spaced at about 5 feet (1.5 m) intervals along the full length of the hull, but if there is a short, heavy ballast keel there must be at least four chocks under it. This means, very often, one solid full length support extending from the toe to the heel of the keel. When the keel is curved on the bottom it is normally essential to have a support which is shaped to conform with the bottom of the ballast. This shape is taken off the plans.

A full set of drawings is needed several weeks before the hull arrives. Experienced builders get two or even four sets of prints. One they use for ordering gear, ticking each item on the plans so that nothing is forgotten or duplicated. This set is also used for general studying, measuring bolt lengths and working out building sequences. It is kept in the office, or what serves as the office, away from the building site. The second set is stuck on ply or hardboard and covered with sheets of polythene or a similar transparent film. These plans are on, or close by the boat at all times during construction. The clear film protects the prints from the oil or paint-stained fingers of the shipwrights, engineers, electricians and everyone else deeply concerned with the finishing work. Without protection the prints soon get grubby and torn.

If the boat is over 40 feet (12 m) a second set of plans stuck onto board and suitably covered is necessary, because there will be so many people involved that more than one person will obviously wish to study the drawings at any one time. If only a few people are building the boat they will take longer and the first set of drawings will be worn out despite the protective film, so another set really is essential.

A few hours spent studying the plans may throw up plenty of questions. Designers are busy people and hate frequent phone calls from builders. The best approach is to list the queries in related groups, putting all the questions about deck fittings on one page, all those about the engine on another and so on. If the questions are typed down the left side of the paper the designer (or sometimes it is the firm supplying the bare hull) can write the answers on the right side and post the lists back.

Since cranes are hired by the hour, the boat must arrive at the building site ahead of the crane, to allow time to unlash the hull, get the slings under, secure

---

Fig. 3   Boatbuilding out of doors
Plenty of precautions should be taken when completing a yacht in a garden. Before the yacht arrives the ground should be levelled, overhead obstructions removed and a firm base laid down if the ground is soft. When the boat is off loaded from the lorry it should be made doubly secure so that there is no risk that it will topple over even in strong winds or when energetic work is going on inside the hull.
It may be advisable to fit a burglar alarm, the owl in the tree may not be a reliable substitute.

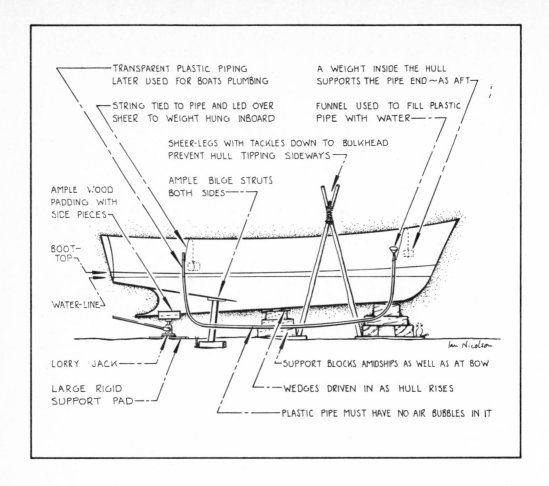

TRANSPARENT PLASTIC PIPING
LATER USED FOR BOATS PLUMBING

A WEIGHT INSIDE THE HULL
SUPPORTS THE PIPE END ~ AS AFT

STRING TIED TO PIPE AND LED OVER
SHEER TO WEIGHT HUNG INBOARD

FUNNEL USED TO FILL PLASTIC
PIPE WITH WATER

SHEER-LEGS WITH TACKLES DOWN TO BULKHEAD
PREVENT HULL TIPPING SIDEWAYS

AMPLE BILGE STRUTS
BOTH SIDES

AMPLE WOOD
PADDING WITH
SIDE PIECES

BOOT-
TOP

WATER-LINE

LORRY JACK

LARGE RIGID
SUPPORT PAD

SUPPORT BLOCKS AMIDSHIPS AS WELL AS AT BOW

WEDGES DRIVEN IN AS HULL RISES

PLASTIC PIPE MUST HAVE NO AIR BUBBLES IN IT

Ian Nicolson

Fig. 4 Getting the hull level

Some builders use the crane which delivers the bare hull to help get the designed water-line exactly level. However, cranes are usually hired out by the hour and are expensive, so a lorry jack under the keel may be a better tool.

If a jack is used there must be quite 2 inches (50 mm) of wood between it and the fibreglass. This chock needs side pieces so that it cannot slide sideways off the keel. The jack must be on a firm base which cannot sink into the ground. Under the hull there should be blocks every 10 feet (3 metres) at the most, with side supports in the form of shores or ropes leading upwards from the sides. If the hull is not in a shed a pair of spars each side, lashed together, with a crossbeam will take tackles port and starboard. As the keel is raised the tackles are tightened and wedges driven in at the keel chocks and side shores. This calls for teamwork or a skilled lone worker.

A length of transparent pipe, which can later be used to link the water tank to the sink and basin pumps or taps, is fitted along the side of the boat. Water is poured in, and the level adjusted till the water-line scribed on the hull is level. On some hulls instead of showing the load water-line only the top of the boot-top is scribed, so a mark on the hull at bow and stern the correct distance down from the ends of the boot-top have to be made, and the water-level in the pipe lined up with these marks.

It may help to colour the water in the pipe with ink or a dye which does not make the pipe unsuitable for drinking water later. Once the hull is level fore-and-aft it must be levelled athwartships.

the slings so that they cannot slip forward or aft, fit ample padding between the slings and the hull, and rig the spreaders. Without spreaders the slings will pinch and may seriously crush the hull. As a rough guide the inner ends of the jaws or V-cuts at the ends of the spreaders should be 2 or 3 inches (50 or 75 mm) further outboard than the hull sides. The spreaders have to be secured to the slings and when metal spreaders are used they must be padded to prevent damage to the deck or cabin top if the spreaders were to drop even slightly.

Where slings pass under fibreglass keels or bilge-keels wood packing is essential because the normal padding of cloths wound round the wire is inadequate. Anyone who lives in a region where there are lots of boats can hire a crane complete with boat slings. The latter are made of wide nylon webbing so that they need little padding, and do not cut into fibreglass edges. They may chafe topsides when grit embedded in the webbing scratches the hull. This is avoided by wrapping clean rags round the webbing where it presses against the boat.

Lifting a boat requires patience and experience so it is always best to get a crane-driver who is used to small craft. He will realise that there must be a rope at the bow and another at the stern held by the boatbuilder and his assistant to prevent the hull from rotating as the crane takes the load. He will have the infinite patience necessary to get the hull located at just the right point on the keel chocks. He may forget to look inside the hull to see if there is an accumulation of rain, so the boatbuilder has to do this. Even if there are only a few inches of water inside the hull it should be bailed out, otherwise it may move about inside during the lifting operation. In extreme cases this can cause the centre of gravity to swim backwards and forwards, so that the crane-driver and his assistants can never get the slings set correctly.

After the boat has been lifted and sat on the keel chocks she should be levelled athwartships. A long straight batten laid from gunwale to gunwale with a spirit level on top is needed to avoid a slight list to port or starboard. On plenty of boats it is impossible to lay a batten across the gunwale because cabin tops and cockpit coamings get in the way. If wooden sawing horses exactly the same height are put at precisely the same distance fore-and-aft, and athwart-ships, on side-decks port and starboard the batten will rest on top of these, clear over the coachroof. Making up a pair of identical sawing horses is another job to do before the boat arrives. They will be used for many other jobs during the course of construction.

As the boat settles on the keel chocks, it also needs side supports. A mini-mum of eight struts or props are required (four each side) even under a small boat. There will be much climbing about, hammering and vibration inside the boat during the weeks when she is being completed, so it is madness to cut down on the supports put under the hull. As a rough guide there should be a strut every 6 feet (2 m) each side. Boats with long overhanging bows and sterns need centre-line props here too.

If the chain-plates are already fitted lashings from them up to beams in the

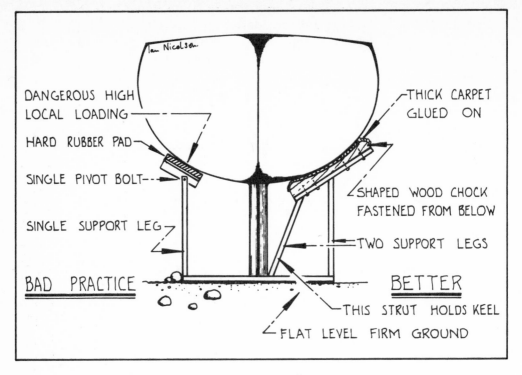

Fig. 5 Boat cradle

It is quite usual for a bare hull to be delivered in a simple steel cradle which has four upstanding legs to support it. Each of these legs has at the top a pivoted angle-bar with a hard rubber pad secured to its horizontal flange. This type of cradle is shown on the left hand side of the sketch. It quite often results in a severe local loading at one point on the hull shell, particularly if the keel slides sideways or forwards when the vessel is being unloaded. Damage often follows.

The right hand side of the sketch shows the same basic cradle frame very much improved. Each support leg is triangulated by an extra leg inside it and a rigid top bar. This top bar has secured on its upper face a carefully shaped hardwood chock which extends at least one eighth of the total girth, that is one quarter of the distance from the sheer or deck edge down to the centre-line of the hull. The wood chock has heavy carpet glued on top, never nailed since fastenings might scratch the gel coat. Each end of the wooden chock is rounded to avoid a hard spot where it impinges on the hull.

roof overhead are handy safety lines provided the building structure is strong enough. If it is not, reinforcing is another job to do before the boat arrives. If the chain-plates are not fitted some builders put them or strong mooring bollards on immediately, and use them for safety lashings. However, these alone are not enough and should only be used as a secondary line of defence.

Even before the hull on the lorry is unlashed, it should be examined carefully all over. If it is imperfect, or has been damaged in transit, often the cheapest and best way to have it repaired is to turn the lorry round and send it back to the moulders. The percentage of bare hulls which arrive at the finishing site in less than perfect condition is startling, certainly over 5 per cent in some areas. A hull on a lorry is high, and road bridges are low. The driver sits close by a noisy engine so he does not necessarily know if the cabin top, or pulpit, or some of the

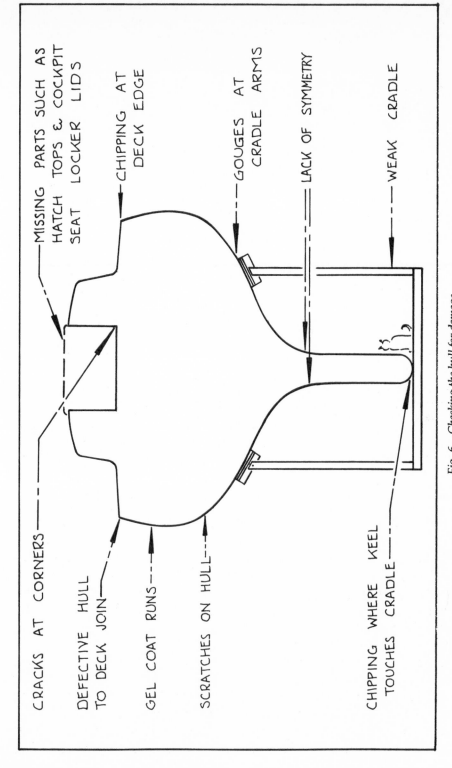

CRACKS AT CORNERS

MISSING PARTS SUCH AS HATCH TOPS & COCKPIT SEAT LOCKER LIDS

CHIPPING AT DECK EDGE

GOUGES AT CRADLE ARMS

LACK OF SYMMETRY

WEAK CRADLE

DEFECTIVE HULL TO DECK JOIN

GEL COAT RUNS

SCRATCHES ON HULL

CHIPPING WHERE KEEL TOUCHES CRADLE

Fig. 6 Checking the hull for damage

Before a bare hull is accepted from a moulder it should be checked all over. If bulkheads or other parts have been glassed in, their joins should be scrutinised to make sure they have stood up to the road journey. The outside of the hull should be examined for damage caused by vandals, or branches of trees overhanging the road.

stanchions have been bashed. Low branches or street lights may have scratched the hull or cabin top. The moulders may have chafed the topsides as they moved the craft out of the fabrication shop, or the shed doors may have swung against the hull.

The first inspection should be a slow thoughtful scrutiny outside, from keel to sheer. Use a powerful light, spend an hour or two or more over the job, lie under the hull, run fingers delicately all over the shell. Look for star cracks and scratches. There is no point in spending thousands of hours completing a shell which is not perfect.

Inside look for bad moulding and damage. The latter is normally easy to spot. Bulkheads may have been carelessly fitted and become loose on the journey, or the chocks on the lorry may have pushed into the hull locally so that there is internal cracking. Check the distance between the bulkheads, and as far as possible check them for alignment athwartships and vertically. This can be done by measuring from one bulkhead to the next at each side, then at top and bottom. All these dimensions should be almost identical but a lot depends on the purpose of the boat and the type of finish. As a rough guide there should be no more than ¼ inch (6 mm) difference, but if no furniture has to be fitted snugly between the bulkheads, or if the bulkheads are unimportant ones near the bow and stern, double this difference is often acceptable. The final checking has to be left till the hull is off-loaded and precisely levelled on its keel chocks.

Just as the outside should be free from blemishes in the gel coat, the inside should be well moulded. There should be no areas where there is a shortage or excess of resin. Too little resin shows up in areas where the glass is dry and straw-like. These areas lack the binding strength of the resin, so a wooden knitting needle can be forced into the shell. This trouble is most often found at the trimmed edges of the hull and deck. Scratching with a wooden spike should not tear up glass strands because they should all be bound tight and solid by resin.

An excess of resin is indicated by a jewelled appearance. (Imitation jewellery is made by pouring resin into suitably shaped containers, to give a glinty, translucent mass with the quality but not the colour of solidified varnish.) Areas of excess resin lack strength. They also suggest that there are other areas where there is a shortage of resin, because it is usual for the moulders to be issued with a fixed quantity of resin for each hull. If they use too much in one area, they have to spread it thinly elsewhere to compensate.

=4 *The moulding process*=

A fibreglass component, whether it is the hull, the deck and cabin top unit, or a small part of the furniture, is made in a three-stage process. First the pattern is built, next the mould is made, and from this the final product is fabricated.

As the pattern has to be full size and an exact replica of the final product it may be costly. It has to be made at least moderately rugged, so that the mould can be made from it without risk of distortion. The finish on the pattern is reproduced on the mould which in turn comes out on the final product. It is essential to get the same grade of smooth finish without undulations on the pattern as is needed on the part to be made from it. When the mould has been made the pattern is seldom of any further use, which is sad and bad for anyone trying to keep costs down.

There are various techniques used for making patterns. For instance, hull patterns have been made from existing boats. All the metal parts like the stem-head fitting, engine stern-gear, and the rudder with its fittings have to be removed. The ballast keel may have to be taken off if the final fibreglass boat is to have an external keel. Next the long meticulous job of getting a perfectly smooth finish on the whole of the hull is undertaken. All the old paint is taken off, dents filled, and a new short-life, high finish coating applied over it. This has to be rubbed down and brought up to a smooth, even surface with no suggestion of cracks, ripples, undulations or roughness . . . nothing which might give the tiniest fly the least foothold. Perfect. It involves so much work that it is now seldom the practice to use an old boat and most hull patterns are specially made, using shadow sections (to define the shape) and planks carefully and closely fastened, with no open seam between because no caulking has to be put in. The aim is just smoothness; watertightness is not needed.

Making the pattern for a furniture part follows the same procedure. Instead of wood it is usual to use hardboard or ply with a super-smooth surface. One of the modern plastic high-gloss laminates on the ply such as Formica is particularly useful here because it needs no surface treatment. It is flat, smooth, free from every kind of microscopic indent or protrusion so a mould made of it comes out with the lovely finish which is the dream of all fibreglass fabricators.

Once the pattern is complete the mould is made without delay, otherwise seams and butts start to open because of drying out or cooling or warping. The mould might be described as the reverse of the pattern. If the pattern is likened to a human body, the mould is akin to a close-fitting rigid leotard. It follows exactly all the contours of the pattern, its inner surface is the same size and of the same proportions as the outside of the pattern. It is made by coating the pattern with fibreglass cloth, then soaking this in a resin which hardens in a few

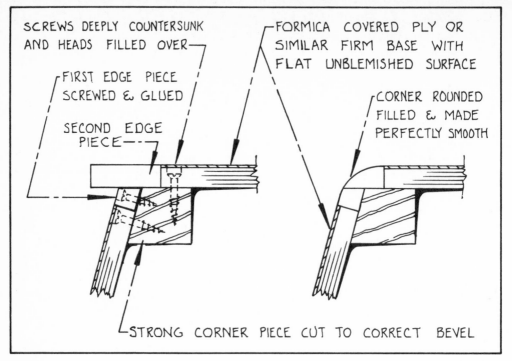

SCREWS DEEPLY COUNTERSUNK AND HEADS FILLED OVER

FORMICA COVERED PLY OR SIMILAR FIRM BASE WITH FLAT UNBLEMISHED SURFACE

FIRST EDGE PIECE SCREWED & GLUED

CORNER ROUNDED FILLED & MADE PERFECTLY SMOOTH

SECOND EDGE PIECE

STRONG CORNER PIECE CUT TO CORRECT BEVEL

Fig. 7   Pattern making

Making a pattern for a fibreglass mould is a straightforward job because the pattern is the same size and shape as the final object. The pattern must have a perfectly smooth surface so the clever thing to do is to use materials which have this characteristic. Sometimes it is a good idea to use smooth sheets of fibreglass for the pattern, sometimes solid wood carefully planed and faired is the answer.

Edges should be very well rounded otherwise the fibreglass cloth will not lie close when it is wetted down with the resin. It is no bad thing to aim for a minimum radius of 1½ inches (40 mm) on all components. This is achieved by having thick wood at the corners and edges, and planing away the wood to give a soft curve, as shown in the right hand sketch. A typical way of building up the right wood thickness is shown on the left.

Each part should be made a neat fit and all joins should be filled with a bedding compound which takes up any tiny gaps. Screw heads are sunk deeply, then covered over with plastic wood or a filler which is compatible with the fibreglassing resins. After the screw hole has been filled it must be levelled off perfectly.

hours. When the resin has set and bound the fibreglass into a continuous solid shape the pattern is extracted. This is possible because before starting the mould a 'parting agent' has been applied to the smooth surface of the pattern to prevent the mould from sticking. Sometimes the parting agent is less than fully efficient. This is the time to apply a little force and leverage and cunning and eventually that special old-fashioned invective which pours out of all boat-builders in times of stress. The mould has to be eased off the pattern without damaging the former, or causing the latter to splinter and scratch the mould.

To help get the pattern out a 'two-part' mould is sometimes used. If the end product is a hull this type of mould divides in two all down the centre, from the fore end of the stem right back to the aft end of the transom. A more important reason for using a two-part mould is the shape of the hull. If it has 'tumble-home' the width a few inches below the deck is greater than the width at the deck. This makes it impossible to pull the pattern out vertically because the mould is inflexible.

The mould is used again and again, perhaps several hundred times. To make it able to stand up to so much usage it is reinforced. The stiffening is often of wood glassed in, partly in the form of athwartships external frames, partly external stringers. This stiffening is to keep the mould the exact shape of the original pattern and to make it able to cope with the inevitable humping and heaving, first to get the original pattern out, and later to get the finished product out.

Instead of having a mould which is split down the middle and held together during use by full length centre-line flanges bolted together, the mould may be in two parts, port and starboard, used separately. One team of moulders make up the port side of the hull in the port mould, while another group make up the other side. When the two components have cured to the correct degree they are taken out of their moulds, the centre-line edges trimmed and the two sides joined, using layer on layer of fibreglass. This way of making a hull avoids trouble with tumble-home and makes the moulds smaller and more portable, usually making it possible for the moulders to work while standing round the outside of the mould instead of perching on movable platforms above it. The advantages are numerous and seldom offset by the extra work of joining the hull up down the centre-line.

All these procedures are followed whatever is being built. It may be a galley unit with integral ice-box, a recess for the cooker or even a sink and draining-board all in one fibreglass moulding. Alternatively, it may be a complete deck with recessed cockpit well, cabin top, wheel-house, upstanding chocks to take the wood or metal hand-rails, shaped chocks for life-rafts, and specially rough-ened surfaces where the crew will walk.

From all this certain conclusions are more than obvious:

1   The pattern must be good and so it is expensive, yet it has a very short useful life.
2   The mould must be above reproach, yet it forms no part of the finished product. Its outside may be rough and crude provided it is tough, but its 'working surface' must cost a lot because it takes so much preparation and finishing.
3   The first fabrication from the mould only arrives after days of skilled and specialised work.
4   Unless the finished product is to be incredibly costly, lots of hulls must be made from each mould; dozens of galley units should come from every galley mould. In short, cost-spreading is important and usually critical.
5   Though many of the moulding processes are easy and call for unskilled or

perhaps semi-skilled labour, there are plenty of opportunities for disaster.

6   What seems like a minor difficulty can result in long production delays and need a lot of money for a full cure. Apparently small crises can turn out to be expensive disasters.

All these factors suggest that making moulds is a specialist job. There is limited logic in a small professional boatbuilding company making its own moulds, and only an amateur with a very special requirement can justify the whole process from pattern to mould and on to the fibreglass assembly. For them it is economical to use a different hull-building technique or buy a standard hull.

Another important consideration is that fibreglass construction is an advancing industry. This year's technology is likely to be out-of-date in the near future. Sometimes a new advance is found to be unsuccessful after a few years service, sometimes cost-saving tricks turn sour once the boat goes afloat, sometimes the chemicals used come from a dud batch.

All this confirms what has been discovered again and again: unless a long production run is planned it is seldom sensible to make a pattern and mould. There are plenty of available moulds in many sizes and shapes. Only rarely is it found that a requirement is so special that a new pattern and mould justifies the cost and production time.

When a new mould is to be built the suppliers of glass cloth and resins should be approached while the lines are being drawn in order to get the latest information and learn about the most up-to-date techniques.

If a builder wants to make up a special furniture unit, or maybe a septic tank, or some relatively minor part, it may be worth completing a pattern and mould, so this is described in the next chapter.

—5 *Moulding a small part*—

An amateur building a boat may buy in all the furniture, as well as the hull and deck, and most of the parts moulded by a hull-maker. But there may be one or two components not included in the kit, or a slightly different shape or style may be preferred. A professional may be in a similar position or he may want to make up a small batch of boats and have his own furniture shapes. For these people the process of making up minor items is described. The aim here is to use simple, almost crude moulds. If the production run is to be more than four or five then normal moulds will be made of fibreglass. The process is the same as that described below except that instead of making a mould first, an exact pattern of the part needed is fabricated. It is made precisely the right size and shape, finished off perfectly but to any colour, and out of any suitable rigid materials, usually wood. From this a fibreglass mould is made, and when this has been finished and polished, then the items are taken from it, just like hull building.

Anyone who has never seen the fibreglassing process being done should move heaven and earth to witness the job in a boatyard or hull moulding factory with a good reputation. This will:

1   Give valuable lessons.
2   Make the following explanations much clearer.
3   Show up the difficulties.
4   Possibly show the newest techniques.
5   Indicate whether the whole idea of fibreglassing should be left to a specialist firm. That is: for an amateur all fibreglass parts are bought in, for a professional the required parts are sub-contracted.

Above all it will show that the dry fibreglass is like a stiff, coarse, awkward-to-handle cloth, such as might be used to line a massive, almost rigid cloak. When it is soaked in the resin this cloth becomes flopping and soggy, so that it is again difficult to handle but in a different way. Now it is sticky, needs coaxing to make it bend into hollows (especially if it is over 1½ oz weight) and it has no strength of its own till it has set hard. The mould is needed to hold the soggy but steadily drying and hardening fibreglass to the correct shape. Once hardening is complete the new component is eased off its mould and it will have as much strength as has been moulded in, which depends on the thickness of the fibreglass and amount of stiffening pieces.

To see how a small piece of furniture is made, the process for making a shower tray is described. A sketch is shown in the chapter on Toilet compartments with additional notes to show how easy the whole job is, provided it is done with loving care, such as is needed for all boatbuilding jobs.

21

At least a rough sketch is needed first. From this an accurate plan to scale should be drawn, though this is sometimes omitted. Details like strengthening and clearances should be indicated. For instance, if making a cover for a life-raft on deck, there must be a gap at each side and each end of about ½ inch (12 mm) so that there is not the slightest risk that the cover will jam.

If a cover for a life-raft was being made, the *outside* surface is the one which would show, so a female mould is used, since this will have a smooth *inside* surface. This surface finish will be transferred faithfully to the *outside* of the part being made. As we are following through the making of a shower tray, we need a male mould, which has a smooth *outside* surface. On this we make our tray, which needs to be smooth on its top, *inside* face.

Before making the mould some builders like to mock up a template from cardboard. This is a good idea if the part has to fit into an awkward recess where the boat is curved and the space tapers in every direction. A template takes such a short time to make that it is worth it if there is any doubt or if the shipwright is treading new ground. Even a three-dimensional template, made up from cardboard and sellotape, will not take more than a few minutes to assemble.

It is seldom a good idea to make up a plan or a template from the boat's drawings, not least because the latter are so often out of date, were never followed accurately or were drawn more with an eye to selling the boat than for building.

Moulds should be as simple as possible. This is to keep down their costs and the time it will take to fabricate a part if there are lots of changes of angle, or lots of recesses and many edges. A mould, regardless of what the finished object is, should have no sharp edges because fibreglass will not easily conform to the shape when wet. The wet glass cloth cannot be moulded easily into sharp cut interior angles, certainly not if they are less than 135 degrees. So all edges and recesses should be made with big radii; an absolute minimum of ¾ inch (20 mm) is a good working basis.

Moulds are made so far as is possible like simple boxes, often with diagonal stiffening. This is put on the outside of a female mould and the inside of a male one. The material used for the mould can be anything which is sufficiently rigid and easily worked. It should have a smooth, glossy surface where the fibreglass is to be applied, so Formica covered ply is favoured. However, the surface can be given the necessary smoothness and polish later, so ordinary, cheap ply may be used. Sometimes hardboard is used, provided it is the type which is totally non-porous and will not soak up fluids. Another favourite material is fibreglass sheet, because it is smooth-faced, strong, easy enough to cut with a jig-saw or band-saw or hack-saw, easy to bond together, not affected by changes in moisture and temperature, and perhaps its only defect is its cost.

Moulds are made with slightly bevelled sides so that whatever is made in them comes away easily. Suppose the mould is for a shower tray; the sides of the tray will all slope outwards at the top. This slope can be as much as 10° off the vertical since this makes no difference to the operation of the tray, but it makes the job of prising the tray off the mould easier. It also reduces the interior angle

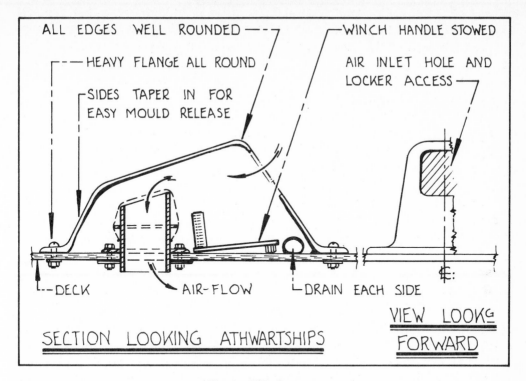

ALL EDGES WELL ROUNDED

WINCH HANDLE STOWED

HEAVY FLANGE ALL ROUND

AIR INLET HOLE AND
LOCKER ACCESS

SIDES TAPER IN FOR
EASY MOULD RELEASE

DECK

AIR-FLOW

DRAIN EACH SIDE

SECTION LOOKING ATHWARTSHIPS

VIEW LOOKᵍ FORWARD

Fig. 8   Fibreglass parts

This drawing shows the features needed for good fibreglass moulding. Whether making a simple ventilator box, as shown here, or building a complete hull or deck or cabin top, the same principles are followed. The total mould is made with sides which 'lie in' at the bottom, so that the finished product is easy to prize out of the mould. All edges, whether interior angles like the one along the root of the bottom flange or external like the ones round the top, are made boldly rounded to avoid resin richness and ensure the glasscloth lies well.

This fitting has extra assets. The sloping ends ensure that ropes will not catch accidentally; the shape is far from rectangular, so it has the strength of a triangulated structure, and it serves two purposes because sheet winch handles, sail tiers and other loose deck gear can be stowed inside the box.

In very severe weather the crew can reach inside the box and slip a tight-fitting cover over the air inlet pipe. In normal weather air and spray enter the box through the access hole but the spray drains out at the bottom and only the air gets into the cabin.

where the sides meet the bottom, so this edge becomes easier to glass round and there is less chance that it will be too rich in resin, and as a result too short of glass cloth. If it does have this defect it is likely to be brittle and have hollows with thin layers of resin over. These 'pop' leaving bubbles which allow moisture to get at the fibreglass.

Interior angles need filling with a solid or malleable material so that when the fibreglass goes in, it forms round a gentle curve. Some people use a mixture of 50 per cent Cascamite glue and 50 per cent Polyfilla made into a firm putty by the addition of water. It is worked in with the thumb and when hard is smoothed and made regular by the application of glass-paper, and also well feathered out at all edges.

23

Wood or plastic strip mouldings are also used for filling interior angles; these can be bought from joiners suppliers and some timber merchants.

Outside edges are faired away with a plane or Surform to the biggest possible radius. All crevices are sealed and if ply is being used it is treated with a wood sealer like a two-pack polyurethane paint. The aim is to get a smooth finish entirely free from all blemishes.

Before beginning to make anything in a mould a release agent is applied all over. It is normally in two parts and must be put on systematically starting at one end and working to the opposite end. To make sure that not even a few square millimetres have been missed it is probably best to work over the whole mould three times, carefully polishing in the final waxy release agent component by hand.

Laying up a component in a mould starts off with the gel coat. This is a clear resin for items which are hidden or unimportant because clear gel is cheaper and less porous. Anything like a shower tray or a cover for a life-raft will be on view, so it will be coloured to suit its job and the surroundings. The gel coat is applied smoothly and not too copiously as it must not 'run' or form 'curtains' like paint put on too thickly. It is left till it is just tacky, then a coat of resin applied, the first pieces of glass cloth applied, more resin and so on, till the correct thickness has been built up. Stiffeners are laid in place and strips of wetted cloth laid over them. Shoddy builders save pennies here by glassing stiffeners with only a single layer of cloth, whereas there should be at least two, and for parts like a shower tray which has to stand up to such stresses as a heavy man jumping about in a jet of freezing water, three layers of 2 oz chopped strand mat are a minimum.

The new component is left in a warm dry atmosphere to harden. The time this takes depends on the resin and mix used, so here the resin makers guidance is needed. If in doubt, leave it for a week. To get it off the mould prise the edge apart with care. The new part will have been made too big so that if the edge is damaged while being taken off the mould it does not matter. However, the damage must not extend beyond the surplus edge, so once separation is started it should be encouraged slowly and with care.

Some professionals use blasts of compressed air. Slow softwood wedges are favourite tools: a couple of energetic men, one pulling the mould down and the other pulling the component up often does the trick. It is usual for the first item off a mould to be difficult to extract and all subsequent ones to be easy. It may help, if a part will not come out, to distort the mould diagonally a little, by applying forces from opposite corners in plan and elevation.

Once off the mould the new component is trimmed all round the edge with a jig-saw (using a fine tooth blade, as recommended on the packet of blades) or a hack-saw. The cut edge is then smoothed with a file, and where it has to be watertight it is coated with resin.

Where possible the part should be made 'seaproof'; that is, sharp corners should be rounded, weak areas stiffened with extra glass cloth, extra stiffeners provided, and perhaps a wood batten or two may need glassing in to take fastenings. There is no such thing as a boat part which is utterly safe and reliable in all sea conditions, so a critical look at each part before it is fitted will make the final boat a happier, more reliable craft.

To take the examples mentioned earlier, the corners of a shower tray top flange should be cut to a bold radius, and someone heavy should stand in the tray to make sure it is not going to sag when in use. A cover for a life-raft should be given a swift kick with a soft boot, to see how it will stand up to a breaking wave or a careless crew. The securing points need a horrendous jolt to ensure they are going to stand up to life afloat.

——6 *Working fibreglass*——

Fibreglass would be no good if it did not adhere easily and set hard. This has disadvantages. If the resin gets on clothes it cannot be washed out and before long it turns what was flexible soft cloth into semi-rigid, scratchy, awkward material, unpleasant to wear and impossible to launder properly.

It is, therefore, only sensible to wear all-enveloping overalls, with aged garments underneath. Shoes should be past their prime by about ten years, and it is best to wear some headgear such as a woollen cap which totally covers the hair. Rubber gloves are usually worn. The best type are cheap because they soon get clogged with resin and have to be thrown away. Sometimes it is possible to buy gloves which can be worn on either hand and these are especially useful. It is best to buy a whole box of them if a lengthy job is being undertaken. I prefer just one glove, on my right hand, leaving my left hand less encumbered. In theory I keep my left hand clean throughout a fibreglassing session and sometimes I succeed. In any case it is important to rub into both hands a liberal measure of barrier cream such as Savlon, made by ICI. It should be well rubbed in not just over the hands and into the nails but up the wrists to well above the level of the sleeve ends. Sleeves are best turned up an inch or two, and no one who has experience of fibreglassing in 'battle' conditions wears a wrist-watch.

Professionals do not wear goggles, but a good case can be made for them, especially if an amateur who is ten-thumbed is involved in his first glassing session. It is not unusual to see splashes of resin on spectacles worn by fibre-glassers, and as this material cannot be washed off with water, clearly a dose of resin in the eye is undesirable.

The outer clothes worn for fibreglassing are kept in the workshop. This is partly to prevent the sticky resin getting onto other clothes and anything else touched, but just as much to keep dust and dirt away from the glassing work.

To achieve success when glassing, the basic rules of cleanliness, temperature and moisture control have to be followed with a little fanaticism. The working area has to start off clean and free from dust and has to be kept that way by regular cleaning and tidying. Inside the workshop the temperature must never fall below 16°C during and after fibreglassing otherwise a permanent under-cure may result. This, in effect, means the glass never gets 100 per cent hard, so it lacks strength and tends to 'creep' under load. On the other hand excessive heat will result in a fast, maybe too rapid cure. Manufacturers give the curing rate for their different resins with the relevant temperatures.

Just as important, everything concerned with the glassing must be at a steady temperature and all at the same temperature. The best way to solve this problem is to store the glass, resin, catalyst, plywood and everything else used including the tools and buckets in the same part of the same building as the boat.

Condensation, like dust, ruins fibreglassing. The building has not only to be kept warm but free from leaks through the roof and dribbles through cracked window-panes. This is, of course, a radical departure from normal boatbuilding practice.

In contrast, it used to be clever to have the saw-milling machinery close by the boat, so that there was no waste of time walking far to cut or plane wood. But this sort of mechanical woodworking equipment generates a lot of dust, so it must either be left unused for a long period before the glassing takes place, or the machinery must be outside the building shed.

Close by the boat (or near the component being glassed) a table is needed for cutting pieces of cloth from the main roll. Cloth comes in big reels which can be suspended like vast toilet rolls. With care the different types of cloth can be arranged one above the other, vertically over one table, so that whichever material is needed is pulled down, sliced off, and the roll rewound to keep the cloth clean and clear of the table. Big scissors and a few sharp, simple knives are needed for this cutting work.

Boards of scrap wood are useful for 'buttering on' the resin to pieces of glass cloth. Generally, these boards are portable and moved to a position close to the job in hand, otherwise the wetted-out cloth drips everywhere. These drips stick wonderfully to shoes, which transfer the goo to decks, neighbouring rooms, inside cars . . . there is no limit to the mess a few drips of resin can make.

=7 Tools for fibreglassing=

The usual container for mixing resin with its catalyst and hardener is a plastic bucket. The principal advantage of this type of container is that the residue of the resin can be left to harden. Once it has become properly solidified the bucket is squeezed sideways, the scrap resin cracks out, and the bucket is bright, clean and ready for use again. There is a moral here: greasy, shiny surfaces are immune to the binding or gripping of fibreglass, so every surface to be glassed must be totally free from grease. This especially applies to stern tubes, rudder tubes and the like.

There is a receptacle which has the flexible plastic properties of a cheap bucket, but has a better handle. It is easier to grip, easier to use in the confines of a small boat, smaller in capacity but adequate. Above all it is specially designed with a wide base and is most unlikely to tip over by accident. It is a child's potty.

Resin should not be stirred by machinery as it moves too fast and this causes bubbles which are very slow to come to the surface. They tend to remain in the resin even after it has hardened, and being little voids they are areas of weakness. A row of bubbles is akin to a line of perforations in toilet paper, a place where the strength is minimal. Stirring is best done with a wood spatula. If it is about 1½ inches by ⅜ inch (40×10 mm) and in length no more than the depth of the container plus 6 inches (150 mm) for a hand-grip it should be adequate. A batch of spatulas made up from freshly planed wood and stored in an airtight plastic bag will be ready when wanted, yet free from dust.

Resin is applied with paint brushes. Cheap unpainted brushes are commonly used but this is doubtful practice because they are likely to be dusty and have loose hairs. A careful builder, trying to be economical while at the same time avoiding weak glasswork, will use his brushes first on unimportant jobs, till they have become free from dust and then he will have 'matured' brushes for important work. Of course, he will clean and tease out the brushes before he uses them at all. Brushes are cleaned with acetone. Immediately after use the brush is stood with its bristles fully immersed in acetone till it is next needed. The acetone is removed from the bristles by brushing on a clean dry surface. In theory the brush should be dipped in resin and again 'brushed out' on a clean, dry surface before starting work, but professionals seldom do this.

A few short-bristle brushes may be used for stippling the glass to remove air bubbles. Another good tool for this job looks like a paint roller but it has a row of washers instead of the fleecy roller. There are various versions of this tool, some have rollers with little spikes all along and all round.

8 *Floors*

Below the cabin sole there are in some boats athwartships frame-like stiffening pieces. They are confusingly called floors but they are not for standing on – they are to strengthen that highly stressed area low down in the hull. Here a sailing yacht has her ballast keel joined. In addition and just as important, the mast thrusts down hereabouts either directly or by way of a mast-support pillar. In all types of boat, power or sail, this is the area which takes the loading when grounding accidentally or on purpose.

Floors also help to distribute the load of the engine; they are important if the hull is bumped sideways alongside a quay wall, or if it is pinched between the wall and another boat. They look insignificant and on plenty of cheap or badly designed boats they are left out, which is often found to be an expensive mistake.

If the hull has athwartships frames it is likely that these will be thickened or deepened for perhaps one fifth of the boat's beam either side of the centre-line. This stronger area is often referred to as a floor. If it is not there a builder is well advised to find out from the designer if he intended extra strength to be built into the vulnerable area.

When there are no athwartships frames the hull moulder may put in floors. Sometimes it is left to whoever is completing the hull, and it may be that the drawings show no floors. Do not be fooled by that extra thickening of the fibre-glass shell along the centre-line. This is needed as well as floors, though shoddy builders may say otherwise. Lack of floors, or inadequate floors is a leading cause of structural trouble in fibreglass yachts. Some boats have these strengtheners too far apart, badly secured, too shallow or too light. As the weight is low down this is an area where weight saving need not be pursued so enthusiastically, even on a high performance boat.

The spacing of floors depends on a dozen factors like the thickness of the hull shell near the centre-line and the loadings. If in doubt it is so obviously better to have more than just enough floors, and only a madman or the meanest penny-pincher puts them in only just strong enough. Two approximate but useful rules of thumb are:

1　Carry the floors right up to close under the cabin sole at least, so that they are as deep as possible. Incidentally depth is more important than thickness.
2　Space them about $\frac{1}{40}$ of the boat's length apart in way of the ballast keel and for $\frac{1}{10}$ of the boat's length beyond the forward and aft ends of the ballast. Have at least three in way of all masts. For power boats space them about $\frac{1}{25}$ of the boat's length apart.

The plans may show no floors, or floors which are neither so deep nor so close as these rough-and-ready rules suggest. Before going for a lower standard of strength give time for thought. If the boat runs aground or suffers any accident, the last place where trouble is acceptable is low down. Here the inrush of water will be greatest because the pressure will be strongest. If the floors are inadequate in service it is an expensive job stiffening them. The furniture and sole will probably have to be taken out to do the job, then put back when the repairs are complete.

In a fibreglass hull the logical material to use for floors is fibreglass. It should be as thick as the hull is near the centre-line and flanged at the top at least $1/250$ of the boat's length. Glassing in must be meticulous, and continuous all round. That is, the glassing must extend down one side of the floor on the fore-side, across the centre-line, up the other side, round the end, and across the whole of the aft bottom edge, turning round at the outside tip. This 'glassing round the ends' is particularly important. Rules for glassing in are misleading, but as a rough guide use at least two runs of well applied $1\frac{1}{2}$ oz chopped strand mat for every 15 feet (5 metres) of boat length, and a minimum of three runs on even the smallest boat. If fibreglass floors are used it is good policy to have them made and fitted at the same time as the hull shell is being made.

Whatever type of floor is installed each one should fit to within at the very worst $1/8$ inch (3 mm) all along the arms where they butt against the inside of the hull. It is true that some rough, fast-working production builders put floors in which just fit roughly here and there, but this standard of workmanship gives trouble. A thin cardboard template to the size of each floor should be made by a beginner, to get the fit tight.

A rot resistant hardwood which does not split and is generally stable can be used effectively for floors. These floors will need bevelling to fit the shape of the hull so the cardboard templates should be made to go at the aft face of forward floors, and at the forward face of floors aft of the widest part of the hull. This ensures that the wood is cut the right shape but with a surplus for bevelling off. Hardwood floors are good in way of a ballast keel because the keel bolts can be fitted through them. The floor thickness should be three times, and better still four times the bolt diameter as a minimum, and it may be necessary to recess the nut in a cutaway section of the floor on the centre-line, so as to extend the sides of the floor as high as possible under the cabin sole.

In passing it is worth worrying about the level at which the floor arms terminate. If all the floors end in line this may result in a highly stressed narrow band in way of the tops of the floors. To get over this every second or third floor is carried up extra high. Just how high depends on how far offshore the boat is going and how hard she is to be driven. For extremely severe conditions it is common sense to extend a few floors up to the deck edge, making them into combined floors and athwartships frames.

The design of each floor should be thought out so that the sides which extend up the hull taper away. This is often hard and sometimes impossible to achieve, but if there is no tapering out the floors may tear away from the shell. What is unacceptable is a lack of tapering out and floors which terminate each side in line.

If hardwood is used for floors it should have the top edges well rounded so that the fibreglass wraps easily around it. A radius of ¾ inch (20 mm) is about the minimum. The same applies to floors made of plywood. This means that plywood floors should have their tops totally rounded. Marine quality ply must be used because floors are down in the bilge and water may get at the wood in spite of the overall glassing.

The glassing in of a floor should be total, not just in the fillet where the floor meets the hull, though it has been suggested above that fibreglass floors should only be secured by glassing in along the fillets, and this is what so many builders do. But a better job is to encase even a fibreglass floor totally. Total envelopment of floors made from other materials is strongly recommended.

Steel floors are used where there is only a limited space between the cabin sole and the top of the inside of the hull shell. The aim here is to gain the extra strength of steel to compensate for the lack of depth. The top of the floor is often flanged about the same amount as a fibreglass floor. It is essential to use stainless steel because mild steel will rust. This process will force off the glassing-in, so that soon the floor will become detached from the shell. When this happens all sorts of frightening things follow, including visible movement of the ballast keel as the boat is moved by crane ashore. There are few things so certain to give an owner a gigantic fright as the sight of a few tons of lead or iron subtly moving and flexing the bottom areas of the hull shell, causing pulsating ridges and hollows. A boat with this defect is less safe than a car with a corroded brake cable.

Whatever type of floor is used, it should be bedded in wet glass as it goes in. There should be at least one substantial limber hole, and one each side is better. These can be made by fitting 1½ inch (40 mm) bore plastic tubing through holes right at the bottom of the floor before it goes in. The tube is extended 2 inches or so (50 mm) beyond the floor forward and the same distance aft, otherwise the glassing in may accidentally block the limber hole. Even a partial blockage is unacceptable, because it will soon gather dirt and form a dam. Just cutting holes in the bottoms of floors is seldom an effective way of making limber holes because the glassing in has to be done copiously with multiple layers and it is almost inevitable that the holes will get at least partly blocked.

9 Ballast keels

There are two distinct types of ballast keel, one is bolted on the outside of the hull, the other is put inside the all-enveloping fibreglass shell. Their assets and liabilities are much argued. Rival designers with different experiences and prejudices will contest the following lists, but this is roughly the way the two types show up against each other:

Bolt-on keels

Good points:
If the boat grounds they resist damage and can stand up to chafe.
If the ballast is lead it cushions the blow when grounding.
If it is dented and gouged it is often easy to repair or trim.
The pattern and mould is cheaper and less complex to make.
Moulding the hull is easier so there are less likely to be mistakes.
It is not too difficult (though it is expensive) to change the whole keel, if for instance more or less draught is required.
The amount of fibreglass is less which reduces its cost.
The fitting of the keel can be deferred till most of the rest of the construction work can be completed. This means the whole hull can be set low down near the ground which makes access and working easier. Shoring up during construction is cheaper and simpler.
The crane which launches the boat can sometimes first be used to lift the hull onto the ballast fin.
Lead or iron can be used; however the low strength of lead does mean that the shape must be compact and there must be ample thickness in way of bolts, etc.

Bad points:
The inside of the boat tends to be flat or shallow with limited space for bilge-water.
Even when there is a moderate amount of space for bilge-water it tends to slosh up the boat's sides, wetting bedding, clothes, books, in time almost everything aboard, especially in severe weather.
The track record is bad, with too many faulty keel-to-hull joins.
The design is more difficult in most cases.
Slight moves in the position of the centre of gravity of the ballast are not easily achieved.

The job of joining the ballast to the hull shell can be difficult; sometimes when the shape of the fin is curved and complex it can be exceptionally awkward.

Poured-in keels

Good points:

Putting in the ballast is easy.

A large proportion can be put in before launching and the rest used to get the correct trim once the boat is afloat.

Later changes are sometimes easy. For instance increasing the weight, or shifting the centre of gravity and adding weight at the same time are especially easy.

In the event of a severe grounding the fibreglass on the bottom may cushion the bumping and perhaps save the ship. Provided water does not penetrate above or round the ballast, many inches of hull may be chafed away before water enters the hull.

Water tanks, sewage tanks and so on can be fitted over or adjacent.

No expensive bolts are needed, bolts which may be hard to obtain.

The ballast can be fitted at almost any time during construction.

Bad points:

Running aground, even slightly, can cause a lot of damage to the glass shell.

Because the damage is on the bottom it is awkward and expensive to repair. Even slight damage should not be ignored.

Careless slipping or lowering from a 'travel-lift' will cause damage on the bottom of the hull shell.

The hull pattern and mould are relatively expensive having more complex shapes.

Moulding calls for more care.

The centre of gravity of the ballast is likely to be slightly higher.

If iron is put into the hull it has to be carefully sealed otherwise it will rust and this causes expansion and various troubles.

Fitting a bolt-on fin

This is not an easy job and so an amateur doubtful of his ability is advised to have the hull moulder do it. Also the tools needed are not owned by many amateurs, nor are they cheap to buy or easy to rent or borrow.

The top of the ballast must be smooth and fair, as must the underside of the hull moulding. It may be necessary to grind off the 'flashing' under the hull along the centre-line, and smooth off the top of the ballast.

Next the top of the ballast must be examined to make sure it has the same profile as the underside of the hull shell. The maximum discrepancy should be well under ⅛ inch (3 mm). It is not easy to discover the difference without lowering the hull down onto the ballast, though a pattern can be used. If there is a difference the builder can either make up a wood packing piece or change the bottom of the hull or the top of the ballast. To make a packing piece it is best to use a piece of clear-grained, fault-free hardwood. Its top face must match the underside of the hull and its bottom face the ballast.

If the hull is to be changed it cannot be ground away, except very slightly in small areas where there are local excrescences. Instead the thickness must be built up with extra fibreglass. Fairing off the top of the ballast is hard work because metal is being cut away, but at least it is down-hand work. If the top of an iron ballast keel is in the form of a flange which is bolted onto the shell, seldom can more that 10 per cent of the flange thickness be ground off. If more has to be taken away either the keel should be rejected and another one obtained, or a packing piece must be used, or the hull thickness built up with fibreglass.

The simplest procedure for fitting an external keel is almost always to stand the fin up, and lower the hull shell onto it. The *fin* must be well chocked off, exactly upright and at the correct rake to the horizontal. The points on the hull shell where the fore and aft ends come are marked on the fibreglass. Mark *both*. This is being pedantic, but if the keel length is wrong, or if there is any risk that the keel is being misplaced, care taken to mark *both* ends should eliminate the error. The location of each side of the keel is marked on the hull shell to avoid ending up with a keel which is not precisely aligned with the hull. It happens . . . examine any hundred or so boats ashore in any boat-yard carefully!

Before lowering the hull onto the fin the top of the ballast must be checked to make sure it is horizontal athwartships. A waterproof bedding compound is put on top of the ballast in lavish quantities so that it spews out thickly all round as the hull comes down. It has to be scraped away to check that the ballast top edge aligns exactly with the marks on the hull shell.

If the ballast has to be taken to the hull shell (and this is not a procedure to tackle without good reason since the other way round is so much easier), handling help is needed. The keel may have athwartships holes drilled in it for bars and securing ropes. These holes are later plugged with wood or fibreglass putty. Lorry jacks are useful for lifting and moving the ballast, but it may well be necessary to bolt lugs or battens to the ballast to give the jacks a secure 'toe-hold'.

To drag the ballast secure a rope to a corner then lead it to a block and hence to a winch. Have the ballast on a wooden sledge with greased baulks of timber underneath to get the ballast into place. Have plenty of muscle-power but make sure that no one lingers on or close to the ballast. By their nature ballast keels are awkward in shape, recalcitrant, and dangerous when self-propelled.

Sheer-legs are set over the ballast to get it upright. Jacks may be used to lift it a few inches but not once the keel is tilted. When the keel is upright, it needs at least three shores or supports on each side.

It is tempting to use the keel bolts to force the hull shell to mate tightly onto the ballast. If this crude technique is used trouble is likely. The keel may move relative to the shell even when the bolts have been strongly tightened. There may be leaking, the hull may be torn, water may work up the glass laminates. Frost will accentuate these troubles.

The construction or keel plan should show the number, size and location of the keel bolts. If the drawings are not available Lloyds' rules are a valuable guide. For those who prefer a rule of thumb: there should be between twelve and sixteen bolts, and if twin fins are being fitted then there should be the same number for each ballast fin. Each bolt on its own should be able to carry the weight of the keel, or the weight of each twin fin. Where possible bolts should be in pairs athwartships or at least staggered either side of the centre-line.

Bolts should be of galvanised mild steel if the keel is of iron. A lead keel is secured with a good quality sea-water resistant bronze having a tensile strength of about 25 tons per square inch. Where the bolts pass up through the bottom of the keel the bottom ends of the bolts should have carrot heads. This type of head has a slow taper which wedges tightly in a matching hole. In practice it is not easy to get carrot-headed bolts and so ordinary countersunk bolts are now often used. Even these are relatively expensive and so the practice has grown up of fitting a nut on the bolt end instead of having a properly formed head. If a nut is used it should be carefully peined or clenched over so that it cannot come off by accident. Whatever type of head is used it must be well recessed into the keel and the recess filled with a waterproof stopping.

Each end of the bolt must be secured in a way that is totally watertight. Traditionalists use a grommet of caulking cotton which they often soak in white lead. Modern boatbuilders frequently use one of the watertight sticky tapes such as 'Sylglas'. On top the bolt has a nut pulled down onto a large plate washer which is bedded in a fully watertight way, often using the same materials as are put on the bottom. The length of washer plate sides should be at least three times the diameter of the bolt and the thickness at least one quarter of the diameter of the bolt. The nuts are hauled up very tight using a socket spanner with a bar about thirty times as long as the bolt diameter. It is not good practice to clench over the top nuts since one or two bolts should be taken out every four years for inspection.

An alternative method of fixing bolts is designed to save money. Instead of going right through the keel the bolts are threaded into it, usually about one third or half way down from the top. The holes are drilled first and then tapped, making sure that the length of thread is at least ten times the diameter of the bolts. The practice has grown up of using threaded rod instead of solid bar with the ends threaded.

It is sometimes necessary, for instance when putting in the threaded rod

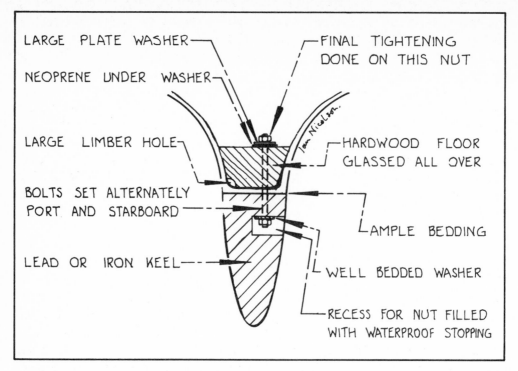

LARGE PLATE WASHER

NEOPRENE UNDER WASHER

FINAL TIGHTENING DONE ON THIS NUT

LARGE LIMBER HOLE

HARDWOOD FLOOR GLASSED ALL OVER

BOLTS SET ALTERNATELY PORT AND STARBOARD

AMPLE BEDDING

LEAD OR IRON KEEL

WELL BEDDED WASHER

RECESS FOR NUT FILLED WITH WATERPROOF STOPPING

Fig. 9   Bolted on ballast keel

External ballast keels are secured by bolts through the bottom of the fibreglass hull. Sometimes the bolts go right to the bottom of the ballast and sometimes they end in pockets as shown here. When the bolts are short, as in this sketch, it is a good idea to have them offset alternately so that the recess is quite small and also the mechanical join between the hull and the keel is better.

The bolt shown in the drawing is made up of a solid bar threaded at each end for a nut. Each nut is tightened on a plate washer and the top nut may be glassed right over once the keel has been pulled up tight. Hardwood floors are not always put in, but they are advisable, especially for a yacht 30 feet (9 metres) long or more.

mentioned above, to use a special technique to secure the bolts. It is no good putting a nut on top and turning this, hoping that the whole bar will turn. The trick is to put two nuts on the top of the threaded bar and lock these nuts tightly together. They then act like the head of a bolt, and a spanner on them will turn the whole threaded rod.

Iron keels with athwartships flanges at the top have become popular over the last few years. They should be secured with countersunk bolts driven up from below, so that the countersunk heads are on the bottom. An alternative is to use threaded rod from above but this is all too often unsatisfactory. What so often happens is that the threaded rod is insufficiently engaged in the flange.

The bolts should be put through floors except perhaps in light craft below about 28 feet (8.5 m). If there are no floors the centre-line structure of the fibreglass shell must be exceptionally strong. A disproportionate percentage of structural troubles in keeled yachts come from a lack of floors. The movement of the fin keel relative to the fibreglass shell causes leaking and structural damage all because there is not enough local strength; this local strength is conferred by the fitting of floors. Sometimes bolts are fitted through the bottom of the fibre-glass shell but not through the floors and this too gives trouble. A fibreglass shell is often not stiff enough to resist the twisting effect of the ballast keel. To overcome the difficulty (if the ballast keel bolts cannot be put through the floors) is not too difficult. For instance, instead of plate washers the builder can use an angle bar with the horizontal flange acting as the plate washer and the vertical flange strongly secured to an adjacent floor. By extending the angle bar extensively athwartships it contributes to the strength of the floor.

It is common practice, once all the keel bolts are in and tightened, to put over the nuts three or four layers of 1½ oz chopped strand mat, so that any leaking up the bolts is localised.

Fitting a poured-in keel

Lead is much the best material for this because it is denser. It packs in low down, the centre of gravity of the keel is lower and the boat's performance is improved. The lead is made into ingots which fit in the space inside the keel. Each ingot is made small enough to handle by the available manpower and equipment. It helps if the ingots have lifting rings but a ring sticking out of the top of an ingot which is going to have another lowered on top of it is bad. Instead strong screw-eyes may be put in the top and taken out once the ingot is down in the fin, or recessed lifting eyes can be fitted. Alternatively a pair of grooves can be made round each ingot and pairs of ropes used to lower them – just as coffins are sent down into graves.

The shape of each lead ingot is determined by making up wood patterns. These patterns can be sent to a lead caster, or the boatbuilder himself can cast his own ingots. The wood shapes are forced down into dry casting sand which is either in a strong box, or in a hole in the ground. The box must be strong otherwise it may burst open due to the weight of the lead. A steel gutter is stoutly secured at a slope of about thirty degrees with its lower end over the hole in the sand. Lead scrap is laid in the gutter and blowlamps or fires or both are brought to bear on the underside of the gutter. As the lead melts it trickles down into the recess in the sand.

When all the lead ingots are in place a sealing over the top of chopped strand mat layers is applied to keep the ballast in place even if the boat inverts. The number of layers of glassing depends on factors like the boat's likely perform-ance, her size and so on. If in doubt use at least three layers of 2 oz chopped strand mat per 20 foot (6 metres) length of boat.

Lead is costly, though worth the extra money. For those who must go for cheaper alternatives there is a choice of iron very carefully glassed in, and ballasting 'systems'. It is a mistake to use concrete and iron or concrete alone.

If iron is used it is packed down as densely as possible and secured with

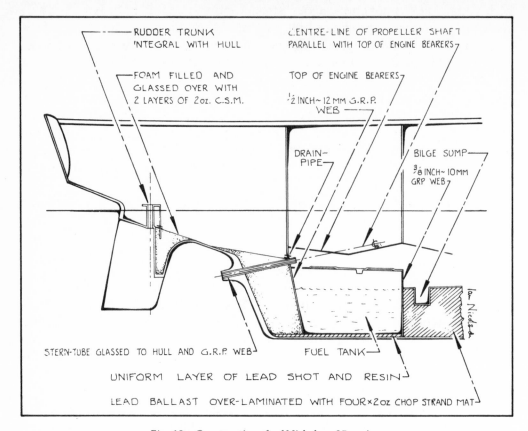

RUDDER TRUNK
INTEGRAL WITH HULL

CENTRE-LINE OF PROPELLER SHAFT
PARALLEL WITH TOP OF ENGINE BEARERS

FOAM FILLED AND
GLASSED OVER WITH
2 LAYERS OF 2oz. C.S.M.

TOP OF ENGINE BEARERS

$\frac{1}{2}$ INCH ~ 12 MM G.R.P.
WEB

DRAIN-
PIPE

BILGE SUMP

$\frac{3}{8}$ INCH ~ 10MM
GRP WEB

STERN-TUBE GLASSED TO HULL AND G.R.P. WEB

FUEL TANK

UNIFORM LAYER OF LEAD SHOT AND RESIN

LEAD BALLAST OVER-LAMINATED WITH FOUR×2oz CHOP STRAND MAT

Fig. 10   Construction aft of Nicholson 35 cruiser

So that bilge-water will not slop high up in the hull when the boat is heeled, it should be channelled to a sump. In this craft the skeg and aft end of the fin keel are filled with foam, then glassed over. This glass gives a measure of local strength, is fairly smooth and not hard to clean.

Each bulkhead has a small pipe through at the bottom by way of a limber hole. The water which gets inboard aft runs over the top of the fuel tank and into the sump where the bilge pump strum box is secured.

Since this boat was designed informed opinion has turned away from built-in fuel tanks, and it is now usual to have either metal tanks or flexible plastic tanks which will fit in the same deep bilge recess as the built-in tank shown here.

If this craft runs aground there is a good chance she will not be holed so that water floods in. The fin either has the ballast in it, or a thin layer of ballast topped by the fuel tank, or a deep layer of foam with glass along the top.

The section of the engine-bearers where the engine feet lie runs parallel with the propeller shaft centre-line. To avoid the bearers tapering out weakly at the aft end, with insufficient depth, they are cranked up slightly and extended to the bulkhead where they are strongly secured. At the next bulkhead forward they are sloped down to save weight, and to avoid excessive height which would obtrude into the cabin accommodation.

layers of glassing in such a way that water simply cannot reach the iron. Either a resin which never lets water through is used, or the glassing in is overpainted with four coatings of two-pot polyurethane paints.

Ballast 'systems' are mixtures which can be shovelled or poured into the keel recess. They are heavy, supposed to be sea-water resistant and are certainly easy to handle in many respects. At first glance they seem to be the answer to everyone's prayer till they are examined in detail. First they tend to be too light; typically they give a keel density of about 350 lb per cubic foot, whereas iron weighs 450 lb per cubic foot, and lead about 700 lb per cubic foot. So an iron filled ballast keel which is not quite perfectly packed in may well have a higher density, and can be cheaper.

'Systems' vary but they are often of iron shot or granules with a resin which solidifies when mixed with a hardener. It may be essential, or at least advisable to hire a cement mixer to be sure that the 'system' is properly churned up before it is poured into the keel. Ballast 'systems' are advertised in yachting magazines and sold complete with instructions for their use.

Whatever type of internal ballast is chosen it is usual to leave out some of the total weight until after the boat is afloat. Before the boat is launched pencil marks are made at the bow and stern to show where she should float. Once afloat the ballast is added till both marks are exactly on the water-line. Just how much is left out of the boat depends on a whole range of factors including the number of identical boats already afloat (not forgetting that no two boats are ever quite identical), the skill of the designer and builder, their courage, and the amount of extra gear which has been put aboard. It would be rare to put less than 70 per cent of the total in before launching, but if more than 90 per cent is put in this does not leave much latitude if the boat is much down by the bow or stern. It may be necessary to pile all the unstowed ballast in a heap at one end to cure a bad trim problem.

The top of the ballast should be finished off so that it slopes, or extends in a series of steps, down to the lowest point of the bilge where the bilge pump strum box is secured. Just occasionally an especially talented builder will make a recess in the top of the ballast at the lower point and drop the strum box down into the hollow, so that almost the very last drop of bilge-water can be pumped out.

=10 *Fitting a moulded deck*=

A hull without a deck lacks strength so that it is slack. Even if it has many more frames or stringers than usual, even if it has lots of well glassed-in, close-spaced bulkheads, without the deck the shell may change shape.

Professional builders like to put into the hull as much of the machinery, furniture, wiring, piping, indeed everything possible, before the deck goes on. To overcome the problem of excessive hull flexiness, they use special cradles. These are made up of a succession of athwartships shapes secured to a back-bone, in a design which is cheap and simple, but good at holding the hull in exactly the right way. Each shape is like a rectangle with a bulkhead cut out. To make up a cradle: assume there is a bulkhead at say 6, 9 and 15 feet from the bow. These bulkheads are cut from rectangles of plywood. The scrap pieces have the shape of the boat at 6, 9 and 15 feet from the bow. The cut-out shapes are enlarged by the thickness of the hull, which varies from the sheer down to the centre-line. This enlargement is increased by say ½ inch (12 mm) and padding of this thickness is secured all round the edge of the cutaway shapes. Next these shapes are set up at the correct intervals, and fixed to a pair of fore-and-aft stringers along the bottom, with more stringers secured to the sides of the shapes. Diagonal straps are added too.

The hull can now be dropped into this cradle, which is like a skeleton female mould. Ideally each external shape should come right at each bulkhead inside the hull so that there is no tendency for the shell to be pushed in at any point. A production boatbuilder will make this cradle early on in the course of building a series of identical boats, as it is such a valuable tool for speeding production. He may well secure many if not all the deck fittings to the deck moulding before it is lifted onto the hull. Working with the deck moulding set up on trestles at a convenient height from the ground speeds up work, reduces mistakes, enables less skilled shipwrights to be used and avoids the need for wandering lead lights in awkward corners under the cockpit. The advantages are so numerous that the snags fade away. One trouble with this technique, however, is that some fittings end up being secured in such a way that they cannot be removed once the deck is on, short of cutting out part of the deck or a bulkhead. The deck is heavier once the fittings are on, hatches may not remain totally watertight if the deck is twisted while it is being fitted, there is a temptation to ignore future maintenance problems. Taking a dispassionate view, these factors are serious but can be avoided with thought and planning.

Amateurs have an entirely different problem. For most of them the extra time taken to put in furniture, piping and wiring, etc., is not so critical. If the deck is not on it is certainly easier to get an engine inboard, and some tanks are awkward to handle through a hatchway. For most amateurs it is a mistake to have a hull delivered without the deck fitted. Few people will want to make a suitable external cradle which will only be used for a single boat. More important, the arrival of a hull which is flexible makes lifting off the lorry more difficult. As the crane takes the load the shell is bound to distort and cracking may occur at the top corners of the transom, or at the bow. If, as is usual, the deck is resting more or less exactly in place, but unsecured, it will be even more pliable than the hull shell. Cracking is likely at hatch and cockpit corners, and at other areas of stress concentration.

If an amateur is very anxious to save money, he might order the hull with the deck bolted down, but with only half or one third the total number of bolts put in. He can use his own labour, and his friends, to put in the remaining bolts. Securing a deck to its hull flange should be carried out like any other job where watertightness is needed, and where one large component is fixed by bolts to another. First all the bolts are secured just hand tight, then they are pulled down progressively, just firmly and far from rigidly, starting from the bow and working aft, port and starboard together. Finally they are taken up tight, again working from forward, both sides together.

If the boat arrives at an amateur's building site with half the bolts in, the holes for the remainder are drilled, then they are put in as described above. During the final tightening the original set of bolts put in by the hull moulder will need tightening up at the same time as the new set.

As the bolts are tightened the waterproof bedding which has been liberally coated on the hull flange spews out. If at some point along the length of the sheer no bedding appears the builder should stop and think – very hard. Did he skimp or worse still miss a short length of the flange when he was smearing on the 'goo'? Surveyors, tracing deck leaks, have more than once found that the bedding is not continuous all round; perhaps lunch intervened when the bedding was being spread, or the supply of material ran out, or there was a distraction. As this type of deck leak is so expensive to cure and so hateful, it is best to make sure during the bolting down process that there is a continuous 'spew' right round the boat. Of course if a tape material like 'Kwikseal' or 'Inseal' is being used, there will be no discharge along the seam edge. To be sure that the seal is wide and continuous, I like to be able to see the edge of a tape seal, so that I can be certain that there is no gap in it. This sort of double-checking makes the difference between a well-built boat and one that may just be satisfactory.

Many craft have a toe-rail bolted down at the same time as the deck is secured to hull. It is a sensible economy to use one lot of bolts to do the two jobs. However, it is not always easy, especially on a large boat, to pin down the toe-rail and the deck onto the hull all in one neat operation. To make the job simple every third or fifth bolt is put in, securing the deck onto the hull. Then the toe-rail is laid in place and its bolts put right through the deck and hull flange.

Whatever procedure is used, there must be continuous bedding beneath the

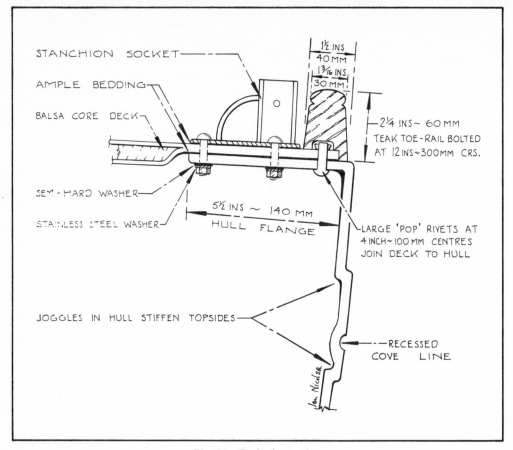

STANCHION SOCKET

AMPLE BEDDING

BALSA CORE DECK

1½ INS / 40 MM

1³⁄₁₆ INS / 30 MM

2¼ INS ~ 60 MM TEAK TOE-RAIL BOLTED AT 12 INS ~ 300MM CRS.

SEMI-HARD WASHER

STAINLESS STEEL WASHER

5½ INS ~ 140 MM HULL FLANGE

LARGE 'POP' RIVETS AT 4 INCH ~ 100 MM CENTRES JOIN DECK TO HULL

JOGGLES IN HULL STIFFEN TOPSIDES

RECESSED COVE LINE

Fig. 11   Deck edge section

An extra wide flange extends all round the top of the hull moulding of the standard Nicholson 24 ft 2 in. (7.4 metre) waterline sloop. It makes a strong base for the stanchion sockets, though some builders would in addition fit a wood under-deck pad for the bolts.

The close spacing of the hull-to-deck fastenings is noteworthy, and even the toe-rail which has only to withstand the side pressure of one or two heavy boots has bolts every 12 inches (300 mm). This small interval between fastenings is the mark of a well-built boat, and one reason why such craft are costly.

The shape of the toe-tail is called 'bottle-top' section and it is traditional, looks good, stands up to chafe, can be bent round the curve at the bow fairly easily, and gives that indefinable 'professional' finish. Even if a spindle moulder is not available to give the side dimples, at least the rounded top and tapered sides should be copied.

It is always a problem getting strength without weight and masses of costly material in a hull. Working on the principle that corrugated iron is much stiffer than flat sheets of steel of the same thickness, this hull has joggles along the full length of the topsides. Apart from stiffening the topsides the false sheer lines add interest to the boat and localise accidental chafe alongside a quay wall.

toe-rail as well as between the hull and deck. Each bolt too should have its squirt of mastic under the head before it is forced down tight.

To lift the deck onto the hull various techniques are used. For amateurs there is the 'beer barrel' method. This is useful for other jobs like lifting the engine in,

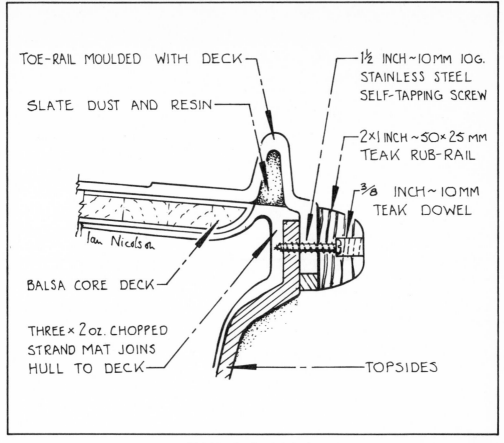

TOE-RAIL MOULDED WITH DECK

SLATE DUST AND RESIN

Ian Nicolson

BALSA CORE DECK

THREE × 2 OZ. CHOPPED
STRAND MAT JOINS
HULL TO DECK

1½ INCH ~ 10 MM 10 G.
STAINLESS STEEL
SELF-TAPPING SCREW

2 × 1 INCH ~ 50 × 25 MM
TEAK RUB-RAIL

⅜ INCH ~ 10 MM
TEAK DOWEL

TOPSIDES

Fig. 12   Fendered deck edge

If a wood rub rail is fitted over a deck edge join, it is possible to use a fairly crude overlap. The teak rubbing band covers unevenness along the bottom edge of the deck flange and prevents the fibreglass from being damaged alongside other craft and quay walls.

For economy and speedy building the toe-rail is moulded in, but if it gets damaged it is hard to repair neatly. However, this one is well designed in that it has well rounded fillets and top edge. On the other hand the taper on the inboard side reduces its efficiency as a device for preventing the crew from sliding overboard.

The self-tapping screws which secure the rub rail help to hold the deck to the hull, but the main strength of this join is in the three layers of 2 oz chopped strand matt. Glassing does the double job of making a strong bond and excluding water. This sort of join should ideally be done with the hull tipped over so that the area being worked is low down and all work is 'down-hand'. This helps the glass cloth stay in place before and during the application of the resin; it encourages the resin to run into the recesses, and stay in the freshly laid cloth instead of dribbling down inside the topsides.

It is not widespread practice to tilt the hull over for glassing up the deck edge, but for small boats the effort involved in lowering the hull over is often worthwhile.

When fitting the dowels over the heads of the self-tapping screws the grain of each dowel is lined up with the grain in the surrounding wood. The colour of each dowel should match the wood near it too. Dowels are made over-long, glued in, and left till the glue has had ample time to set. The final dowelling job is the cutting of the dowel end off flush with the surrounding wood, this being done with a sharp chisel. A rub over with glass-paper gives the perfect finish, fair and smooth.

or manhandling a completed hull out of the shed. It works like this: a suitable number of strong men who are experienced in small boat affairs (but who are not necessarily skilled as amateur shipwrights) are invited to have a beer or two or three in the building shed. When they arrive there indeed is the barrel of beer and glasses, but before the drinking begins, everyone gathers round the deck and on the command, 'Lift', all heave together. The men are arranged in lines,

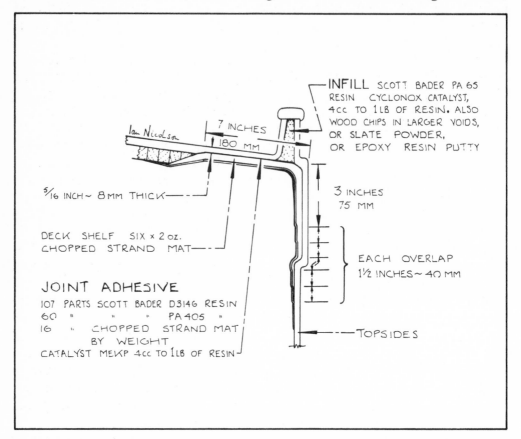

Fig. 13   Nicholson 35 construction detail

This is a typical deck-to-hull join. No mechanical fastenings such as bolts are used here, just multiple layers of fibreglass, carefully tapered out by carrying each layer 1½ inches (40 mm) further down and across than the previous one. This not only avoids a strong ridge which is likely to fracture if bumped, but it also looks neater.

The deck is made of a top and bottom layer of fibreglass separated by balsa wood. This very light timber is used with its grain vertical to achieve the best bond between the glassfibre and the wood. All round the sheer the deck edge turns up, to mate with the top of the hull. After applying infill a toe-rail capping is fitted. This may be a standard plastic extrusion or a hardwood such as teak or afrormosia. The former is much the best but costs a great deal more than most other timbers. However, the total quantity of wood used is so small that the extra expenditure forms a tiny percentage of the total cost of the boat.

Between the outboard edge of the balsa and the toe-rail there is a width of solid fibreglass, and this is where the stanchions are secured, as well as many other deck fittings. There should be a hardwood pad under the deck at each fitting. If a fitting comes in way of the balsa, this soft wood must be replaced by hardwood to take the through bolts.

port and starboard down the deck edges; they approach the hull from aft, with the deck pointing forward and raised just above the sheer; the bedding material has already been put on the sheer flange. The men walk forward until the fore end of the deck is over the bow of the boat; they lower the fore end of the deck onto the hull, then the next lot of men aft lower their section, so that progressively the deck descends onto the hull, gently and under control. Great care is taken to get the fore end exactly placed because once the deck is lying in place it sometimes cannot be shifted even slightly without effort. Once it is seen to be exactly where it should be, the beer barrel is broached.

For professionals it is not economic to use large numbers of men. Instead overhead lifting gear is needed with a long beam almost the length of the deck. This beam has pieces of rope tied to it every 3 feet (1 m) or maybe every 5 feet (1.5 m) for a large boat. The middle of each piece of rope is tied to the beam, and the two ends are tied to lengths of wood passed athwartships under the deck. When the long beam is lifted it in turn lifts the deck which is supported at closely spaced intervals. The deck is lowered onto the hull so that the fore end of the deck is exactly over the stem of the hull. The ropes from the long beam to the cross-pieces are untied; one by one, starting from the bow, the cross-pieces are pulled out sideways. In this way the deck is gently laid onto the hull. The bedding material must be put onto the hull flange before the deck is lowered. To prevent the cross-pieces from sticking to the bedding some polythene sheeting is put over the bedding, this sheeting being pulled away progressively as each cross-piece is removed.

It is common but not universal to fibreglass over the join of the hull to the deck, the glassing being inside the hull, never outside. The aim is to make the join stronger and, more important, make it totally watertight. To ensure that the join and surrounding fastenings are totally watertight the glassing is worked over the bolt ends under the deck edge. Cheap builders put in bolts 12 inches (300 mm) apart and sometimes almost double that distance, so the internal glassing is essential. It is normal good practice to have the bolts spaced 6 inches (150 mm) and sometimes even 4 inches (100 mm) apart.

One trouble about glassing here is that it makes repairs more difficult since it is awkward and expensive to take the deck off. Admittedly a repair is a drastic one if the deck has to be lifted away from the hull, and it is quite often more economical to build a new boat; even when it costs more to build anew it is sometimes a better procedure, especially if there are amateurs such as the owner and his friends available to take off the old fittings and secure them to the new hull and deck.

The designer will show on the plans the type and number of glass runs to put on the deck-to-hull join. If in doubt use three layers of 1½ oz chopped strand mat as a minimum with an extra run for boats over 40 feet (12 metres) and another for boats over 55 feet (16.5 metres). The mat has to be put on upwards, so it is best to use a thick or thixotropic resin, and quite small pieces of glass, say 12 inches (300 mm) long, at least to start with.

The work should be started at the bow and worked port and starboard together. Joins should be staggered and the glass worked carefully over each nut. Some builders glass in a plastic tube with electric cables inside close into the recess where the topsides meet the deckhead. Resin which runs down the topsides must be wiped off before it dries if the hull lining is the type which is glued on direct.

11 Deck finish

The top surface of a fibreglass deck is normally made smooth where fittings are to be bolted on, and smooth along the scuppers and the edges of the cabin coamings. Wherever the crew walk an attempt is made to give a non-slip finish. 'Tread patterns' are moulded in alongside decks, over the full extent of fore and aft deck, on cabin tops and sometimes even on wheelhouse tops. However, fibreglass by its nature is slippery even when left nominally rough, so these so-called non-skid surfaces are far from ideal.

To give a true grip in wet weather it is necessary to apply a gritty paint. Special compounds are sold for this purpose by companies which advertise in marine magazines. The choice can be for a material which is relatively smooth, or at the other extreme a paint which is so rough that anyone who sits down in oilskins on the surface for quite a short period will find his oilskin will no longer keep out the water! The technology here improves year by year so it is worth finding out about the latest blend.

Whatever paint is used it must be put on a completely clean, dry deck, so it may be necessary to wash then blast the surface for an hour or maybe more using a warm electric fan before applying each coat. The last coat is put on just before commissioning, after all the walking about by builders is complete.

In contrast to paint there are various materials sold in sheet form which are glued to the deck. Typical of these is 'Treadmaster,' available world-wide and wonderfully versatile. It comes in sheets 4 ft×3 ft (1,220 mm×915 mm). It is about one eighth of an inch thick (3 mm) and feels akin to cork tiling but it is a man-made substance. Different finishes are available, from almost smooth to a rough diamond pattern, and the choice of colour is green, grey, blue, fawn, orange and stone. Treadmaster is not particularly cheap so far as first cost is concerned but taking the long term view it can be most economical. The sheets are sometimes laid edge to edge all over the deck but this calls for a certain amount of skill and time. Usually the sheets are laid with gaps between which may be of the order of 1 or 2 inches (25 or 50 mm). Gaps are also left around the deck edge and around fittings to allow the material to be laid without very precise fitting.

This deck covering gives not only a remarkable non-skid finish but it also protects the fibreglass, adds a little insulation and takes the thump when some-body drops an anchor. It is hardly surprising that it has become so popular.

Treadmaster is used on yachts and commercial craft, on fishing boats and on racing machines. It is seen on foredecks and on cockpit seats, in the bottom of anchor lockers and on the main cabin steps. It is used in shower compartments and on the treads of steps up through the fore-hatch. Perhaps its main disadvantage is that it will not fold over the sharply rounded edge of a cabin top. Being something like cork it breaks if pushed around a tight radius. The makers supply a good leaflet showing how the material is glued down, so it is not surprising that Treadmaster is popular with professionals and amateurs.

A half cousin to Treadmaster is 'Trakmark' made by the Dunlop Company. This is a canvas woven material with a plastic diamond pattern finish on top. It is relatively cheap but not completely stable dimensionally and tends to shrink after a time. It has not achieved a great deal of popularity on fibreglass boats but anybody applying a plywood deck to a fibreglass hull might well select this economical material. It is particularly convenient for sealing seams and butts on plywood, it comes in a wide variety of colours, it does not need painting (at least for several years) and it stands up to a good deal of wear and tear. The manufacturers supply a leaflet describing the use of this material and it too can be used on cabin soles, particularly on commercial craft, or in the fo'c'sle or working area such as on a plywood sole in an engine space.

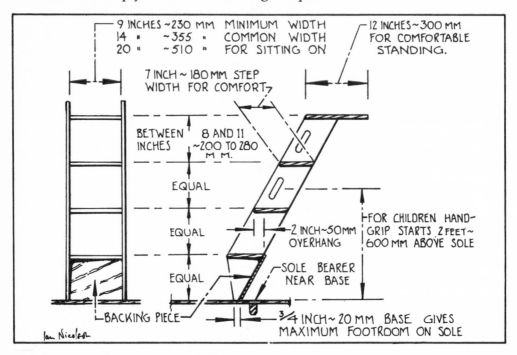

Fig. 14 Comfortable cabin steps

In a small boat the steps may have to be crammed into a small space. Where possible the dimensions and details shown here should be followed to make the steps easy and safe to use in all weathers.

It is often comfortable and convenient to sit on the steps, provided they are wide enough. The same applies to standing on them for long periods. The top step is one of the favourite positions in the ship, but it should not be so narrow that it requires the skill of a monkey to stay put.

By having a backing piece across the bottom the whole set of steps is prevented from distorting athwartships or 'wracking'. This backing piece is not always extended right up partly to save material costs and weight, partly to allow toes to go right through at each step.

The side pieces are narrowed as much as possible at the bottom to give the best foot-room on the sole in an area where it is often needed, near the galley or chart table.

Just occasionally fibreglass decks are covered with wood and this is where teak is by far and away the best timber. The aim here is to give a very fine appearance, improve the insulation, make the deck relatively non-slip, maybe stiffen the deck somewhat and also protect it from dropped anchors.

Since the wood is secured by screws driven upwards through the fibreglass there must be sufficient thickness of timber for each screw to grip tightly. Sometimes half inch wood is used, but this seems to me to be an unjustified risk. The wood deck will be scrubbed and occasionally scraped so that the tip of each screw must not be too near the surface otherwise the screw ends will become exposed after the boat has been in use for a few years. As a result the wood has to be ¾ inch (20 mm) or more in thickness. It is usual to keep the planks quite narrow to give the best appearance and 2 inches (50 mm) is a fairly typical width. The planks should be fastened to the deck edge and traditionally rebated into a joggled king plank which is down the centre line of the fore and aft decks.

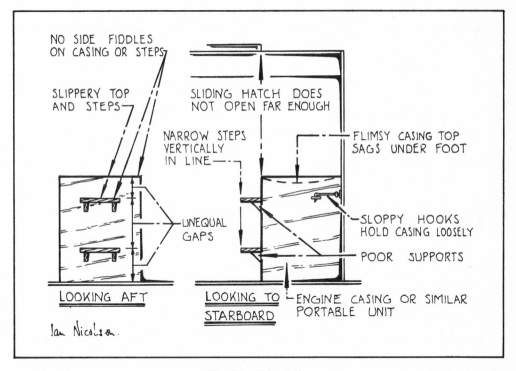

Fig. 15 Bad practice

Grouped here are all the troubles to avoid when designing and making cabin steps. The hatch which does not open far enough will result in bashed heads. If there is no way to avoid a hatch opening which is not well forward of the top steps, some padding is needed to minimise the bruises.

Steps are often fitted up engine casings, and as a man may crash heavily on the steps in an emergency, everything must be strong enough to take the thumping without flinching.

All the steps should be the same distance apart, even though in this case the top one is much wider, and even though the bottom one is the sole. Steps without side pieces are dangerous when a boat is heeling or rolling as feet slip off sideways, especially if the steps are not made skid-proof.

To save money and time the king plank may be made with straight edges, but it will lack the professional touch.

To cope with the varying shape of the deck from forward to aft the planks may be tapered but this needs some skill since each plank must taper the same amount as its neighbour. If all the planks start off 2 inches wide then they must all be exactly 1¾ inches wide at a particular line across the deck, and they must all be exactly 1½ inches wide at another line right across the deck. This precise tapering requires careful pre-planning and measurements. The deck width is divided up into an even number amidships and into the same number at stations forward and aft. Anyone not used to this work is advised to draw out the deck plan to the largest possible scale and mark in each plank before cutting any timber.

The wood must be very copiously bedded in a waterproof compound so there is no risk of leaks at each screw hole. Round headed brass or better still bronze screws are used and each one should first be fitted with a hard washer and then a semi-hard washer. Because the planking is relatively thin and it must be held down very tightly, each plank needs a screw at about 8 inch (200 mm) centres. Also since the screws must grip well they should not be less than 12 gauge. All this means that a teak skin on a fibreglass deck is very expensive in both materials and labour. Sometimes the cost is cut by skinning the deck with teak in limited areas such as on the cockpit seats, on the short length of the side deck where the crew walks most, and on parts of the fore-deck where the anchors lie, also possibly round the mast on a sailing boat where the crew needs a good grip and tend to be stamping about a good deal.

To give the wood deck covering a really good appearance each plank must be bevelled to form a seam which is filled in the traditional way, but not caulked. Modern two-part, rubber-like deck seam filling compounds are used, never the old-fashioned seam glue which has to be melted and poured in. In addition the covering board round the edge should be two or three times as wide as the other deck planks and the king plank down the centre-line of the fore and aft decks should be as wide, or even 50 per cent wider than the covering boards.

Anybody unfamiliar with the appearance of a traditional yacht deck may have some trouble producing the same effect. A visit to a big marina may be well worthwhile, armed with a camera. There is absolutely no mistaking the true professional finish. All the planks sweep in unison from bow to stern, without blemish, mathematically exact, a sight to raise envy and admiration.

===12 *Stiffening the hull*===

There are two contrasting attitudes towards hull stiffness. One view is that the whole hull shell should be of uniform thickness, with substantial strength over every part. The aim is to make the whole hull strong enough to stand up to rough seas, the impact of flotsam and the results of careless handling with no internal stiffening parts.

The opposing view is held just as strongly, and by the same kind of people. There are designers, stress calculators, accountants, boatbuilders and owners who contend that a hull of roughly uniform thickness (admittedly with graduations of increased thickness down towards the keel) is a wasteful and inefficient way of building. They favour a relatively light shell with a framework inside. This strong internal structure may be in the form of stringers or athwartships frames or a combination of these.

In practice most boats are built in the form of a compromise. There are some boats (mostly cheap and fairly small) which have no internal stiffeners. There are some hulls, mostly racing machines, which have wafer-like shells with a complex 'rib cage' of internal supports.

As the dominant factor in most boatbuilding is the final cost, builders work to a price and compromise all through the construction. One way to cheapen a boat is to minimise the work of fitting internal stiffening. This is done by thickening the shell a little, by using bulkheads and furniture as shell stiffeners, and sometimes by cutting down the internal stiffeners till there is only a small reserve of strength to deal with crises.

Boats to be used for long range voyaging and boats which are expected to last a long time without trouble are given extra stiffness over and above the designer's standard specification. Modern production boats are built in a climate of intense financial competition, so an amateur completing a hull, or a professional keen to establish a reputation for fine workmanship may sensibly decide to space the stiffeners 20 per cent or even 40 per cent closer together than the standard plans indicate. This particularly applies in the areas which are highly stressed, such as in way of the mast and ballast or centre-board of a sailing yacht, and by the engines and propeller shafts of a power boat.

That criss-cross web of floors and longitudinal stringers below the sole amidships on the typical modern sailing yacht, sometimes called the 'spider', is very often designed with a view to cheap fabrication, and seldom with severe grounding in mind. When it is remembered that modern sailing yachts so often have steeply sloping leading edges to their keels it is appreciated that grounding at speed results in a severe shock to the whole boat. She is brought up short, unlike old-fashioned yachts with gently sloping keels which rode up over the underwater obstruction and caused a fairly gradual slowing down. So even if the main part of the boat is not given any more stiffening than the plans require, it is good practice to beef-up the 'spider' for peace of mind, to achieve a good resale value and to reduce the chances of a rupture or leak when grounding.

To ensure that fore and aft stringers drain into the bilge they are stopped and restarted with an overlap, so there is no local weakness (see Fig. 9). This technique is reliable, whereas attempts to fit limber holes through stringers seldom work for long. Part of the trouble is that it is hard to keep limber holes clear and open during the glassing in. A more important difficulty is that the holes are seldom large enough to remain free of dirt so blocking up occurs, usually within months of launching.

Fore and aft stringers add to the complications of fitting bulkheads, so athwartships framing is sometimes preferred. In boats with ballast keels it is logical to run frames in line with the floors supporting the keel bolts. Frames are also put in at chain-plates if there is no bulkhead to carry the high loads. Just occasionally stiffeners are run inside the hull diagonally, starting at the sheer and extending aft and downwards. This avoids the problem of water lodging

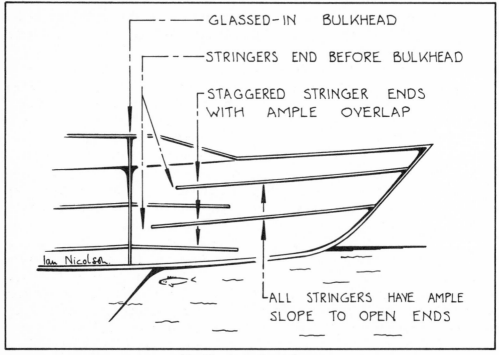

Fig. 16 Arranging stringers

Stringers which stiffen a hull should be fitted in such a way that no water lies above them. Some stringers are made with sloping top faces, but even these will trap water when they are located below the turn of bilge. One way to allow water to escape to the bilge sump is to fit drain holes but too often these become blocked. A better technique is to stop and restart the stringers so that water runs off them. Each stringer is carefully installed on a gentle slope with plenty of overlap so that there is no line of weakness. Stringer ends are not in line otherwise there might be a weak region where the strength of the stringers ceases. Ideally each stringer should taper out at the end though this is seldom seen.

above stiffeners and uses a smaller total length of stiffening to cover the whole inside of the hull, when compared with normal athwartships frames.

Stiffeners are made by glassing over a core material. The core generally has no function except to hold the added fibreglass away from the hull shell. For anyone with no engineering knowledge the way a stiffener works can be summed up in this simple example. Suppose we start off with a hull shell 4 mm thick and we find that it is not stiff enough; we double the thickness of the shell by adding more fibreglass, and the stiffness goes up not to double the original thickness, but to about four times. Now suppose we strengthen the hull a different way; we start off with the 4 mm thick shell, then add 8 mm of core material, then put an extra 4 mm of fibreglass, giving a total thickness of 16 mm. This stiffened hull is about sixteen times as stiff as the original 4 mm thick hull, even though the core material has a negligible stiffness. What matters is the separation of the two layers of fibreglass. As this goes up the stiffness goes up in proportion to the 'square' of the increased total thickness dimension.

As the strength of the core is unimportant, a light cheap material is chosen. Some people use cardboard tubes, cheap rope, plastic tube, or aluminium alloy channel with a series of cuts to make it bend effortlessly. One of the best materials is Polyisocyanate* because it is so cheap, light and easy to slice up into strips any required width. It is cut with the edges at 45° so that glassing over is as easy as possible. It is a temptation to recommend making the edge slope 30° because then the glass cloth would lie even more easily, but perhaps it is better to stick to 45° as this will show air bubbles if insufficient trouble is taken forcing in the resin and coaxing out all entrapped air. White bubbles indicate that there is air locked in the glass cloth and therefore a local weakness.

Occasionally wood is used for the core of stiffeners partly because it has some strength of its own; just as important, it does not easily compress. This makes it ideal in way of bolts which hold fittings. If a soft core material is used it crushes as the nuts are tightened. Because incompressibility is needed the wood used should be marine ply or a rot resistant hardwood.

So often in fibreglass boats bolts are put through the *edge* of stiffeners, either because of careless workmanship, or because the designer has not appreciated that boatbuilders do not have X-ray eyes, so they cannot see where an internal stiffener is when working on the outboard side of the hull. The moral is to make wood stiffeners two or three times as wide as the fittings, and take care to locate them exactly where the fitting is to go. As a final precaution, drill the first hole from the inside. If a bolt is put through the edge of a stiffener it is largely ineffective and may tear the shell, it is likely to crush the edge of the stiffener and let water in, and it advertises to anyone observant that the boat has been shoddily built.

*Polyisocyanate is sold in some countries under the trade name of 'Purl Board'. It is also called 'Rigid urethane board' and is available in different thicknesses typically 20 mm (nominally ¾ inch), 25 mm (nominally 1 inch) and 35 mm (nominally 1⅜ inches). It is rot-proof, acts as a good insulator and is exceptionally light. The weight varies according to the density but is about 1.4 kg/metre^2 in the 25 mm thickness. That is, the 1 inch thick board weighs about 0.3 lb per square foot.

The cost of putting in the bracing is high because it is a slow job. So it is logical for anyone buying a bare hull to get an unstiffened shell and put in the framework himself. The job can be conveniently combined with the fitting of bulkheads and some of the furniture. It requires care and patience rather than special skills. The main problem is getting the floppy, unstiffened hull to the completion site and unloaded without damage.

To achieve the maximum stiffening with the minimum material and hours of work fore and aft stringers are put in. They start off running parallel with the sheer, and taper together at the bow and stern. This results in better panel stiffness at the ends of the boat, just where the stresses are highest. If the girth round the belly of the boat amidships is much more than the girth at bow and stern, some stringers are kept short and extend only over the middle length of the boat, while others run full length, or nearly so.

Stringers are made with their top and bottom edges sloped at 45° to the hull shell, so that water will not lie above the stringers, besides making the glassing in quicker and easier. Unfortunately below the bilge water is trapped outboard of a stringer even if the edges are steeply sloped. These puddles result in mustiness inside the boat, gear gets wet, and occasionally no amount of ventilation entirely clears up the problem.

The procedure for fitting stiffeners is:

1   Grind the fibreglass back till the fibres are exposed. An electric drill fitted for disc sanding is a good tool for this or a Surform or rasp may be used. If there is doubt about the new glass bonding on, for instance if there is weathering, the surface is painted with acetone.
2   If wood is to be used for the core it should ideally be freshly planed all over to make sure it is free from grease and dust. Its inner edges should be rounded but this is not always done. Whatever core material is used it must be clean and free from dirt and oil.
3   Core material should be primed with resin thinned with between 10 per cent and 15 per cent styrene, though some commercial builders do not do this because it takes time and they argue that what matters is the bond of the new glass to the old, and a bond between the core and the new glass is important. Some would even say that once the new glass has set the core could be removed if there was a simple and economic way of doing this.
4   On the hull both sides of each stiffener are marked to avoid the mistake of putting the core on the wrong side of a single marked line. The stiffeners are usually put in place at the same time as they are glassed, and not in a batch ahead of the glassing work. This is because so many types of core material will not stay exactly where laid till glass is worked over them.
5   Electric cables or water pipes may be laid through or under the core prior to glassing in.
6   Resin which is compatible with the one used to build the shell is painted onto the hull each side of the stiffener, then the first layer of chopped strand

mat, carefully pre-wetted, is laid over the stiffener and well pressed with a wetted resin brush down onto the hull. It is best to start with pieces of glass not much more than about 10 inches (250 mm) long. With experience longer pieces of mat are used. The first layer of mat will extend perhaps 1½ inches (30 mm) each side of the stiffener.

7   At least two and sometimes four layers of chopped strand mat are put over each stiffener. Each layer extends about ¾ inch (20 mm) for every 20 feet (6 m) of boat overall length. For example the stiffeners of a 40 feet (12 m) boat might be 2 inches (50 mm) wide, and 1 inch (25 mm) high. To cover the stringers the first layer of cloth would need to be 4 inches (100 mm) wide. To this must be added ¾ inch each side (20 mm), making a total of 1½ inches (40 mm) so the first lot of chopped strand mat would be about 5½ inches (140 mm). The next layer would be at total of 1½ inches wider (40 mm) giving 7 inches (175 mm) and so on.

8   The longitudinal joins in the cloth are staggered, and care is taken to build up the glassing in a neat way taking special care to cover over each end of each stiffener.

═══13 *Making bulkheads*═══

Bulkheads and partial bulkheads are made from plywood. Though some commercial builders use exterior grade ply, there is a risk that water will cause delamination, especially at the bottom. This results in accelerating soakage, so that the bulkheads come apart into weak wafers. This deterioration develops faster and faster. The discolouration creeps up the wood and the loss of strength in the delaminated areas is total. It is thus very poor economics to use anything but the best marine ply.

Bulkheads have so many jobs to do that they have to be yet another 'boat-building compromise'. Normally they form an important part of the structural strength of the craft, resisting wracking and distorting strains, preventing the hull from denting inwards, resisting blows when coming alongside a quay wall and resisting forces which try to change the shape of the hull. In addition, the bulkheads carry principal strains like mast loads and ballast keel weights. They form a principal securing point for cabin soles, chain-plates, furniture, and sometimes for engine bearers. They divide the cabins, they usually form an important part of the interior decoration, they keep out the weather, block the travel of noises and smells and sometimes even limit the flow of bilge-water.

Part of the 'bulkhead compromise' is in the proportion of ply and stiffening pillars. To cut down labour the professional will have a stiff bulkhead with no pillars because the latter need cutting, finishing, fastening and trimming. Even if he stoops to using screws between the ply and the pillar, and so throws away parts of the available strength, the fitting of pillars still involves enough labour to make the job costly. However, there should be no visible ply edge showing, so some form of edge moulding has to be laid along the sides, top and bottom of the doorway. This might as well be combined moulding and pillars, especially beneath a sailing yacht's mast where the downward loads are so severe. So in practice most bulkheads have a pillar each side of the doorway. Partial bulkheads are normally pillared on the inboard edge unless they abutt onto a galley front or some similar piece of furniture which covers the edge and provides local stiffening.

By far the most popular thickness of marine ply for bulkheads is 12 mm (nominal ½ inch). This material is used for racing and cruising craft, for fishing boats and commercial vessels. It is a good compromise between cheapness and strength, between lightness and rigidity. It is adequate for divisions between cabins where a degree of privacy is wanted; it is generally stiff enough to need pillars only at doorways; it is thick enough to hold fastenings well provided these are driven first through the play and then into the pillar or floor-bearer, or other component. It is strong enough to carry major furniture items; it is light enough to handle reasonably easily inside a hull – no wonder it is used so much.

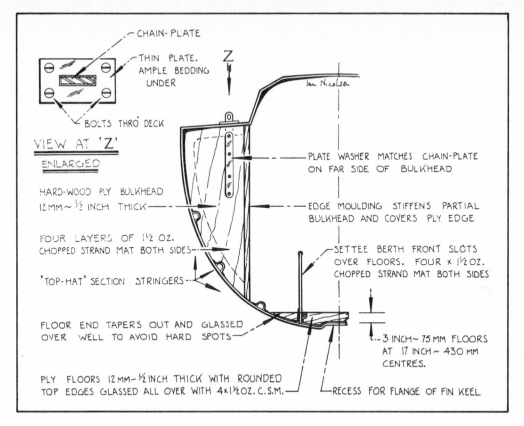

CHAIN-PLATE

THIN PLATE. AMPLE BEDDING UNDER

Z

Ian Nicolson

BOLTS THRO' DECK

VIEW AT 'Z'
ENLARGED

HARD-WOOD PLY BULKHEAD
12 MM ~ ½ INCH THICK

FOUR LAYERS OF 1½ OZ. CHOPPED STRAND MAT BOTH SIDES

'TOP-HAT' SECTION STRINGERS

FLOOR END TAPERS OUT AND GLASSED OVER WELL TO AVOID HARD SPOTS

PLY FLOORS 12 MM ~ ½ INCH THICK WITH ROUNDED TOP EDGES GLASSED ALL OVER WITH 4×1½OZ. C.S.M.

PLATE WASHER MATCHES CHAIN-PLATE ON FAR SIDE OF BULKHEAD

EDGE MOULDING STIFFENS PARTIAL BULKHEAD AND COVERS PLY EDGE

SETTEE BERTH FRONT SLOTS OVER FLOORS. FOUR × 1½ OZ. CHOPPED STRAND MAT BOTH SIDES

3 INCH ~ 75 MM FLOORS AT 17 INCH ~ 430 MM CENTRES.

RECESS FOR FLANGE OF FIN KEEL

Fig. 17   Securing a bulkhead and chain-plates

Though this section is of the 'Bolero' ¼ tonner, the techniques shown can be used on all sizes of boat. The method of securing chain-plates is widely used. Some builders put only common washers on the chain-plate bolts, but these 'pull in' and crush the wood, causing a local weakness. On boats over about 35 feet (10 metres) overall length it is usual to double the bulkhead in way of a chain-plate, if building to a good standard.

An exposed ply edge is ugly and not seen on well-finished craft. Hardwood rebated edge pieces are usual; in this sketch the edge moulding considerably stiffens the bulkhead provided there are plenty of screws or better still bolts holding it. On the best craft as well as the metal fastenings there will be a waterproof glue.

The 'top-hat' section stringers add enormously to the strength of the hull, but water will lie above them unless there are limber holes at the lowest points along their lengths. Sometimes a stringer is stopped near its low point, and restarted a short distance further on. This allows water to drain off the stringer. To bridge the gap, there will be a short length of stringer clear above or below the main length of stringer, and overlapping it.

In craft between about 23 feet (7 m) and 50 feet (15 m) it is not unusual to find all the bulkheads are of 12 mm ply. Where lightness matters some bulkheads will be of 8 or 10 mm ply, especially in craft under about 33 feet (10 m). For boats under about 28 feet (8.5 m) intended for racing bulkheads may be as light as 6 mm, especially if the area is small. For instance, the end bulkheads within the forward and aft one sixth of the boat's length may be made of this light material. Or a partial bulkhead under berths may be as light as 6 mm.

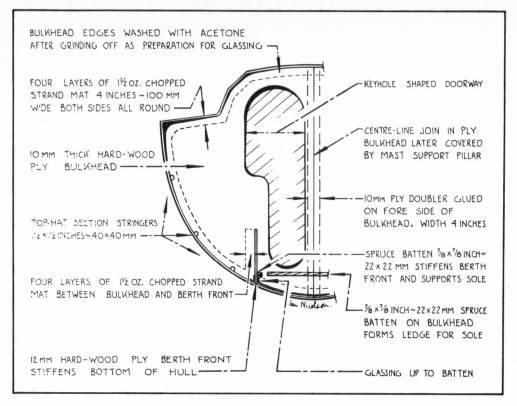

BULKHEAD EDGES WASHED WITH ACETONE
AFTER GRINDING OFF AS PREPARATION FOR GLASSING

FOUR LAYERS OF 1½ OZ. CHOPPED
STRAND MAT 4 INCHES ~100 MM
WIDE BOTH SIDES ALL ROUND

10 MM THICK HARD-WOOD
PLY BULKHEAD

TOP-HAT SECTION STRINGERS
.2 × .2 INCHES ~40×40 MM

FOUR LAYERS OF 1½ OZ. CHOPPED STRAND
MAT BETWEEN BULKHEAD AND BERTH FRONT

12 MM HARD-WOOD PLY BERTH FRONT
STIFFENS BOTTOM OF HULL

KEYHOLE SHAPED DOORWAY

CENTRE-LINE JOIN IN PLY
BULKHEAD LATER COVERED
BY MAST SUPPORT PILLAR

10MM PLY DOUBLER GLUED
ON FORE SIDE OF
BULKHEAD. WIDTH 4 INCHES

SPRUCE BATTEN ⅞ × ⅞ INCH~
22 × 22 MM STIFFENS BERTH
FRONT AND SUPPORTS SOLE

⅞ × ⅞ INCH ~22×22 MM SPRUCE
BATTEN ON BULKHEAD
FORMS LEDGE FOR SOLE

GLASSING UP TO BATTEN

Ian Nicolson.

Fig. 18   Mast supporting bulkhead

Looking forward at the mast support bulkhead of the quarter tonner 'Bolero', a successful David Thomas design, it is clear that there is no excess weight. The settee-berth front stiffens the hull and the sole support battens stiffen the settee fronts. To make the bulkhead take its edge glassing the teak facing (which is oily) is first ground off, then the wood is treated with acetone.

The keyhole doorway is designed to make it possible for the crew to get forward without cutting away so much of the bulkhead that it would be weak and without having the settee front obstructing the doorway. This sort of technique is common on racing boats of all sizes but is seldom acceptable on cruising yachts or commercial craft above about 40 feet (12 m).

Sometimes a bulkhead may be made of two layers with vertical or horizontal stiffeners between. Sometimes there is a pattern of vertical and horizontal battens onto which the two layers of ply are secured. The gap between gives a degree of extra sound and heat insulation, and the resulting bulkhead is strong for its weight, but usually expensive.

An amateur, not costing his labour but acutely conscious of the price of marine ply might well select one or two thicknesses lighter than usual, and criss-cross the whole bulkhead with stiffening pieces. These reinforcing parts are usually of hardwood; they should be glued and bolted, fastenings being spaced between 5 and 8 inches (125 and 200 mm). In practice many builders use screws to secure the stiffeners, except for the items like the pillars on mast-supporting bulkheads on boats over 33 feet (10 m) but this is symbolic of the current enthusiasm for second-rate work.

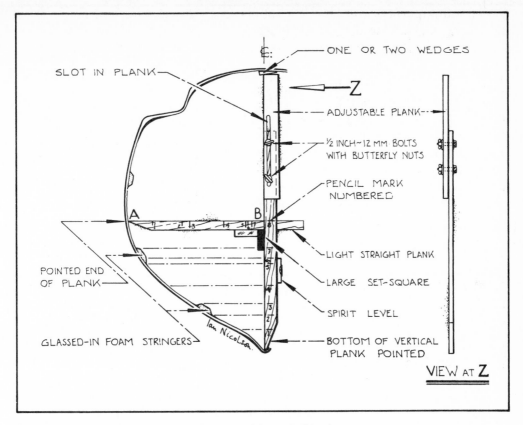

ONE OR TWO WEDGES

SLOT IN PLANK

Z

ADJUSTABLE PLANK

½ INCH ~ 12 MM BOLTS
WITH BUTTERFLY NUTS

PENCIL MARK
NUMBERED

A B

LIGHT STRAIGHT PLANK

POINTED END
OF PLANK

LARGE SET-SQUARE

SPIRIT LEVEL

Ian Nicolson

BOTTOM OF VERTICAL
PLANK POINTED

GLASSED-IN FOAM STRINGERS

VIEW AT Z

Fig. 19   Making a bulkhead

This drawing shows how the shape of a plywood bulkhead which has to fit inside a hull is obtained. The technique can be used for other things such as the shape of fitted furniture, or athwartships engine-bearers, or Formica covering for a bulkhead.

A vertical pillar is secured exactly on the centre-line of the boat. This pillar is made in two pieces which slide on each other. The two bolts are slackened, the top piece is slid up tight and the bolts tightened. A wedge or two tapped in the top jams the pillar securely.

The horizontal plank needs to be light to handle easily, but two people are needed to work it properly. It is held at various heights and pencil or chalk marks are made on the pillar and on the horizontal plank. These marks are numbered. A set square makes sure the horizontal plank is exactly level, just as a spirit level ensures the pillar is precisely vertical.

The pillar and cross beam are laid on the ply to be cut into the bulkhead, and the marks are used to give the height and distance off. When a set of points have been marked on the ply they are joined with a smooth curve, which the saw follows. Allowance must be made if a length of foam plastic is to be fitted round the outer perimeter of the bulkhead.

The stiffeners can often be designed to do two jobs: they may not only make the bulkhead stronger but also support berth ends or fronts, or hold up one end of the cabin sole, or be part of a bookshelf, or the doubler for a row of hooks holding oilskins. Stiffeners are often fitted round cut-outs in bulkheads in the form of edge mouldings which are L-shaped in section.

Almost always the grain of a ply bulkhead is vertical. If the ply is covered by Formica, or the bulkhead is painted or hidden in a locker, the direction of the

59

grain is unimportant. In theory if a cabin is high and narrow to the extent that the designer wants to disguise the fact he might specify bulkheads with their grain running athwartships, but the effect would offend most people.

Ply is sold in boards 8 feet (2,440 mm) long and 4 feet (1,220 mm) wide, but occasionally it may be found 5 feet (1,525 mm) wide. Where the hull is less than 4 feet wide one piece of ply is enough. Where it is less than 8 feet wide there is no difficulty joining two pieces down the ship's centre-line. Problems arise when the width is just a little more than 4 feet or 8 feet or 12 feet. If the hull width is say 2 or 3 inches (50 or 75 mm) more than the ply the deficiency may be ignored. This results in a bulkhead which has a small hole between it and the inside of the hull at each top corner. These holes are useful for passing through electric cables and the gaps are small enough to be bridged by the glassing in. Bigger gaps can be made up by joining on pieces either with scarphs or butt straps. The former take time and are not needed if the join is hidden. Butt straps should be wide enough to allow a row of well staggered fastenings to be driven in each side of the join, and so a strap width of about sixteen times the ply thickness should be used. Normally the strap will be made of the same material as the bulkhead, but where extra strength is needed a thinner ply may be used with butt straps on *both* the fore and aft sides of the bulkhead.

Centre-line joins are strengthened by solid wood beams across the top, and floors twice the bulkhead thickness or more across the bottom. In way of sailing yacht masts both the beam and the floors may be doubled, being on the fore and aft sides of the bulkhead.

The shape of the bulkheads may be taken from templates or measurements. Templates are usually made by production boatbuilders because they turn out a series of identical boats, and to save time they make a set of templates from the first set of bulkheads. An amateur can sometimes borrow these templates to mark out the bulkhead shapes on his ply or on large sheets of paper. Occasionally, the bulkhead templates or sets of dimensions are lifted from the mould-loft floor. It is risky to make bulkheads from tables of offsets provided by the designer unless ample allowance for later trimming is made all round.

A professional producing the first of a series, or an amateur building a single boat, will often get the bulkhead shapes from the inside of the hull, either making templates or taking sets of dimensions. The precise location of each bulkhead is marked first, taking the dimension from the plans.

Some designers work from the fore end of the water-line because this is a precise dimension, others start from the fore side of the stem, which may be a rather less precise point, especially if the boat has a sharply raked bow and the stem-head is a feathery mess of unfinished fibreglass. If the datum mark is the fore end of the water-line this point has to be transferred to the inside of the hull or marks at the sheer made port and starboard in line with the fore end of the water-line. One way to carry the critical mark from the outside to the inside of the hull is to drill a tiny hole right through, sealing it up later. Another trick is to shine a bright light outside the hull and hold up a knife blade so that it throws a

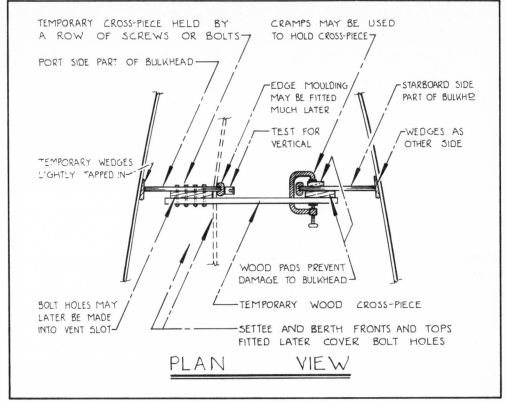

TEMPORARY CROSS-PIECE HELD BY
A ROW OF SCREWS OR BOLTS

CRAMPS MAY BE USED
TO HOLD CROSS-PIECE

PORT SIDE PART OF BULKHEAD

EDGE MOULDING
MAY BE FITTED
MUCH LATER

STARBOARD SIDE
PART OF BULKHD.

TEST FOR
VERTICAL

WEDGES AS
OTHER SIDE

TEMPORARY WEDGES
LIGHTLY TAPPED IN

WOOD PADS PREVENT
DAMAGE TO BULKHEAD

BOLT HOLES MAY
LATER BE MADE
INTO VENT SLOT

TEMPORARY WOOD CROSS-PIECE

SETTEE AND BERTH FRONTS AND TOPS
FITTED LATER COVER BOLT HOLES

PLAN VIEW

Fig. 20 Two-part bulkhead

When fitting a bulkhead which has a doorway through, or which is in two halves, it is important to have a cross-piece like a beam. This strengthens the bulkhead, preventing it from being too floppy to handle. It also ensures that the bulkhead goes in without bending and it gives the shipwright something to hold, when working the ply into position.

Once located the bulkhead is held till the glassing can begin by a series of wedges all round. If these are tapped in too hard the hull will distort locally, and the distortion will be permanent if the wedges are left tight in while the glassing sets. It is often possible to withdraw the wedges successively as the glassing in is completed.

Alternative ways of holding the cross-piece to the bulkhead are shown. A clamp or two each side is quick, but not so reliable as a row of large screws or small bolts. To be sure, fastenings need holes through the bulkhead, but these can be disguised or hidden below the tops of berths or settees or under galley work-benches.

While the bulkhead is being worked into position it must be checked for vertical on the aft face, and on the doorway jambs. The location of the bulkhead is pre-marked on the hull, exactly athwartships.

sharp shadow through. Measurements taken from the bow aft to the two marks on the sheer should be identical port and starboard.

Having established the datum, the position of the forward AND AFT sides of each bulkhead are pencilled inside the hull shell. If only one side is marked it is too easy to make a mistake, glassing a bulkhead's forward edge to a line when it should be the aft edge, or vice versa. The bottom and top points inside the hull where each bulkhead goes is marked, and for bulkheads more than 4 feet

(1.2 m) deep there should be intermediate points marked too. Measure from forward to the first, the second, the third bulkheads and so on. Check the distance from the aft bulkhead to the stern, as this is a good way to confirm that no error has been made. It is likely that this last dimension may be perhaps 1 per cent adrift. There are various reasons for this: the hull overall length may not be precise, the designer will have been working from a drawing which may have stretched or have been to a small scale. Before telephoning the designer or hull moulder it is best to study the drawing and check the dimensions carefully. Almost certainly it will be seen that the critical dimensions are the distances between the aft face of number 1 bulkhead and the forward face of number 2, between the aft face of number 2 and the forward face of number 3. Check that the bulkhead thicknesses are correct, and above all check the distances between the bulkheads. On most boats small discrepancies ahead of the forward bulkhead and aft of the last one are of no importance.

—14 *Glassing in bulkheads*—

Just before glassing in a bulkhead, the edges of the wood should be ground off with a disc sander. This is to take off the outer dusty, greasy layer of wood, and expose new clean wood onto which the fibreglass can bond well. If an electric drill with a coarse disc cannot be used, a Surform with a new blade is a good if slower substitute. The work should not be done days before the bulkheads go in, or a new layer of dust will settle on the bulkheads.

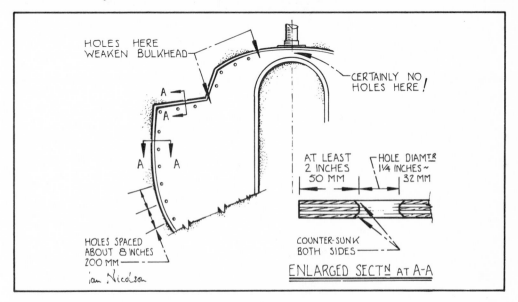

Fig. 21 Improved bulkhead glassing

A recurring source of weakness in fibreglass boats is the joining of the bulkheads to the hull. It is not always easy to get the glass to bond onto the wood even though the ply is harshly abraded to scour off the outer laminate, especially if it is of an oily wood like teak.

A simple way to be sure the glass bonds on well is to drill a series of holes round the edge of the bulkhead so that the glassing on one side bonds to the glassing on the other. This gives a mechanical 'key' and avoids a smooth, flat glass bond which once broken from the ply may progressively part with the ease of a piece of toilet paper tearing along the serrations.

To help the glass bond well and fit effortlessly through the holes countersinking is used. This makes it easier for the glass to sag through the holes, which incidentally should never be smaller than 1¼ inches (32 mm) diameter, regardless of the boat size. Larger holes are to be preferred.

The sketch shows the bulkhead in place but before glassing in has started; both sides must be glassed within a short time to ensure that the two sides of glassing are both wet when they mate through the holes. Keeping the holes away from high stress areas is common sense, as few bulkheads have much reserve strength beneath a mast or where the cabin top coaming meets the side-deck. Additionally the holes are kept away from the extreme bulkhead edges to avoid 'tearing out', but of course the width of the glassing-in strips has to be sufficient to reach well inside the line of holes.

This 'line of holes' technique can be used when glassing in other components. The line of holes is not drilled till the bulkhead has been cut to just the right shape.

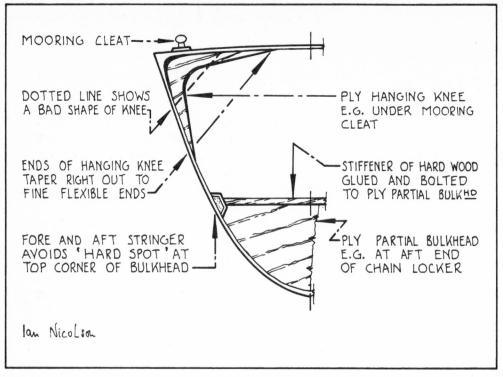

MOORING CLEAT

DOTTED LINE SHOWS
A BAD SHAPE OF KNEE

ENDS OF HANGING KNEE
TAPER RIGHT OUT TO
FINE FLEXIBLE ENDS

FORE AND AFT STRINGER
AVOIDS 'HARD SPOT' AT
TOP CORNER OF BULKHEAD

PLY HANGING KNEE
E.G. UNDER MOORING
CLEAT

STIFFENER OF HARD WOOD
GLUED AND BOLTED
TO PLY PARTIAL BULK<u>HD</u>

PLY PARTIAL BULKHEAD
E.G. AT AFT END
OF CHAIN LOCKER

Ian Nicolson

Fig. 22   Avoiding 'hard spots'

Throughout construction the builder has to avoid too much concentrated local strength otherwise 'hard spots' occur. These result in local cracking when the boat pounds into rough conditions or runs aground, or meets some similar crises.

'Hard spots' are caused by introducing stiffening which ends too abruptly. For instance, the hanging knee shown dotted (under the mooring cleat) has a corner on the topsides; above the corner there is ample local strength, below it only the unassisted strength of the topsides. As a result when the boat is heeled over and she thumps into a steep wave, the topsides are well supported, but only for the depth of the knee. So the gel coat cracks at the bottom of the knee, and maybe on deck at the knee upper end too.

This sort of trouble is avoided by having knees which have long tapering arms. The arm ends are spindly so they flex when heavily loaded. Not shown in the sketch is the glassing in of the knee and the glassing of the partial bulkhead.

Where the top line of the bulkhead meets the topsides would be another 'hard spot' but this is avoided by running a stringer fore-and-aft. So the local high stresses are dissipated by the stringer over a good length of topsides.

Sometimes a row of 1 inch (25 mm) diameter holes well countersunk both sides is drilled near the edge of the bulkhead, all round the perimeter, so that the glassing can get a really good grip. The glassing on one side is poked through the holes so that it bonds onto the glass on the other side.

When lifting the bulkheads into the hull greasy dirty hands are kept away from the newly scoured edges. A supply of short lengths of fibreglass cloth, somewhere between 9 and 18 inches (225 and 450 mm) long are cut or torn off the roll of cloth and stacked inside the boat close to the bulkheads' final position.

A minor bulkhead is fitted first, partly because it is light and easily handled, partly because if there are going to be problems, it is best to have them with a component which does not matter so much.

The hull is prepared by grinding away with a disc sander in an electric drill or very coarse dry glass-paper on a rubber or cork block till the surface layer of resin is chafed off and glass strands exposed.

The area where the glassing will go is wiped with acetone and the edges of the bulkhead where the glass will go primed with a mixture of resin and 12 per cent styrene. When this has set the bulkhead is put in place and held by wedges or props or even clean, dry sandbags on either side, or cramps, or a combination of these. Sometimes a few strips of glass cloth are used to hold the bulkhead before the main glassing in is carried out, but more usually the glassing goes forward in the usual way.

It is important to glass bulkheads on both the fore and aft faces. If this is not done, the strength of the join between the bulkhead and the hull drops off dramatically. In practice it is sometimes difficult to get *all* round both sides of some bulkheads for the whole distance, and if one face has glassing only round 60 per cent of the perimeter, it will normally be strong enough. However, the lengths glassed-in should be spread all round the bulkhead. In some cheap boats bulkheads are not secured to the deckhead at all nor down at the keel. Both these areas are every bit as important as the sides and sometimes much more important.

If a bulkhead is put in tight against the hull shell there is a possibility that it will cause a local distortion or 'hard spot', so that by sighting along the topsides outside, it will be possible to detect from outboard where the bulkhead is. In time cracking of the hull is likely, especially if the hull bumps against a quay wall or another ship.

To avoid this trouble the hull may be built up locally with extra layers of glass. However, this alone is seldom satisfactory. It is usual to arrange that the bulkhead either bears against a strip of ply laid round inside the hull or more usually a foam plastic strip is fitted continuously or intermittently all round between the bulkhead and the ply. If the ply strip is used its width should be 25 times the thickness of the bulkhead and have edges bevelled at 45°. It should be fully glassed in before fitting the bulkhead and the glassing prepared by grinding like the hull. The bulkhead size is reduced to compensate for the ply thickness. If foam plastic is used it should have bevelled edges, so that the fore and aft sides are at about 45° to the face of the bulkhead. This makes it easier for the fibreglass to lie neatly with no air pockets between it and the surface with which it is required to bond.

Regardless of boat size it is best to use 1½ oz chopped strand mat for bonding in bulkheads. Heavier glass will not bend and stay in the sharp angle between the bulkhead and the hull, especially if there is no fillet, that is, if the foam plastic is not bevelled. The first layer of glass will be quite narrow, perhaps 3 or 4 inches (75 or 100 mm) wide, and spread as far as possible evenly either

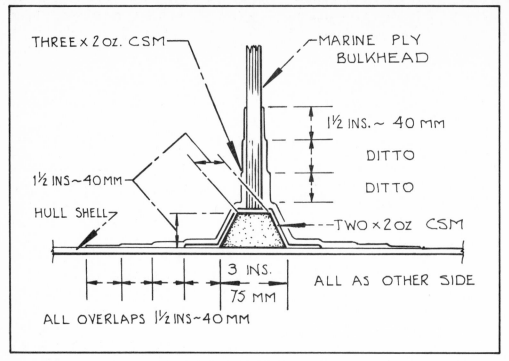

THREE x 2 OZ. CSM

MARINE PLY
BULKHEAD

1½ INS. ~ 40 MM

DITTO

DITTO

1½ INS ~ 40 MM

HULL SHELL

TWO x 2 OZ CSM

3 INS.

75 MM

ALL AS OTHER SIDE

ALL OVERLAPS 1½ INS ~ 40 MM

Fig. 23   Typical bulkhead construction

So that the plywood bulkhead does not press hard on the hull and make a vertical ridge round from sheer to keel, a foam plastic stringer is first glassed in using two layers of 2 oz chopped strand mat. Three layers of the same weight of glass are used each side to hold the bulkhead in place. This construction is typical of a boat between about 25 and 38 feet (7.5 and 11.5 metres).

For a boat which is hard driven, or likely to see service far offshore in rugged conditions, all the glassing may well be increased by 50 per cent or even 100 per cent. All glassing should be done so that each successive layer is larger than the previous one. Then if by accident one layer does not bond well, the next one, being larger in all directions, will bond in the previous layers as well as itself.

Some builders use a final layer of woven cloth or even 'finishing cloth' to give a neat appearance. This is good practice if the boat is built with no lining or other covering over the glassing in, so that the workmanship is visible all the time.

side of the join line. The next layer will be about 3 inches wider, and the next 3 inches again. This means:

1. If any one layer does not adhere well, the next layer will overlap it and bond itself and the layers beneath well.

2. The join will taper away which looks tidy, but more important, avoid 'hard spots'.

There are plenty of builders who secure bulkheads with only two layers of glass each side, and some shoddy builders who use only one layer. Most surveyors (those hawk-eyed fellows who see everyone's boatbuilding sins) insist that even in a small boat there should be at least three layers of 1½ oz chopped strand mat on each side of each bulkhead.

A rough rule for really strong building is that the maximum thickness of the glassing up should be about half the thickness of the topsides. And another one is that for every 20 feet of a boat's length (6 metres) the glass should extend about 3½ inches (88 mm) across the bulkhead and along the topsides. Of course, like all boatbuilding rules, this one needs adjusting according to the type of boat being built. For far-ranging offshore it is sensible to increase all these dimensions by perhaps 30 per cent. It seldom pays to reduce them.

Where the bulkhead edge is concealed by a locker perhaps, or a settee, the glassing can be run boldly in from the edge, along the hull. However, where the edge is exposed to view some technique must be used to give the edge of the glass a neat line. Some builders stick newspaper to the bulkhead with masking tape. This tape is run round the periphery parallel with the inside of the hull and at the correct distance from it; the glassing is carried up to and over the masking tape; when the resin is tacky the newspaper and all the tape is removed by slicing round the outer edge of the tape with a sharp knife. The trick here is to ensure that the knife is taken in a steady smooth unwavering curve parallel to the inside of the hull. Also the blade should be pressed so that it *just* slices through the masking tape but does not cut deep into the wood.

Another trick is to cover the penultimate layer of chopped strand mat with woven cloth or broad ribbons of fibreglass cloth. With care and practice this can be arranged so that the edge of the glass follows the hull neatly with no wriggles in the run of the weave. Yet another approach is to let the glass end in a rough way and conceal it with wood facing pieces, or a vinyl or leathercloth skin, or Formica or some other covering.

15 Cabin soles

A 'sole' is the board or a set of boards on which the crew walk. It is sometimes wrongly called a 'floor board'. A floor board is a set of slats secured to cross-pieces which lie in the bottom of a dinghy. One essential difference between a sole and a floor board is that the former is level and well above the inside of the hull shell, whereas floor boards lie directly on the inside of the hull. Another important difference is that a sole is designed for the maximum comfort and convenience, so that it is level athwartships as well as fore-and-aft; floor boards are principally to distribute the weight of a man's foot, which might otherwise strain the hull shell and cause a local rupture.

It is usual to fit the cabin sole early in the hull finishing schedule. Once the sole is in it forms a good working platform; it prevents tools and fastenings slipping into the bilge and getting lost; it forms a base for some of the furniture, it even cuts down the chances of injury when working because the inside of a fibreglass hull can be slippery.

Virtually all cabin soles are fitted so that they are parallel with the water-line. An exception is the forward cabin sole which may slope up slightly towards the bow, to give a bigger sole area at the expense of headroom. In the same way, an aft cabin sole may slope up aft. These slopes are unlikely to exceed about 1 in 7 otherwise the crew will tend to trip, especially in severe weather conditions. If the sole is required to extend well up into the bow it is usual to have a small step up, or a series of steps. Where possible these steps should be at bulkheads and not across the middle of a compartment.

Plywood is the most common material for cabin soles because it is quick to lay, strong, consistent in quality, easy to cover or treat and it does not expand or contract much, so that portable sections or access hatches are less likely to swell and jam.

However, it is expensive when costed by the square foot of laid sole. A well seasoned hardwood such as mahogany is sometimes used to save money, and on cheap boats, especially commercial craft, fully seasoned pines are used. If solid timber boards are used, they must be quarter sawn (or rift sawn) to minimise warping and to reduce wear.

The accompanying table shows typical sole thicknesses.

Sole bearers are often of a cheap soft wood, but as they get wet, they should be cut from a wood which is at least moderately rot resistant. Generally they are made like beams (but without camber), with their ends glassed onto the hull. Sometimes they are in the form of floors glassed in and designed to strengthen the hull as well as support the sole. This type of dual purpose floor is usually of marine ply.

Bearers have to stand a certain amount of abuse, for instance one of the crew may jump down through a hatch. Wood with knots which occupy more than 20 per cent of the cross-sectional area cannot be used, and major knots must be in the end third of the bearers. Typical bearer dimensions are given in the accompanying graph.

Each end of each bearer is cut at a slant, so that it fits on the inside of the hull neatly. This sloped cut spreads the load of the bearer over a reasonable area of the fibreglass shell, avoiding hard spots. It also makes it easy to glass in a useful length of the bearer. If the width of the sole is quite small, under 20 inches (500 mm) or thereabouts, there may be no sole bearers athwartships at all. Instead fore-and-aft bearers are glassed in each side, precisely at the same level and the ply sole lies on top. When this sole is lifted there is uninterrupted access to the bilge which is particularly handy if a tank or anchor is kept down there.

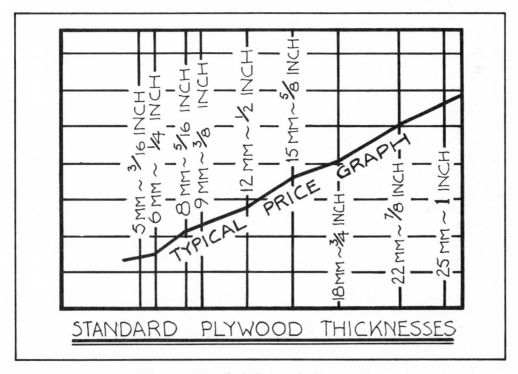

Fig. 24 *Marine ply thickness and price comparisons*

Marine plywood is made in nine different thicknesses, and sold in standard sheet sizes 2,440×1,220 mm (8×4 feet). This graph shows the sizes available, and also indicates how the price rises with increasing thickness. By substituting 22 mm ply for 25 mm, a cost saving of about 17 per cent is achieved. This is fine provided the boat is not unduly weakened.

An increase from 12 to 15 mm thickness puts the price of a bulkhead up by over 25 per cent so it may be better to use the lighter ply and stiffen it with vertical and horizontal pillars and beams. If the builder is an amateur the extra labour and material may be to his advantage, but professional labour is costly so a boat factory may go for the heavier, unstiffened ply.

Using this graph various design ideas can be assessed. For example, a double bulkhead made with two layers of 6 mm ply separated by pillars or beams or both will be cheaper (so far as ply costs go) than a single thickness bulkhead of 15 mm. It is also likely to be more rigid and a better sound and heat barrier.

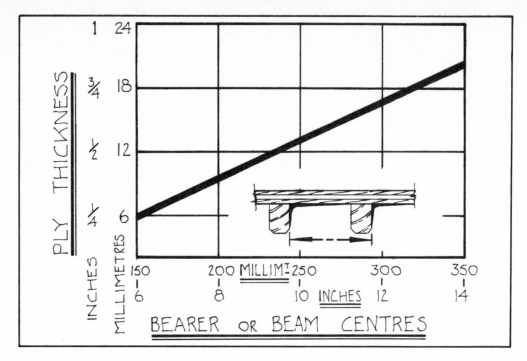

Fig. 25   Cabin sole, cockpit sole and plywood deck bearers

The spacing of bearers or beams under any ply cabin sole or other ply area which is walked over depends on the ply thickness. This graph is an indication of the distance (centre to centre) of bearers which are close enough to avoid a nasty 'spongy' feeling when the ply takes the weight of a heavy foot.

The graph is based on a good quality marine ply and firm bearers about 1 inch (25 mm) sided. If a fibreglass boat is to have a ply deck this graph is valuable for selecting the beam spacing against the ply thickness. A deck is assumed to be glued to the beams beneath it, cabin soles are laid loosely. It is also assumed that no narrow access traps are fitted in the sole, or if they are they are stiffened on the underside.

Another type of sole is fitted between berth or settee or galley fronts. The procedure here involves first fitting the vertical parts of the furniture. They are glassed onto the hull shell. On the inboard faces of these upright fronts of the berths (or whatever it is) there are ledge pieces for the sole. These supports are likely to be 1×1 inch (25×25 mm) section wood, glued and screwed or bolted at 8 inch (200 mm) intervals. The outboard edges of the ply sole rest on these narrow shelves. If the sole sags when it is tested a few athwartships bearers are added or stiffeners are glued on the underside of the sole.

Where the distance athwartships is more than about 20 inches (500 mm) a combination of fore-and-aft and athwartships bearers may be used. When athwartships bearers are used the forward and aft one in each compartment are ledge pieces secured to the bulkheads. These two bearers are fitted first and great care is taken to make sure they are exactly horizontal. A spirit level 24 inches (600 mm) long is preferred for all this work, rather than a diminutive level which looks as if it has escaped from a child's tool set.

Once the forward-and-aft bearers are in strings are stretched between them each side and all the other bearers lined up with the strings. Alternatively straight battens can be laid on top of the end bearers, and the other bearers secured so that their top faces just touch the battens. To make sure the battens do not sag they should be made of something like $4 \times \frac{1}{2}$ inch (100×12 mm) timber, set with the greatest dimensions vertical. If after all the glassing in is complete one bearer is too high it has to be planed down. Any that are too low have to be built up with packing pieces along the top.

Professionals building a series of identical boats make up templates. The bearers are cut to match these patterns and laid on a flat floor in the workshop the correct distance apart. Two fore-and-aft pieces are screwed or nailed on top of the row of bearers, making a sort of grid. This whole grid is laid inside the hull where it will be found to fit with reasonable but not sensational accuracy. It is glassed in at both ends of each bearer, and the fore-and-aft pieces (which hold the bearers together while they are lifted into the boat) now form bottom rails to support the berth fronts, or galley fronts or whatever the vertical pieces of furniture are which lie above the bearers just fitted.

When screwing ledge pieces to a bulkhead or berth front, the screws have to pass first through the bulkhead (or berth front) then into the sole support piece. If the screws are put in the other way they will pass right through the bulkhead and emerge on the other side, ready to catch clothing or fingers or stored equipment; they will look dreadful and they will not hold as well as they should. The way sharp screw ends so often protrude into lockers in production boats is an affront to civilisation. It is also a curse-inducing nuisance when these screws jag the plastic bag which contains the last dry clothing aboard, so that the crew have to stay cold and damp for another forty-eight hours.

If after it has been installed an athwartship bearer is too flexible, so that it sags when two people stand adjacent over it, a vertical support can be bolted to the front or back, and glassed in round the foot. This support need not be in the middle. Even if it is one quarter the length from one end it will reduce the unsupported length so that the bearer should be rigid enough.

Where the bearers have to be long and the builder is trying to save weight, it is worth putting in pairs of vertical pillars under each bearer. By reducing the length of unsupported bearers in this way the cross-section, and therefore the weight, is brought right down.

Access to the nether regions under the cabin sole is needed to store gear and to get at hull damage, to check piping and to clean out tanks, to hide hard liquor and to remove accumulations of dust or muck. For all these reasons there must be portable sections of the sole and ideally the whole sole should be removable. No piece of the sole which is designed to lift should butt up against a vertical surface, otherwise as the sole board is pulled up its edge will scratch the adjacent berth front or bulkhead. If the sole board rests on a ledge piece there should be a strip of wood fixed along the edge of the ledge against the vertical surface.

All the edges of the portable parts of the sole should be planed to a bevel of about 10°. This prevents the board from binding if it swells. To lift the portable pieces there may be finger holes (for cheapness) or recessed lifting rings on more expensive boats. Bolts through the board are needed to hold these rings because screws will pull out after three or four years – or months.

Fingers holes are not ideal because only a single finger can be poked down them; they are usually ¾ or 1 inch in diameter (20 or 25 mm) so occasionally hand slots are cut in the sole. Another idea is to drill a pair of 3/16 inch (4 mm) holes about 4 inches (100 mm) apart and have a light terylene loop as a handle. This looks a little untidy even though it is practical so slotted metal plates are sometimes bolted down to take T-keys.

Whatever form the cabin sole takes, it needs protection during construction otherwise it will get splattered with paint and varnish, oil and spilt coffee. Some builders tape over pieces of carpet, and others put down lengths of canvas held with staples or drawing pins. Another technique is to make the sole of the cheapest marine ply about ⅛ (3 mm) too thin and have this down all during construction. Just before the boat is commissioned the whole sole is lifted and each piece laid on decorative ply such as the type which has imitation deck planking, complete with thin black or white lines running fore-and-aft on a teak top veneer. This attractive ply is cut out to the exact shape of each piece of sole, and glued onto the top of the cheap ply sole sections. Before gluing the sole boards which have been walked over during construction need careful cleaning.

16 *Interior lining*

The purpose of a lining is to improve the appearance and the comfort in the cabins. It also gives a measure of insulation, helps to deaden sound, and makes the boat more habitable particularly in unpleasant conditions. Racing boats have little or no lining because it contributes nothing to the speed. Cheap boats have the minimum lining located only where it shows to advantage. The more expensive the boat the more extensive the lining. Some boats even have lined cockpit lockers, lined engine spaces, lined stern lockers but virtually none have lined fore-peaks and lazerettes (aft peaks).

In general the lining is not put into areas which are likely to get dirty or are used for stowing hard or heavy equipment, but this is not a universal rule. It is very seldom fitted below the cabin sole, but some craft are lined throughout before putting in any furniture and so they have what is virtually a total interior skin.

The idea of putting lining in lockers is partly to give that finished appearance which impresses buyers at a boat show. However, lining in lockers also protects clothes. For instance, if a boat is rolling downwind for two or three days on end clothes which are hung up can rub against the rough interior of a fibreglass shell and become badly chafed and useless. A semi-soft lining in a locker prevents gear like anchors damaging the fibreglass. The lining in lockers also contributes to the reduction in condensation and helps to keep the whole boat warmer in winter, cooler in summer and quieter all the time.

The strongest reason for reducing the amount of lining is its cost both in labour and material. Many types of lining, and there are a large variety, are expensive and take many man-hours to finish. A further disadvantage is that it makes access to deck fitting fastenings, chain plate bolts and sea cock bolts more difficult.

The interior of a boat is often damp and sometimes wet so whatever is used for lining (or indeed furniture or anything else) should be suitable for moist and even saturated conditions. Ordinary cotton and wool cloths are not much good unless very successfully waterproofed. In large vessels these materials may be used if secured on semi-portable panels which can be easily changed and taken out for cleaning.

Whatever form the lining takes it should not be secured with steel screws, not even the type which is chrome plated. Sooner rather than later the rust will come through and there is no place on well-built craft for mild steel screws in any form.

In Europe the job of selecting suitable materials is made easier in some of the bigger cities where there are Design Centres. Here it is possible to choose patterns and colours from a wide selection.

Linings are most conveniently divided into two basic **types: the first** is applied direct to the inside of the hull and might be called 'direct application lining', while the second is fitted with a gap between it and the hull and might be called 'spaced lining'.

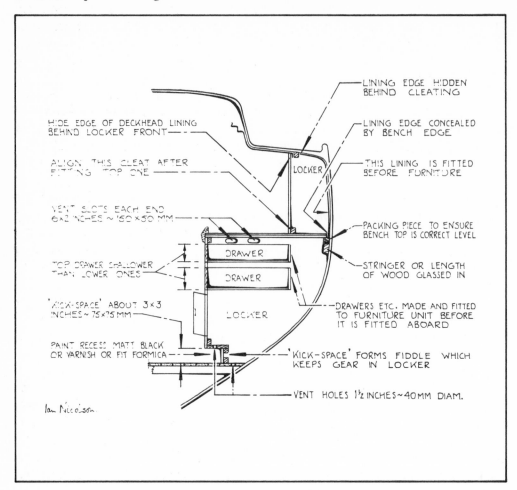

Fig. 26   Lining and furniture

Where possible the lining is put in before furniture, so that as the woodwork goes in it conceals the lining edges. Furniture is usually made up into units away from the boat and carried aboard for fitting. Each part has to be small enough to go through the hatchway unless furniture is installed before the deck is secured down.

Furniture may be bolted to bulkheads, screwed to glassed-in stringers, or glassed in. Sometimes one unit will have all three methods of fastening. At least three edges of each furniture part should be secured.

Working tops such as the cooking table, often called the 'galley bench' are normally horizontal but chart tables are often sloped between 5° and 15° towards the navigator's seat to make the charts easier to read. Furniture fronts are normally vertical but not always parallel with the centre-line of the boat.

The 'kick-space' allows the cook's toes to extend under the galley front, so that cooking is easier and it is not necessary to lean forward to work. A 'kick-space' weakens a furniture front unless there is a strongly joined panel at each end, or unless the front is secured to a bulkhead each end.

Direct application lining

The simplest of this type is paint. Special compounds are available for the inside of fibreglass hulls. One which used to be popular but which is now dying out is a speckled paint, which is usually off-white or cream and has in it brown or blue-grey flecks of different sizes. This paint has to be applied with a spray-gun and it gives a simple finish which can be washed down and is quite effective in an inexpensive boat or racing craft.

A better type of lining is glued to the hull and may be in the form of a leather-cloth or plastic sheet. These materials are available in a good range of different colours and surface finishes. The cloth on which the plastic finish is applied should be knitted not woven since the former stretches well and works into awkward recesses and round corners. A woven backing cloth is relatively stiff and less practicable though it is often cheaper.

Some of these cloth materials are what is called 'foam backed'. That is, on the hidden side of the material there is a thin layer of foam plastic cushioning, varying in thickness from about $\frac{1}{16}$ inch (1.5 mm) up to about $\frac{1}{4}$ inch (6.5 mm). This foam backing improves the insulation greatly and also helps to take up any unevenness on the inside of the hull. It is in short a forgiving material which hides a multitude of sins!

The edges of the lining present difficulties and where possible the material should be tucked out of sight. It may be slipped down behind berth tops, finished inside lockers, run down to just below the cabin sole or allowed to run in under the edge of the engine box. This technique, which consists of extending the lining material into a hidden area, or running it into some obscured recess saves a lot of time and work. Lining may be put on virtually throughout the boat before bulkheads and furniture and the cabin sole are fitted. In this way relatively few edges have to be worked carefully. The bulkheads and furniture are secured to lugs glassed onto the hull. The lining is cut away at each end. Round windows and doorways there are some problems but it is often possible to put the lining on first and then fix the door frame or window frame next, neatly covering the lining edge.

Leathercloth can be finished with a neatly cut line well glued down. Round windows the lining material can be brought just up to the edge of the glazing and then stopped with a precisely cut edge. A razor blade is useful here for giving a good clean line. To make the window fastenings look smart Plasti-domes may be used on bolt heads or even on small nuts. These Plastidomes were originally designed for use with screws and are nothing more than decorative plastic cups which clip onto nylon washers fitted under the bolt heads.

For areas low down near the sole which may be walked over, Treadmaster or Trakmark may be used. These are deck covering materials, available in different colours and finishes and designed for continuous hard wear (see Chapter 11).

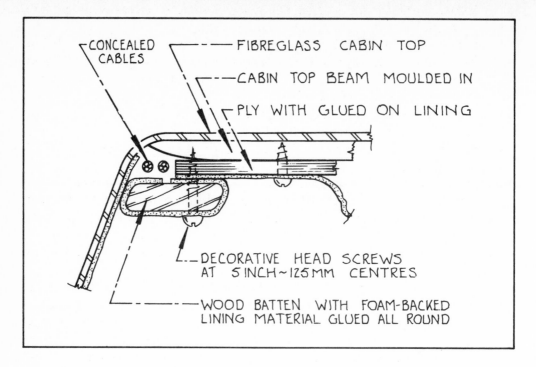

CONCEALED CABLES ———— FIBREGLASS CABIN TOP

——CABIN TOP BEAM MOULDED IN

——PLY WITH GLUED ON LINING

——DECORATIVE HEAD SCREWS
AT 5 INCH ~ 125MM CENTRES

——WOOD BATTEN WITH FOAM-BACKED
LINING MATERIAL GLUED ALL ROUND

Fig. 27   Interior lining

Fastening lining, and concealing its edges is a constant challenge. Whatever technique is used it should be quick, not demand much skill because a lot of the work is in awkward corners and overhead, and be easily dismantled.

This section through the top outer edge of a cabin top shows ideas which can be used in various parts of a boat. The side lining is glued to the flat fairly smooth face of the cabin coaming. As the deck-head has glassed-in beams it is uneven, so it is covered by a piece of light ply. Before putting the ply up with self-tapping screws into the beams it is covered with lining material glued all over. The foam-backed type gives extra insulation as well as covering local minor irregularities on the surface.

To conceal the join a batten is screwed up after it has been covered with lining material which will normally match, but may be a contrasting material or colour.

Whatever lining material is used it should be glued with the compound recommended by the manufacturers. Before buying both the lining and the glue it is important to make sure the supplier realises just how rugged conditions afloat are.

Spaced lining

This takes the form of a rigid material like plywood secured to stringers or beams or other moulded-in stiffeners, or onto glassed in lengths of wood or cleatings.

The ply itself is treated to give the correct balance between decoration and ruggedness. On a commercial boat one wants something like a really good varnish finish which is quickly touched up and can stand scuffing and general chafe. Varnish can be refurbished in odd moments and there is no problem with matching colours.

In contrast a boat which might be described as 'marina-fodder' will probably have some rather decorative, artistic, almost feminine lining which will look good, at least for a few years. It may not stand up to hard sea-going conditions, but such is the modern fashion.

Each panel is best made small enough for one person to handle easily, and the limit here is about 5×3 feet (1.5×0.9 m). However, where two people are working together a full ply panel 8×4 feet (2.4×1.2 m) can be managed and it covers a big area quickly. When working shorthanded two or three pliable wood props are most useful since they can be used to jam a panel in place, while screws are put in round the edge and across the middle. In cheap production yachts it is usual to put in very few screws and as some of the screws are mis-drilled panels sag away and even drop off when the boat starts to thrash through a lumpy sea far offshore. The correct number of screws for a given size of panel is given in the accompanying graph.

The ply which should be marine quality can be painted or varnished to give a very reasonable finish particularly for a commercial vessel. However, repainting or varnishing will be necessary every three or four years whereas a long lasting plastic does not need treating for many years. If the panels are covered with a leathercloth, or one of the modern plastic lining materials the reverse side should be given two or three coats of paint or varnish to prevent mildew growth and to prevent water soaking in.

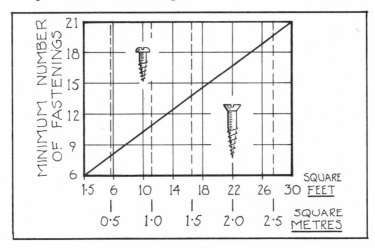

Fig. 28   Lining panel fastenings

The minimum number of fastenings needed to support a lining panel are given by this graph. Virtually all panels need at least six screws, partly because these fastenings are often driven in 'blind' and some may not get a good grip of the cleating or stringer hidden behind the panel.

Along the bottom of the graph the upper figures are the panel area in square feet, the lower line in square metres.

Where one edge of a panel is lodged behind some form of continuous support, such as a facia piece, the number of fastenings can generally be reduced by 25 per cent.

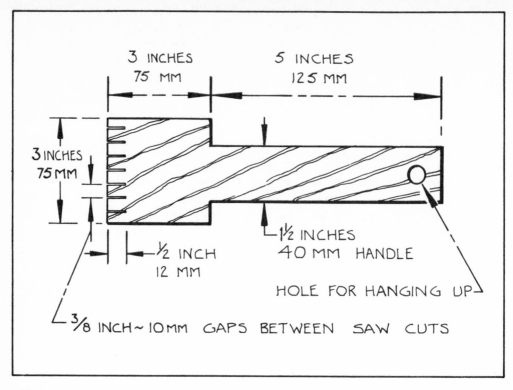

3 INCHES
75 MM

5 INCHES
125 MM

3 INCHES
75 MM

½ INCH
12 MM

1½ INCHES
40 MM HANDLE

HOLE FOR HANGING UP

⅜ INCH ~ 10 MM GAPS BETWEEN SAW CUTS

Fig. 29   Glue spreader

To spread the glue on cabin lining material or on the inside of the cabin, or indeed on any fibreglass or wood, this home-made tool is most useful.

The saw cuts ensure that there is a series of thin lines of the glue all over the area yet there is never too much glue in any one patch. Before any spreading job it is well worthwhile making up a batch of sticks like this from scrap ply. The best thickness is 8 or 10 mm ply (⁵⁄₁₆ or ⅜ inch thick).

If a batch of these spreaders is made up a long time before they are to be used they should be stored in a clean polythene bag otherwise they will collect dust and this inhibits good gluing.

When taking glue from a container, only a little is scooped up at a time, just enough to cover the end 'teeth'. If a piece of cloth lining is being covered it should be laid flat on a clean table. Once the lining has been covered in glue it is usually necessary to smear a second lot of glue onto the cabin surface where the lining is to go. This work should be done from the top downwards, with ample glue at the edges because a surplus can be wiped away after the lining has been secured in place.

Any of the different lining materials described under the 'direct application lining' may be glued to the panel to give an attractive appearance and good insulation. Before gluing on these materials the edges of the ply must be well rounded.

Panels are screwed up to wood battens which have been previously glassed onto the deck-head or onto the ship's side. Sometimes foam plastic stiffeners instead of wood battens are asked to carry the weight of a panel, and quite often they succeed. But the foam has no strength, so the only grip which each screw has is where it passes through the fibreglassing over the foam. The glass may be only two cloth layers thick, maybe only one on some shoddy hulls. This means that even with heavy gauge self-tapping screws the grip is poor.

On no account should the panels be screwed to a single thickness fibreglass deck or hull. Hollow stiffeners sometimes take the screws, but here the situation is like foam stiffeners, and the only grip each screw has is through the thin wall of fibreglass over the hollow. It is obvious that screws in this sort of position must be put into precisely the right diameter of pre-drilled hole.

Sometimes panel edges are secured by wood battens. For example, a lining panel may extend along the topsides and its forward edge lie along a bulkhead. To keep this edge in place a wood batten varnished or polished to match the rest of the decoration is screwed onto the bulkhead. The batten can have a quarter-round or rectangular section, or indeed any attractive section provided that outstanding edges are well rounded or bevelled.

Panels should not be glued or glassed in place for the following reasons: electric wires run behind them and these need periodical attention, panel covering needs renewing at intervals, repairs are more likely because when the boat flexes in use the bonding may fail and the panel become loose.

Screws through a panel must be evenly spaced, ideally round all four sides, with at least a few fastenings across the middle. Where there are no wood strips glassed in to take the screws the person completing the hull will have to add them. In this case it is common practice to secure the wood battens by 4 inch (100 mm) wide strips of glass cloth across the battens, at 12 inch (300 mm) intervals. This is adequate, but not the best practice and not recommended for hard used craft. These should have continuously glassed-in battens.

A trick which helps sometimes is to secure panels to wood blocks or chocks which have been put in for quite a different purpose. For instance, a lining panel under a foredeck might be screwed up to the wood under-deck chocks in way of the mooring bollard, stanchions and anchor chocks on top of the deck.

=17 *Interior decoration*=

The interior of a boat has to suit the job, the character of the owner, and yet it must not be too complex or too delicate or too refined for the people who have to make it, fit it, and use it. For instance, for offshore racing there is stark, tough, glinting aluminium alloy. This also suits some expensive, fast commercial craft like high speed pilot boats, police boats and coastguard launches.

At the other end of the scale there is the blatant luxury produced by firms like Heals of London. For sheer beauty and comfort a firm like this turned loose inside a bare hull is unbeatable. For many owners the cost is also impossible.

Between these extremes there is a variety of tastes and styles. Scrubbed teak is easy to keep clean – tough and seamanlike, but too sombre for some people and the price of this wood is four or six times the cost of lesser woods. A mixture of large areas of painted wood with edges of polished or varnished teak or mahogany used to be popular. The paint was almost always white or a very light colour so that the overall effect was trim and cheerful. It was easy to keep clean as most of the wear and dirty finger marks occurred on the polished or varnished edging. Some builders fitted the edge pieces so that most of them were simple to take off, and repainting the big areas was very easy. In spite of its advantages this style has fallen out of favour, the general feeling being that it looks too unsophisticated, too much as if a semi-skilled shipwright has completed the work.

A modern style which is used in a variety of small craft, by professional and amateur, is based on the use of plastic leathercloths and similar decorative materials. The fibreglass hull inside may be lined with one of these materials and the same cloth, or a contrasting one, used to cover bulkheads, berth fronts, sometimes even locker doors and occasionally main doors too. These materials are stuck in place with a glue sold by the same wholesalers who market the cloth. Because they require no painting or finishing, cloth finishes are not expensive, though it takes plenty of time and care to fit them well.

Some of these materials are about ⅛ inch (3 mm) thick, or more, either because they are naturally bulky, or because they have a thin layer of plastic foam backing. This gives several bonuses. It results in a degree of sound and heat insulation, it fairs over unevenness so often found on the inside of a fibreglass shell, and it covers hollows and humps in the mouldings, provided these are not too blatant. The extra thickness also gives an attractive 'feel' and minimises bruises when the crew are flung about in severe conditions.

A whole cabin finished with one type and colour of cloth is dreary, so there should be some contrast like wood trim, or polished wood bulkheads at least above waist level. The leathercloth can also be put in the upper parts of the bulkheads and the lower halves can be polished or varnished. If very large areas

80

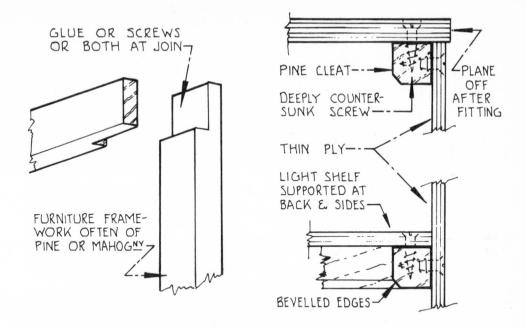

GLUE OR SCREWS
OR BOTH AT JOIN

FURNITURE FRAME-
WORK OFTEN OF
PINE OR MAHOG^{NY}

PINE CLEAT

DEEPLY COUNTER-
SUNK SCREW

PLANE
OFF
AFTER
FITTING

THIN PLY

LIGHT SHELF
SUPPORTED AT
BACK & SIDES

BEVELLED EDGES

Fig. 30   Furniture joins

On the left is the simplest type of join, a 'halving' or 'halved join'. This is useful for amateurs who are short of skill. The ends may be left too long and finished off after the glue has set, though great care is needed to avoid splitting the edges. This type of join is useful for all sorts of furniture parts.

The right sketch shows a section looking outboard through a galley bench, or chart table or similar structure, with a shelf beneath. Since the ply is thin it cannot be recessed. Instead cleatings are glued, or screwed (or both) on the vertical sides to take the top and shelf. These cleatings stiffen the thin ply substantially. Screws must go through the ply first, into the cleatings. At the top the screws are well countersunk so that Formica can be glued down on the finished bench top.

As the shelf is of very thin ply, to make it light and cheap, it needs supporting each side and across the back. If a back support cannot be worked in, the front fiddle may be strongly secured to give the shelf strength.

are covered with a plastic or woven cloth it usually makes sense to have contrasting cushions.

A source of inspiration for suitable materials is the Design Centre, found in major cities. Pattern samples are available here, as well as the addresses of suppliers. However, before venturing boldly into a courageous decorative scheme a guarantee is needed from the manufacturers that the material is suitable for life afloat.

Another source of ideas is any boat show, where the serried ranks of craft offer a variety of styles. A critical eye is needed as boats are often decorated just to attract buyers; many of these people are either not used to conditions afloat, or carried away by the carnival atmosphere and the sales talk. A cabin should be looked at with the head tilted, so that it can be seen as it will be when the boat is

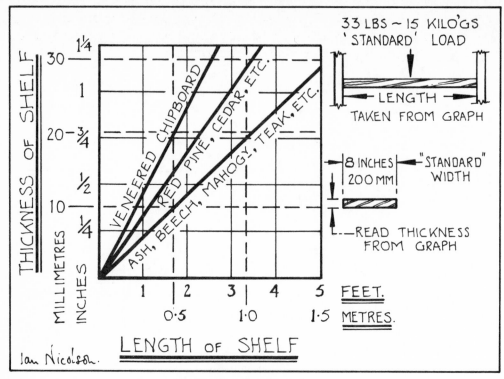

Fig. 31   Shelving design

When making up shelves for books, radio and other gear it is useful to know the safe thicknesses of material. Dr M. J. Fletcher devised this graph as a guide, based on a 'standard' load of 33 lbs. (15 kilos) and a 'standard' width of shelf equal to 8 inches (200 mm).

The graph shows up a number of valuable side issues such as the weakness of chipboard (which is one reason why it is not used in good boats) and the better strength of hardwoods as compared with softwoods. This confirms the principle that wood strength is roughly proportional to its density.

In practice boatbuilders do not always use these thicknesses of timber, but instead make sure that shelf fiddles and doublers well screwed on give something like three times the total section depth indicated by the graph.

heeled to leeward, or rolling wildly. Will the back-rests swing away from the panelling? Is the cabin sole too slippery? Will the locker doors stay shut even when there is a locker full of heavy gear behind them? Does the panelling make the whole of the skin including wiring, piping and even seacocks hard or even impossible to reach?

As with everything else on a boat, the furniture should be viewed with two conditions in mind: force 1 and force 12. If the components are suitable for these extremes, the intermediate weather and sea conditions will give few worries. In light conditions there are problems from too much sunlight, too much heat, a lack of ventilation, and a shortage of stowage space. In bad conditions the boat has to be imagined inverted, with her keel waving in the air and the crew shaken like peas in a drum. It happens. Not often, but every year a few boats find themselves with the deck where the cabin sole should be. Under rugged conditions the furniture must be free from sharp edges and corners, liberally supplied with hand-grips at about 4 foot (1.2 m) intervals and tough. Plain tough. A galley which detaches itself and hastens about the cabin complete with hot stove and a confetti of jam pots is a nuisance.

=18 *Moulded cabin furniture*=

Just as the main hull is made from fibreglass, so can furniture be fabricated from this material. The procedure is the same: a pattern is made exactly to the right size, with all surfaces smooth, all joins tight, edges rounded (normally with a radius of at least ¾ inch (20 mm) to avoid resin rich or resin starved areas) and the basic shape tapered so that the mould can be pulled off. Patterns are often made of cheap ply faced with a hard smooth plastic laminate which does not need further finishing. Next a strong mould is made from fibreglass amply stiffened so that it is reliable enough to be used again and again. If in doubt, as a rough guide, space the stiffeners for furniture components about a foot (300 mm) apart and make them about 2×1 inches (50×25 mm). Using these moulds furniture is fabricated just the way as a hull. The drawings will show how many layers of glass cloth are to be used to make up each part. Typically four or five layers of 1.5 oz (0.04 kilos per sq. metre) chopped strand mat is right for many parts provided extra stiffening is used round locker doors, and at about 8 inch (200 mm) centres under seats. The stiffening will be about 1½×½ inch (40×12 mm) glassed in wood or foam plastic strips, with at least two layers of the 1.5 oz glass over the stiffening. The stiffening will be laid on after say the third or fourth main layer, then a localised length of mat wetted over it, before the final layer of cloth goes on over the whole surface.

If only 1.5 cloth is used this simplifies the buying, reduces waste and with such thin cloth there is no excuse for having areas which are not fully wetted. A particular attraction of this cloth weight is that it can be worked into sharp angles and awkward corners. Even one weight heavier tends to be too stiff, too intractable, so that it cannot be wetted and bent into an angle of 90° or worked into features like a moulded fiddle.

Professional builders, aiming to work fast and keep down all possible costs, make moulded furniture so that one unit includes all the seats and lockers and often the cabin sole, the side and deckhead lining in one compartment. The moulding extends exactly from bulkhead to bulkhead and is fastened to these ply boundaries. It is essential that the bulkheads are exactly the right distance apart, precisely parallel both athwartships and vertically and accurately at right angles to the ship's centre-line. If either of the bulkheads is slightly misplaced the moulding may not fit. Correcting an error here may take days; usually the only course is to cut out one of the bulkheads and reglass it in. Sometimes both bulkheads need repositioning.

These big furniture mouldings suit professional builders because they minimise the fitting-out work. All the big mouldings have to be put in before the deck goes on. Even if a moulding is small enough to go through a hatch it

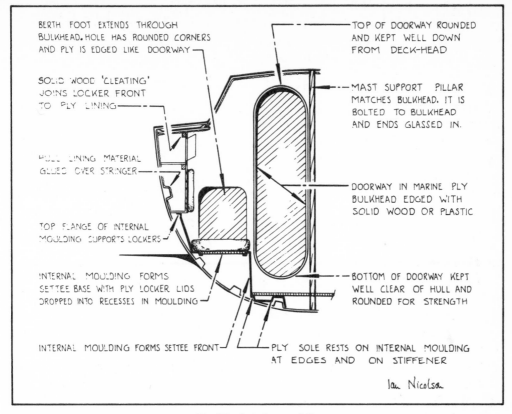

BERTH FOOT EXTENDS THROUGH
BULKHEAD. HOLE HAS ROUNDED CORNERS
AND PLY IS EDGED LIKE DOORWAY

SOLID WOOD 'CLEATING'
JOINS LOCKER FRONT
TO PLY LINING

HULL LINING MATERIAL
GLUED OVER STRINGER

TOP FLANGE OF INTERNAL
MOULDING SUPPORTS LOCKERS

INTERNAL MOULDING FORMS
SETTEE BASE WITH PLY LOCKER LIDS
DROPPED INTO RECESSES IN MOULDING

INTERNAL MOULDING FORMS SETTEE FRONT

TOP OF DOORWAY ROUNDED
AND KEPT WELL DOWN
FROM DECK-HEAD

MAST SUPPORT PILLAR
MATCHES BULKHEAD. IT IS
BOLTED TO BULKHEAD
AND ENDS GLASSED IN.

DOORWAY IN MARINE PLY
BULKHEAD EDGED WITH
SOLID WOOD OR PLASTIC

BOTTOM OF DOORWAY KEPT
WELL CLEAR OF HULL AND
ROUNDED FOR STRENGTH

PLY SOLE RESTS ON INTERNAL MOULDING
AT EDGES AND ON STIFFENER

Ian Nicolson

Fig. 32   Interior moulding

The furniture moulding of a Weatherly 8.5 includes the support for the cabin sole, the settee berths and their backs, also the foundations for the lockers outboard. Each end of the moulding is secured to the bulkheads with stainless steel self-tapping screws.

Holes for doorways, locker doors or berth ends which are cut through strength bulkheads like the one under the mast should never have square cut corners, nor should they be near the hull shell, otherwise the bulkhead will be seriously weakened. After such holes have been cut the raw ply edges are covered either with strips of solid wood, or with plastic extrusion secured at about 5 inch (125 mm) intervals.

This drawing shows the advantages of a furniture moulding; once it is in the rest of the furniture is quickly and easily added; large areas do not need lining; the moulding needs no painting or varnishing; it forms useful supports for minor items and even some quite big parts.

will be too big to get into the correct space, turned the correct way round, between bulkheads.

Some amateurs buy hulls for completion with sets of interior furniture mouldings made by the hull builder. If the boat is sent by road with loose furniture mouldings inside damage will almost certainly result. As the lorry bumps along, especially over those last few hundred yards to the typically remote building site off the main road, loose fibreglass furniture will grate and grind against the inside of the hull. Edges will chip, flanges will break, smooth surfaces will be scratched.

So either the hull maker must wrap the furniture parts carefully and lash them down, or he must fix them fully and finally in place. Securing is by bolts or self-tapping screws into the ply bulkheads and by glassing along the edges which butt onto the hull. Three runs of 1.5 oz chopped strand mat are needed as a minimum and for furniture parts which have glassed-in edges longer than 3 feet (1 m) four runs is not being overcautious.

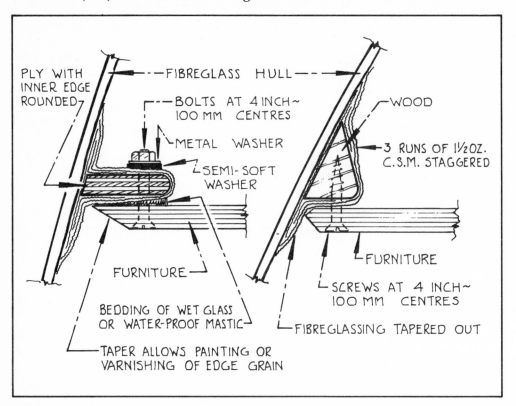

Fig. 33   Joining furniture to hull

The techniques shown here in section can be used to join furniture or even bulkheads to the fibreglass shell. This might be described as the secondary method of securing wood (and occasionally metal) parts to the basic hull. Instead of glassing the bulkhead, or seat or whatever it is, to the hull, a minor piece of structure is glassed in well and the component screwed on when the glassing has set hard.

An advantage of this technique is that the furniture can be taken out easily for cleaning, repainting or changing. Some amateur builders may get the hull moulder to fit the bonded-in wood strips, so that whoever completes the hull has no glassing work, and none of the mess that often goes with it.

Bolts are generally best for holding the furniture in place, but in some areas such as a cramped end compartment, it may be impossible to get nuts on a row of bolts. Here screws are used. To keep the damp out of the join the faying surface between the bonded in strip and the new component is either wetted with glass and resin just before the join is made, or a non-hardening material like Secomastic is used to exclude moisture. As the first job a run of glass is put along the shell partly to spread the loads and partly to make sure the wood or ply strip seats well. Three or more runs of 1½ oz chopped strand mat are used for glassing in because this is about the heaviest gauge of mat which folds and wets well in an interior angle.

All wood used has well rounded edges to give a good bond onto the glass, and semi-soft washers under the metal ones ensure there is good bonding and no crushed glass.

Here as everywhere the glassing in must taper well, so as to avoid 'hard spots'. One area which often gives trouble is the junction of the forward berth tops to the hull topsides. Sailing craft are especially vulnerable. In this area the hull tends to be fairly flat, with plenty of depth between the deck and the curve of the bilge. When going hard to windward, this large flat area pounds into the sea, so that the hull above and below the berth top pants inwards. Along the line of the berth there is a strong edge which cannot flex inwards so in time cracks in the gel coat show up on the outside of the hull. To avoid this the topsides need reinforcing with 'framelets' or extra thickness, or stringers. If the plans show nothing in the way of reinforcing here the designer should be reminded of the risk (see Fig. 22).

If a hull is to have moulded-in furniture, and the boat is amateur completed, it makes double sense to have the hull moulder fit the fibreglass furniture. First the work can be done before the hull has left its mould, when it is still 'green'; secondly, the hull builder will know exactly how and where each part goes. Even with a good plan it is sometimes difficult to get some parts exactly right. Often enough if one part is put in just slightly adrift, several others will not lodge in place. This is a three-dimensional jig-saw puzzle.

When a fibreglass furniture unit is screwed or bolted to a ply bulkhead, or onto a glassed-in length of wood, there should be at least three fastenings at each join line. Where the flange is more than 16 inches (400 mm) long there should be at least five fastenings. Often self-tapping stainless steel screws are used, and they should never be less than ⅛ inch (3 mm) diameter. To secure a major part, such as a berth, self-tappers about ³⁄₁₆ inch diameter (5 mm) are needed. They are normally pan head or round head screws. It is the almost universal practice to put them in on their own, but a meticulous builder would put a semi-soft washer under the head, or better still a metal washer followed by a soft washer. Sometimes light bolts are used and they should be brass or stainless steel, though professionals often use the cheapest form of galvanised bolts in their scrabble to save pennies. Whatever fastenings are used, they should be staggered.

The furniture moulder often makes up a complete berth or galley unit with the glass extending right across the locker doors. The doorway is cut out when the compartment is well cured, usually by a mechanical jig-saw fitted with a fine-toothed blade. This leaves a clean cut so that only a little rubbing over with emery paper is needed to take away the sharp edges.

Locker door holes are cut with their corners rounded. The radius here will be about 2 inches (50 mm) and seldom under 1½ inches (40 mm). This is partly to avoid a weak interior angle which might crack when stressed, partly because a mechanical jig-saw works more quickly and easily round such corners. The outline of each doorway is marked by good builders on their patterns; these outlines are reproduced on the moulds, and they show up again as a thin groove line on the final furniture component. It is this sort of detail which makes fibreglass furniture quick to produce and cheap. However, some builders with efficient production runs, turning out many boats every year, claim that they can make up wooden furniture as cheaply as fibreglass moulded furniture. They say this knowing that wood furniture has to be finished and polished, whereas fibreglass furniture only needs polishing once it is out of the mould, apart from the addition of locker doors and fiddles and so on. Much depends on the cost of the patterns and moulds and the length of the production runs.

Doors for lockers (and often drawer fronts) are made to fit on the outside of the locker, not flush fronted with the furniture unit, because of the rounded corners of the doorway. Fitting the doors on the front like this means their precise size is not critical, and as there is no fine fitting there is a further time-saving here.

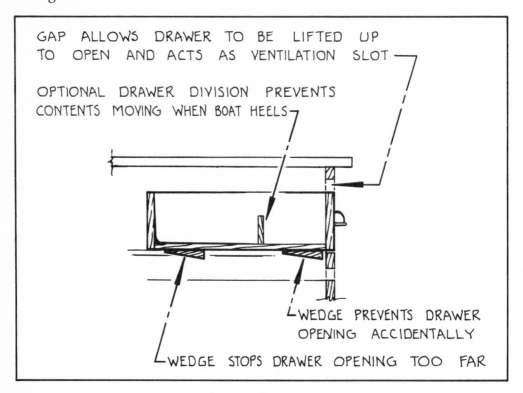

GAP ALLOWS DRAWER TO BE LIFTED UP TO OPEN AND ACTS AS VENTILATION SLOT

OPTIONAL DRAWER DIVISION PREVENTS CONTENTS MOVING WHEN BOAT HEELS

WEDGE PREVENTS DRAWER OPENING ACCIDENTALLY

WEDGE STOPS DRAWER OPENING TOO FAR

Fig. 34   Drawer design

Every drawer which opens athwartships on a power or sailing boat needs a device to prevent it opening accidentally. If no catch is fitted every time the boat goes to sea all the drawers will slide out as the boat heels or rolls.

Sometimes a wood or metal turn-button is used, but it can be a nuisance as it has to be strong, and it needs one hand to open while the other hand pulls the drawer. This is dangerous if the boat is rolling, because under these conditions everyone aboard needs one hand to steady himself.

Shown here is a traditional way of securing drawers. A hardwood wedge holds the drawer safe. To open the drawer it is raised slightly, and for this it needs a good handle. Then it is pulled out till the second wedge stops it.

If the drawer has to be taken out to be cleaned it is lifted so that the second wedge clears the bottom sill, and pulled clear. The wedges should be screwed from above and possibly glued as well.

Hinges have to be bolted on for reliability, and a backing strip of wood is needed behind the fibreglass to take the crushing strains when the bolts are tightened, also to spread the load of the door. For a door no more than a foot square (300×300 mm) a backing strip (of hardwood) about 1×¼ inch (25×6 mm) the full depth of the opening will do. But for doors up to around 4×2 feet (1,200×600 mm) the back strip should be about 2×½ inch (50×12 mm).

Fiddles are sometimes moulded in, sometimes made of hardwood. The latter are secured from beneath by screws spaced about 3 inch (125 mm) centres, and with never less than three screws. The screws should penetrate about two thirds into the fiddle. Just occasionally fiddles are made of light alloy angle, usually just round galleys. These are bolted in place.

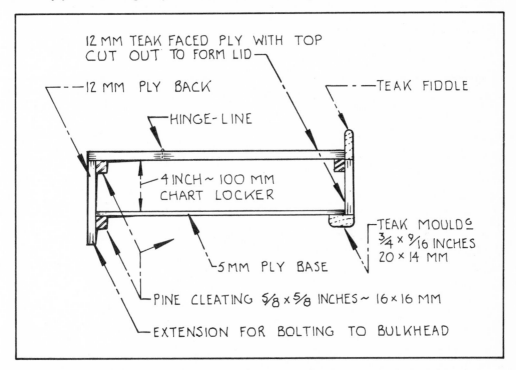

Fig. 35 Furniture construction

This section through a chart table shows how one firm puts its furniture units together. An amateur might go for fillets twice the size shown and should bevel the exposed edges, especially those inside the chart locker.

The locker lid only forms three quarters of the length of the chart table, and the fillet by the fiddle is stopped in way of the lid opening. All the fiddles are glued and have screws at 6 inch (150 mm) centres. These screws are 8 gauge, countersunk brass.

A hole in the bottom of the chart locker about 2 inches (50 mm) diameter makes it easier to get charts out by pushing them up. Another improvement would be a recessed hinge which would avoid a lump under the chart. The join of the fiddle might be stronger, since it is screwed and glued to the edge grain of only 12 mm ply, but it is finished this way to give a flush front to the locker.

To cover the edge grain of the front ply there is a teak moulding which also doubles as a joining piece to the bottom ply. Here as throughout this furniture carcase, there is no rebating or recessing, which keeps the cost to a minimum.

The fiddles which hold the berth cushions in place also secure the lower edges of the leeboard. Access to the lockers under settees and berths is usually through the top because this is the cheapest way and also because the berth front needs extra strengthening if locker door holes are cut in it. Berth fronts are frequently glassed along the bottom so the lockers end up by being watertight. This stops bilge-water getting in, but puddles from condensation or deck leaks or water which sneaks in through open hatches cannot get out.

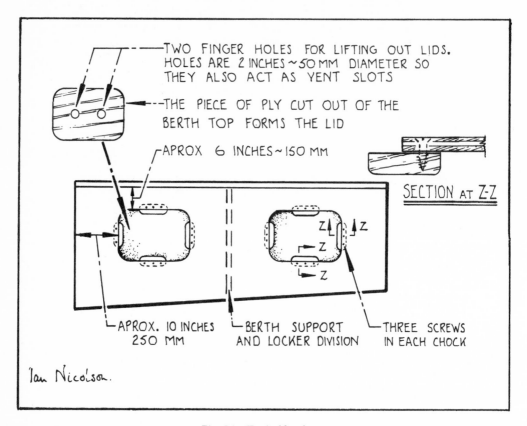

Fig. 36 *Typical berth top*

Many berth tops are made of marine ply, with the space below forming lockers. The cheapest form of locker access is in the form of portable lift-out panels under the berth cushion, and this sketch shows the plan view of the berth with the cushion off and the hatches taken away.

Before fitting the ply berth top the hatches are marked in pencil using a paint tin or similar round container to draw round, so giving the corner radii, which should be about 2½ inches (65 mm). With careful cutting the piece removed needs very little cleaning off to make it the lid. Hardwood chocks all the same size are screwed or bolted on each side of the apertures to prevent the lids dropping into the lockers.

The lids and the berth base should be treated with paint or varnish otherwise mildew growth will soon start. Before putting on the first coat of varnish all edges are slightly rounded with glass-paper.

Berth tops are typically of 12 mm ply for a normal cruiser but of 8 or 6 mm ply and in extreme cases of 4 mm ply in racing boats. The use of ply under 12 mm calls for light stiffening battens typically of 1½×½ inch (40×12 mm) spruce glued and screwed, the larger dimension being vertical.

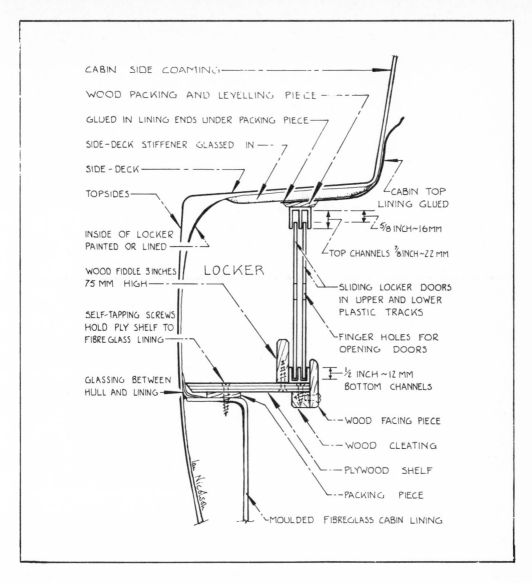

CABIN SIDE COAMING

WOOD PACKING AND LEVELLING PIECE

GLUED IN LINING ENDS UNDER PACKING PIECE

SIDE-DECK STIFFENER GLASSED IN

SIDE-DECK

TOPSIDES

INSIDE OF LOCKER PAINTED OR LINED

WOOD FIDDLE 3 INCHES 75 MM HIGH

SELF-TAPPING SCREWS HOLD PLY SHELF TO FIBREGLASS LINING

GLASSING BETWEEN HULL AND LINING

LOCKER

CABIN TOP LINING GLUED

5/8 INCH~16MM

TOP CHANNELS 7/8 INCH~22 MM

SLIDING LOCKER DOORS IN UPPER AND LOWER PLASTIC TRACKS

FINGER HOLES FOR OPENING DOORS

1/2 INCH~12 MM BOTTOM CHANNELS

WOOD FACING PIECE

WOOD CLEATING

PLYWOOD SHELF

PACKING PIECE

MOULDED FIBREGLASS CABIN LINING

Fig. 37   Making a locker

The space under the side-deck is often filled with lockers. In this section view the galley locker of the Weatherly 28 foot (8.5 metre) cruiser is shown, but this layout will suit large and small craft. Locker doors can be of ply or plastic. In this case they are of coloured translucent Perspex, sliding in plastic channels. Because the top channels are much deeper than the bottom set, it is easy to fit the doors; they are slid into the top channel and dropped down into the bottom ones. Once the lower wood facing piece has been screwed in place the doors cannot fall out even if the boat inverts, but to get the doors out for cleaning or painting or repairs it is only necessary to remove that facing piece.

The shelf is set on a packing piece to lift it above the glassing of the cabin lining, but instead the underside of the shelf could be bevelled away so that it would lie flat on the flange of the lining.

A fiddle is needed inside the locker to prevent things falling out when the locker doors are opened. If the locker was lined with a glued in cloth, the top edge of the lining will be hidden by the top packing piece and the bottom edge by the outboard side of the shelf.

A look through the lockers of a hundred boats with fibreglass furniture will show lockers with puddles in eighty of them. Lack of ventilation is at least partly to blame. An induced draught is needed through all the lockers and this can only be achieved if:

1   There is a hole for the wind to blow in, and another for it to waft out.
2   The holes are so big that the gentle breezes trickling through the cabin get through easily. Holes less than 6×3 inches (150×175 mm) are suspect.

Because lockers beneath berths so often have puddles some builders fit deep trays which drop into the lockers. These trays are moulded of fibreglass, with the smooth side inside, so they make excellent clothes stowage lockers. Bilge-water can sluice up the ship's side and it should not reach the clothes until conditions almost reach the stage when it's time to call out the lifeboat. The deep trays are made portable so that the hull beneath the berth is accessible; low-cost boats have the trays moulded in and if an accident occurs the regions beneath the berths can only be approached by wielding an axe.

19 Windows and ports

The shape and location of the windows and ports are marked on the cabin plan, or on the construction plan. Occasionally a meticulous designer draws out a special window plan; conversely some draughtsmen omit any dimensions or information about the windows, and so the builder has to do all his own measuring on the plans.

The cabin coaming mould may be marked with thin lines which come out on the cabin coamings, indicating where the builder is to cut out the windows. Such lines can be hard to follow with a saw, especially in the traditional gloom of a boatbuilding shed, so the careful shipwright draws over the lines with a felt tip pen or similar instrument.

Windows should be small if the boat is to be taken far offshore. Just what is 'small' depends on the person considering the problem. Anyone who has cowered below while a 6 foot (2 metre) deep, breaking crest of green-white water thunders in roaring uncontrolled torrents against the boat will say that no window should ever have any dimension larger than 5 inches (125 mm). This is in strong contrast to modern boats of all types, which so often have vast, vulnerable windows. A few of these are bashed in every year.

A reasonable compromise might be: stick to the designer's drawings for normal coastal work; for extended offshore voyaging ask the designer's opinion about smaller windows; if he is not available keep windows down to about 10×5 inches (250×125 mm) for boats over 35 feet (10 m) and to about 7×3 inches (180×75 mm) for smaller craft. Window size in this context is the length and height of the opening. In makers' catalogues windows have two sets of dimensions, the 'overall size' which is to the outside of the framework and the glass length-by-breadth.

The size and shape of a window or set of them is a matter of personal taste. High short windows tend to look dated, but they suit fishing boats and commercial craft with bold, boxy cabin tops or wheel-houses. So many modern yachts have high topsides that they simply demand long, slinky, low windows to give emphatic horizontal lines.

To give a modern, sleek look some boats have two or more apertures cut through the coaming covered by a single long length of coloured transparent plastic. This gives the appearance of one long, shallow window, but because the coaming has several relatively small holes instead of one long slot cut out of it, there is no great loss of strength.

This technique depends on the use of the coloured glazing material. A serious disadvantage of the colouring is that it makes the inside of the boat dark. Some builders favour a smoky, dark bluish-grey plastic which looks superb from the outside. In the cabins the effect can be totally depressing. At boat shows (where many craft are sold) the inside of the cabin is brilliantly illuminated with artificial light, so the buyer never realises the gloom he is purchasing till he starts to use the boat. Of course, for hot climates where the sun is often too fierce, this coloured glazing is an asset. In temperate climates coloured glazing is like some women's fashions, eye-catching but uncomfortable.

The choice of glazing materials lies between glass and modern plastic. Glass does not scratch when wiped or accidentally chafed, does not craze with age, and as it is only used in a toughened form it is hard to break. On the other hand it is heavy, must be fitted with a frame, and so it is expensive. Windows which have wipers on must be of glass. Windows which open are almost always of glass, but wise owners have very few openers – they nearly always leak. If a window has to open like one at the forward end of a wheel-house where visibility in fog must be as good as possible, then it should be located where a leak is not important. Electrical equipment must be kept away.

There is a choice of plastic materials, including Perspex, Luctite and Polycarbonate. In different countries various trade names are used. These materials can be cut with electric jig-saws or wood-working tenon saws. They are easy to drill, but they must be given slightly oversize holes for bolts, and not pinched by pulling bolts up tight.

When the windows have been marked on the coamings they can be cut out, but if the boat is a prototype, or the windows are non-standard, or there is even the tiniest doubt about the appearance, they should first be painted in on the coamings. This is done with any old cheap left-over paint, or even with coloured tape. Anything will do to make the windows stand out clearly. If the cabin coaming is a light colour the windows are made dark and vice versa.

Once the windows have been coloured they should be studied slowly. Go well aft, stand amidships, move forward. Do the windows look right from all angles? Climb up high, squat down, shift around a lot. Get a trusted helper with an artistic eye to give an impartial view. Spend time on this job because it affects the whole appearance of the boat all her life. It can change the character and the value of a boat. If necessary take some photos of the boat and pin them up above the shaving mirror, above the dining room table, above the office desk, just about anywhere which gives ample time for thoughtful study.

When the windows are correctly marked in, they are cut out, normally with an electric jig-saw. If a window is very low down near a deck the guide-plate of the saw will make it impossible to cut out the shape. It is poor design to have a window so low, not least because its aperture weakens the coaming, and leaves too little margin for fastenings. However, some coamings have quite a big radiused sweep down to the deck, and this may interfere with the jig-saw.

If a window is to straddle a bulkhead it is best to cut it out before the bulkhead is fitted. In any case windows should be cut out early in the building operation to let light, air and the electric cables for tools into the hull. Another important reason for cutting the apertures in the coamings early is that window makers cannot hold stocks of windows. Most windows are specially made, and this is not a quick job, so orders have to be placed long before launching day.

To cut out a window a hole about ½ inch diameter (12 mm) is drilled through the coaming from the outside. This hole is made in the coaming where the aperture will be and close to the marked outline. A jig-saw blade fits easily into this size of hole, and the cut is taken diagonally up to the marked line, then round it, working down the middle of the line. Once the aperture has been cut out the sharp inside edge of the coaming is faired off, but the outer edge will normally be left sharp.

Professionals have patterns which they make from the prototype and use on each succeeding boat. An amateur may be able to borrow the patterns or get the hull moulder to mark the outlines of the windows using his pattern. The best type of pattern has legs down to a horizontal bar which rests on the deck, with another leg extending aft or forward to the coaming end. These legs position the pattern exactly, so in a few minutes the shipwright has his windows marked in with adequate accuracy, and he is sure they are in the right position, at the right tilt, and the correct shape.

When the window apertures have been cut out, the various pieces of scrap are the exact size and shape of the glazing needed, except that they are smaller than the apertures by the thickness of the saw blade. If glass windows are to be fitted, these cut-out shapes are sent to the window maker, since he can have no better guide – but there are snags. Window makers get orders from the four corners of the globe, and like other sections of the boatbuilding industry they suffer from booms and slumps. Experienced builders take precautions accordingly. They put their name and address and the boat's name or number on each piece. They mark the appropriate edges boldly with the words TOP and FORWARD, and PORT or STARBOARD and SECOND WINDOW FROM FORWARD or whatever is appropriate. They also add such useful information as THIS PATTERN IS ONE OF A SET OF SIX, and WANTED BY FEB. 10th 19** and ORDER NO. 1234/J REFERS.

Before cutting and sending pattern pieces to a window maker his catalogue has to be studied because there are limitations to what can be done. The framework extrusions used for window making cannot be bent round tight radii, and the catalogue will give the limits. There will be a choice of window frame material; aluminium alloys are the cheapest and lightest but some versions corrode within three years. Brass is reliable but relatively costly. For heavy duty commerical craft the frames are cast bronze and very much more expensive than brass extrusion, but such frames often outlast the hull. They should, bearing in mind their weight and price.

Window makers advertise in trade and yachting magazines, and a few exhibit at some boat shows. Some of them offer standard windows, which can occasionally be used without spoiling the appearance of the boat. These semi-mass produced windows are cheaper than specially shaped ones.

If the windows are of transparent plastic the builder can either buy sheets of the material and cut out the windows himself, or have the supplier do the cutting. The boatbuilder sends patterns of the exact size of window needed. This is normally the size of the aperture with an extra 1 inch (25 mm) all round for the bolts. The outer edges of the plastic need rounding or bevelling partly for appearance, partly to avoid damage to anyone brushing against the sharp edges.

Whatever type of window is used, the corners should be radiused to prevent weakening the coamings. If in doubt use a minimum radius of 1½ inches (40 mm).

On very cheap boats used solely on protected inland waters the windows, of

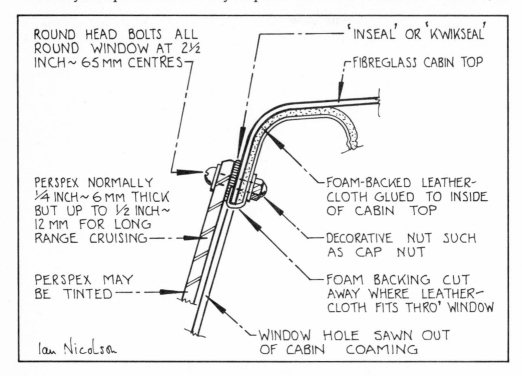

ROUND HEAD BOLTS ALL ROUND WINDOW AT 2½ INCH ~ 65 MM CENTRES

'INSEAL' OR 'KWIKSEAL'

FIBREGLASS CABIN TOP

PERSPEX NORMALLY ¼ INCH ~ 6 MM THICK BUT UP TO ½ INCH ~ 12 MM FOR LONG RANGE CRUISING

FOAM-BACKED LEATHER-CLOTH GLUED TO INSIDE OF CABIN TOP

DECORATIVE NUT SUCH AS CAP NUT

PERSPEX MAY BE TINTED

FOAM BACKING CUT AWAY WHERE LEATHER-CLOTH FITS THRO' WINDOW

WINDOW HOLE SAWN OUT OF CABIN COAMING

Ian Nicolson

Fig. 38   Window fabrication (section at top of window)

A boat well known for its simple light-weight construction is the David Thomas designed 'Bolero' quarter tonner, built by Nick Stratton. Each window shape is cut out of the cabin top and the same shape with an extra inch (25 mm) border all round is cut from Perspex. The window thickness depends on the service the boat performs; for racing one selects the lightest material, about ¼ inch (6 mm) thick, for normal cruising say 5/16 inch (8 mm) and for rugged deep sea operations ½ inch (12 mm) material.

The cabin lining is glued up first, with cut-outs in way of the windows. Where the leathercloth passes through the windows the foam backing is stripped off, and the cloth pushed through to cover the rough sawn edge of the window aperture.

The edge of the leathercloth is trimmed to fit under the middle of the 'Inseal' or 'Kwikseal' strips. These sealants are bought by the roll or by the box and come in different widths and thicknesses to suit windows, hatches, etc. This type of seal very seldom leaks but if it does, rebedding is quick and cheap.

It may be argued that a window without a frame is less smart, but it is lighter and cheaper by far than a framed one.

glass or plastic, may be secured by a rubber extrusion. This has one groove which embraces the fibreglass coaming, and another groove which holds the glazing. This rubber strip dispenses with the need for a frame round a glass window. However, no boat which is used at sea, even in an estuary, should ever have windows held by this form of seal. It will not hold the glass or plastic against a breaking wave or even against an accidental blow from a heavy boot. This rubber extrusion is supplied by wholesalers of vehicle spares.

Normally windows are held by bolts through the coaming. Very occasionally screws put in from the outside may be acceptable provided they have a good grip through the coaming into a strong frame, and provided the boat is not intended for serious venturing in deep water. Bolts are spaced about 2 inches (50 mm) apart and drawn up slowly and evenly, so that the frame or plastic is pulled onto the coaming all round at the same time. If one end is tightened down before the other cracking is likely.

Very ample bedding is used, but with plastic it is best to use a continuous strip bedding material like 'Inseal' because it looks so much better. Decorative nuts are usual, and they may be on the inside or the outside of the window, according to the effect required. Careful builders turn a hose on each window in turn, working the hose close to the edges, and using the full force of water – the sea is no less relentless.

20 Rudders

In a vessel with a counter the rudder must have a stock which passes up through the bottom of the counter. This type of rudder has a fibreglass blade made in two halves, port and starboard. Each half needs its own mould and is made just like any other fibreglass component. Once these halves have cured they are put together on the stock which is a metal rod or tube. The stock has straps, made from the same metal, welded on its aft side. Without these straps, when the stock is turned, the bond of the blade onto it may not be strong enough and so fail. This failure results in the stock rotating while the rubber blade does not. The straps are bonded inside the blade with a resin dough. Partly to save weight and partly to make a better bond, large holes are drilled in the straps. The rest of the hollow space in the blade is often filled with expanding foam plastic.

In practice most people completing bare hulls buy the rudder already bonded onto the stock from the hull moulder. Because rudders are vulnerable, and because fibreglass rudders have a bad reputation, it is a good idea to ask for extra fibreglassing round the edges of the rudder if the boat is to be used in harsh conditions. It might be thought that a worthwhile precaution would be athwartship fastenings through the fibreglass blade and the straps. In practice such fastenings crack the fibreglass sides of the blade due to the high local loading.

The stock extends up into the counter via a gland which acts both as a bearing and to exclude water. Sometimes there is a fibreglass or metal tube from the bottom of the counter upwards to the gland. This tube may be extended up to or near the deck, so that its top is well above the water-line, in which case no gland is needed. As glands are expensive to buy and fit this layout is favoured on cheap boats. On small racing boats glands are unpopular because of their weight.

Where the stock emerges from the top of the gland or tube there is a quadrant or tiller, sometimes held in place by a key, and sometimes on cheap craft by a simple through bolt or two. Neither of these techniques are recommended for long life and reliability, though if the stock is enlarged by a stout sleeve the through bolt method may be used where metal machining facilities are not available. The best technique is either to weld the quadrant or tiller fitting in place (and cut it free when the time eventually comes to take the rudder off), or use the traditional technique of machining the top of the stock square. Tubular stocks, which are used to save weight, need a well-secured metal bar fastened down inside the top, so that there is solid metal for machining square.

If a quadrant is fitted the square section must be continued above it to allow space for an emergency tiller to be slipped on. This tiller consists of a socket which fits the top of the stock and a handle long enough to give reasonably easy steering even in severe conditions. There may be an athwartships bolt, pin or clamp to hold the tiller onto the stock.

There are proprietary brands of steering gear which link the steering wheel to the stock. Some of them need a tiller rather than a quadrant. They are adver-

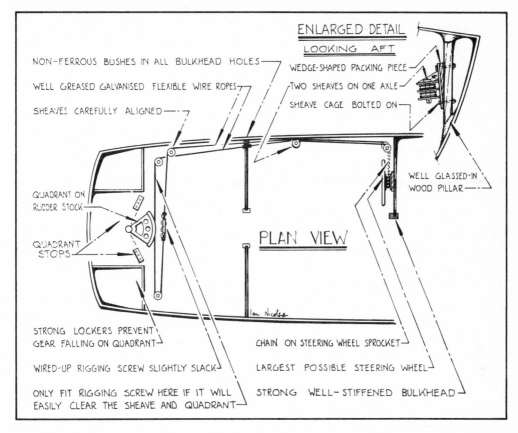

ENLARGED DETAIL
LOOKING AFT

NON-FERROUS BUSHES IN ALL BULKHEAD HOLES
WELL GREASED GALVANISED FLEXIBLE WIRE ROPES
SHEAVES CAREFULLY ALIGNED

WEDGE-SHAPED PACKING PIECE
TWO SHEAVES ON ONE AXLE
SHEAVE CAGE BOLTED ON

QUADRANT ON RUDDER STOCK

QUADRANT STOPS

PLAN VIEW

WELL GLASSED-IN WOOD PILLAR

STRONG LOCKERS PREVENT GEAR FALLING ON QUADRANT
WIRED-UP RIGGING SCREW SLIGHTLY SLACK
ONLY FIT RIGGING SCREW HERE IF IT WILL EASILY CLEAR THE SHEAVE AND QUADRANT

CHAIN ON STEERING WHEEL SPROCKET
LARGEST POSSIBLE STEERING WHEEL
STRONG WELL-STIFFENED BULKHEAD

Fig. 39   Steering gear

A simple form of steering gear is shown here. Chandlers supply standard steering wheels which are complete with drums for flexible wire on the front, or better still chain sprockets. When the wheel is turned the drum or sprocket turns too because they are secured to the same axle. Twin wires lead aft by way of blocks, to a quadrant which is rigidly fixed on the rudder stock, often by a key. Sometimes the top of the stock is machined square and the quadrant has a square socket which is tightened on the rudder stock by a pair of bolts. These bolts like everything else in a steering gear linkage, must be locked so that vibration or age or excessive use of the helm or tough sea conditions do not loosen any part.

The wires must be led without any obstruction, and render easily round sheaves. This means the sheaves must be carefully aligned and prevented from drooping. In short, blocks shackled to eyebolts are seldom safe for very long because the weight of the block tends to cause them to sag, and the wire will in time chafe the sides of the block. If the wires are tightened so that such blocks do not sag, steering will be hard work. The rigging screw should be left slightly slack to ensure effortless steering, and this is where it is necessary to experiment to get the right tension.

To prevent the quadrant from going over more than 35 degrees each way there must be stoutly bolted chocks, or a chain fixed to the quadrant and to a nearby strong-point such as an overhead beam.

tised in yachting and commercial small craft magazines. As with other equipment which is designed, made and marketed to a keen price, the cheapest is not necessarily the best. The size recommended by the manufacturer is not always the one to select; experienced builders often choose the next size up, for added reliability, longer life and peace of mind. Fitting instructions are supplied with the gear.

A device to prevent the rudder going over more than 35° may be built into the steering gear. If not, something should be fitted which can stand up to rugged conditions, never needs maintenance, and cannot be broken even by a panicky helmsman. Sometimes a short length of chain is secured to the middle of the quadrant or tiller, with the other end made fast on the ship's centre-line. The length of the cabin is adjusted by cutting off links until it just allows the right amount of helm, and the chain sited so that even if the boat rolls prodigiously it cannot jam the steering mechanism.

Sometimes chocks of wood are glassed in each side with hard rubber pads where the tiller or quadrant bears. Glassed in steel brackets or short lengths of angle-bar may be used. Or there may be a bulkhead athwart the tiller cut away a limited amount to restrict the tiller's swing. Doubling pads at the points where the tiller bears are well bolted through the bulkhead.

The weight of the rudder is taken either by a heel fitting on the skeg, or by a collar on the stock which rests on a bearing. On vessels over 50 feet (15 metres) there may be two weight-carrying bearings, one at the top and one at the bottom. It is necessary to have renewable wearing surfaces at these bearings and a modern plastic is more likely to be used than a traditional bronze.

The heel fitting on the rudder takes the form of a well-secured bracket with a vertical pin which pivots in the mating fitting on the rudder skeg. As these two fittings, one on the rudder and one on the skeg are so close they must be of the same material. The latter is a simple bracket embracing the skeg and fastened through it, with a socket to take the rudder pin. Sometimes this pin is the extension of the stock, possibly machined down. This machining gives a shoulder on the bottom of the stock which forms the bottom bearing.

Skeg fittings are notorious for working loose so they should have four or better still six fastenings of the same material as the surrounding metal. Except on a flat out racing craft where weight saving is pursued with unalloyed fanaticism, the fastenings should be solid bolts or rivets. Hollow fastenings are acceptable on racing machines because inspection occurs, or should, monthly. There may be a metal strap or two round the stock about half way up the skeg, to prevent the rudder blade from flexing sideways when it is hard over and the boat is moving fast. This strap should be a smooth working fit on the stock, and to achieve this there may be some shimming of a bearing material such as nylon between the stock and the strap. Here as elsewhere below the waterline if a plastic compound is used the manufacturer's recommendations should be followed; he should be asked to specify a material which does not become waterlogged or expand when immersed for a long time, and his recommendations for working clearances should be used. In practice many excellent bearing materials soak up water too much and cause partial seizure. Expansion due to water absorbtion is difficult to avoid, so an initial clearance is made to allow for the swelling.

Anyone new to boatbuilding may think that the rudder skeg will be exactly on the centre-line of the boat. Someone trained in engineering may expect that the skeg misalignment to be of the order of four to ten thousandths of an inch. Fibreglass boatbuilding is not that precise. We all pray long and fervently that errors are less than ⅛ inch (3 mm) but hopes are often crushed. The assembly procedure should therefore be:

> Fit rudder up through the counter and gland, or tube. Slip on the skeg fitting, packing out one side and/or grinding away the skeg on the other, till the fitting can be secured without bending the stock or blade.

If the tube or gland has not been fitted by the hull moulder, the procedure will be:

> Pass the stock up into the counter.
> Slide the gland down the top of the stock.
> Put on the skeg fitting.
> Make sure that the rudder blade is vertical, and on the centre-line.
> Secure the skeg fitting.
> Bolt down and glass in the gland.

Holding the rudder in place while its fittings are fixed firmly will call for some ingenuity. A massive table or work bench under the blade, with a heavy block or two of wood on top can be used as a good basis. A wedge under the rudder blade will hold it, with perhaps one or two clamps gripping both the blade and stout battens which are nailed to the table. Clamps should never be screwed up onto fibreglass without softwood pads under the jaws; also the clamps should not be tightened fiercely. It is easy to crush a rudder blade so any temporary grip on it should be just tight enough to hold.

Inside the boat a crossbeam may be wedged in temporarily if there is no convenient bulkhead. Lashings, perhaps tightened by driving in a wedge or two, will hold the stock to the beam till all the fastenings are in and the glassing has set.

One disadvantage of a rudder under a counter is that it can be difficult to fit because the stock is so long. The blade may have to be lowered far down before the top of the stock can be entered in the hole in the bottom of the counter. Ways to cope with this difficulty are:

1   Fit the rudder as the boat is being lifted off the lorry which delivers her. With the hull up in the air the stock is pushed in place and the rudder lashed temporarily.

2   Fit the rudder when the boat is lifted onto the lorry for transport to the sea, or during the launching.
3   Dig a hole under the counter.
4   Using a lorry jack, raise the stern of the boat. At the same time the bow may be lowered so that the whole hull is angled. It may be necessary to dig a shallow hole under the counter as well.
5   Reduce the length of the stock inside the boat either by having the quadrant (or tiller) very close above the gland, or by fitting a coupling on top of the gland and continuing the stock upwards with an extension piece.
6   Have a coupling just below the counter. This is commercial power boat practice. It looks crude but saves money during major refits.
7   Having external rudder straps so that the stock is fitted first, then the blade (see sketch).
8   Fit the stock first then assemble the blade onto the stock. This introduces endless problems especially with the glassing round the forward edge of the blade if a skeg is fitted. With no skeg this approach is still awkward, so a complete beginner should be wary.

So as to be sure that the gland fits the stock, and the packing fits the gland, they should all be bought from the same source. Sometimes there is no way in which the gland can be bolted as well as glassed down. In other boats a wood chock is glassed in using at least five layers of 2 oz c.s.m. and the gland is glassed and bolted to this. The top edge of the gland flange should be machined or filed to a soft radius, then the glass will lie easily and snugly on it. If the flange is circular it is particularly important to have bolts through it, otherwise if the glassing works loose the whole gland may rotate when the helm is put over. What is needed is some arrangement whereby if the glassing over becomes slightly loose the glass still embraces some protrusion. This excrescence must be locked inside the glassing and so prevents the gland turning with the rudder stock. One trick is to machine or saw away part of the sides of the round flange; another is to tap in some studs which stand up and are gripped by the glass; another is to put two or three stainless steel hose clamps round the body of the gland, and carry the glass up to lock round these.

All that has been said about the gland applies to the rudder tube and its flange, if no gland is fitted. On boats intended for long range offshore work a fibreglass tube may need supporting at half height. All tubes should be substantially secured to the deck.

Transom hung rudders

A rudder pivotted on a transom is less efficient than one under a counter. It is favoured on some less expensive boats and on craft used for such work as deep sea cruising, where daily inspection even when at sea, reliability, ease of repair and similar considerations are paramount.

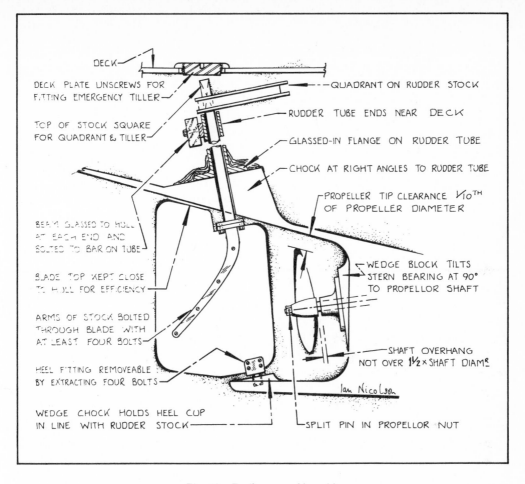

DECK

DECK PLATE UNSCREWS FOR
FITTING EMERGENCY TILLER

TOP OF STOCK SQUARE
FOR QUADRANT & TILLER

BEAM GLASSED TO HULL
AT EACH END AND
BOLTED TO BAR ON TUBE

BLADE TOP KEPT CLOSE
TO HULL FOR EFFICIENCY

ARMS OF STOCK BOLTED
THROUGH BLADE WITH
AT LEAST FOUR BOLTS

HEEL FITTING REMOVEABLE
BY EXTRACTING FOUR BOLTS

WEDGE CHOCK HOLDS HEEL CUP
IN LINE WITH RUDDER STOCK

QUADRANT ON RUDDER STOCK

RUDDER TUBE ENDS NEAR DECK

GLASSED-IN FLANGE ON RUDDER TUBE

CHOCK AT RIGHT ANGLES TO RUDDER TUBE

PROPELLER TIP CLEARANCE $\frac{1}{10}$TH
OF PROPELLER DIAMETER

WEDGE BLOCK TILTS
STERN BEARING AT 90°
TO PROPELLOR SHAFT

SHAFT OVERHANG
NOT OVER 1½ × SHAFT DIAMS

Ian Nicolson

SPLIT PIN IN PROPELLOR NUT

Fig. 40   Easily removable rudder

As the blade is bolted to the fork arms on the bottom of the stock, and the bottom pin side-plates, it is only necessary to remove four bolts to take the rudder off. This is useful if the propeller shaft has to be taken out, or the rudder mended. The stock can be dropped out too, provided it is shorter than the distance from the bottom of the counter to the skeg.

To save money no gland is fitted for the stock. Instead the tube is carried almost up to the deck. Sometimes it is taken right up to the deck and even through it. However, the design shown is in some ways easier to assemble as there is so little precise fitting.

To support the top of the tube there must be some strong structure. Instead of the beam shown there might be a bulkhead or a bracket extending from the cockpit well. The bottom of the tube in all but the smallest, cheapest boats should be secured with metal fastenings as well as the multiple layers of fibreglass chopped strand mat.

The same machined square part of the stock which takes the quadrant is extended up to take the emergency tiller too. The quadrant cannot be simply dropped over the square section; there must also be a clamping arrangement to grip the stock fiercely.

A variation of this arrangement has one bar on the bottom of the stock *inside* the rudder blade. To remove the blade the bolts on the circular coupling flanges just below the counter are removed and the heel fitting bolts, then the blade slid out aft. All these bolts should be locked in, or wired, or otherwise safely secured. Other technical information is included in this sketch including the correct clearance of the propeller blades under the hull (and above the skeg, though this is less important) and the shaft overhang limitation.

For an amateur this type of rudder is sometimes simpler to hang especially if there is no heel fitting. Heel fittings are less easy to buy or make than straight-forward dinghy style pintles and gudgeons. A simple approach is to have three standard sets of pintles and gudgeons, with the lowest set near the bottom, another set about a third of the way down the transom, and the middle one biased more closely towards the bottom than the top, because the loads on a rudder are at a maximum at the bottom.

In practice the pintles will have to be fitted so as to avoid the propeller aperture. They have to be where fastenings can be put easily through the transom, or where the stern-post is the right width and construction for a gudgeon.

On craft under 24 feet overall length (7 metres) just two sets of fittings may be acceptable if coastal voyaging is to be undertaken, or if weight-saving is critical. In the latter case the design is carefully engineered, with hollow pintles, lightening holes in the straps, and with the flanges cut away round the bolts, aircraft style.

The conventional arrangement of fittings is: a heel pin on the rudder pivoting in a cup fitting which is part of the aft end of the keel or skeg, and two sets of gudgeons and pintles. On craft over about 40 feet (12 metres) there may be more than two hangings as well as the heel fitting, especially if the boat is expected to take a thrashing far offshore. Because it is a moving part and because it is vulnerable to breaking waves, the rudder often gives more trouble during the life of a boat than other parts.

The rudder blade is bought from the moulder, and it may well have the heel fitting and pintles already in place. If the fittings are not secured they are likely to be the type which has arms to fit on either side of the blade with bolts right through. It is essential to put such parts in exactly the right location where the inside of the blade has been strengthened and made solid right through as shown on the rudder plan. The bolts must be of the same material as the fittings and have their nuts clenched over. This is done by cutting the bolt off after the nut has been put on and tightened, leaving just enough of the threaded length beyond the nut to allow for a rivetting process to be carried out. The bolt end is battered with a round-ended hammer (sometimes called a ball-pein) so that the edge curls over the nut and prevents it coming off.

If the rudder blade arrives in two halves from the moulder it is assembled as described for a rudder under a counter, and the work should not be attempted without a detailed drawing. Before beginning, the two sides of the blade should be checked for straightness by looking along the leading edges, with the component lying on a work-bench. If the side of the blade is seen to be flat it should then be turned over and resighted, just in case its own weight was tending to eliminate an unfairness. If the blade parts are not straight and well made they have to be sent back and a new set obtained.

When the rudder is supplied assembled it should be checked for straightness before any attempt is made to fit it on the boat. Sighting along the leading edge

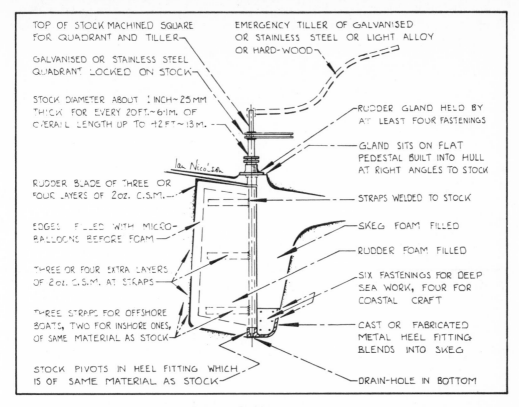

TOP OF STOCK MACHINED SQUARE
FOR QUADRANT AND TILLER

EMERGENCY TILLER OF GALVANISED
OR STAINLESS STEEL OR LIGHT ALLOY
OR HARD-WOOD

GALVANISED OR STAINLESS STEEL
QUADRANT LOCKED ON STOCK

STOCK DIAMETER ABOUT 1 INCH~25MM
THICK FOR EVERY 20FT.~6·1M. OF
OVERALL LENGTH UP TO 42FT~13M.

Ian Nicolson

RUDDER BLADE OF THREE OR
FOUR LAYERS OF 2oz. C.S.M.

EDGES FILLED WITH MICRO-
BALLOONS BEFORE FOAM

THREE OR FOUR EXTRA LAYERS
OF 2oz. C.S.M. AT STRAPS

THREE STRAPS FOR OFFSHORE
BOATS, TWO FOR INSHORE ONES,
OF SAME MATERIAL AS STOCK

STOCK PIVOTS IN HEEL FITTING WHICH
IS OF SAME MATERIAL AS STOCK

RUDDER GLAND HELD BY
AT LEAST FOUR FASTENINGS

GLAND SITS ON FLAT
PEDESTAL BUILT INTO HULL
AT RIGHT ANGLES TO STOCK

STRAPS WELDED TO STOCK

SKEG FOAM FILLED

RUDDER FOAM FILLED

SIX FASTENINGS FOR DEEP
SEA WORK, FOUR FOR
COASTAL CRAFT

CAST OR FABRICATED
METAL HEEL FITTING
BLENDS INTO SKEG

DRAIN-HOLE IN BOTTOM

Fig. 41   Rudder construction

Rudders are commonly made of fibreglass in the same general way as hulls. Two moulds are needed, one for the port and one for the starboard side. The two sides are bonded together, and in the best yards special care is taken to apply two, three, and even four extra runs of glass along the leading edge join, because it so often fails in service.

This sketch shows a typical rudder for a sailing yacht of between 25 and 50 feet (7.5 and 15 metres). There is a strong back-bone in the form of a solid or tubular stock with 'ribs' welded on, in the form of metal plates. These extend aft about two thirds or three quarters the width of the blade, and for economy are often made all the same length even though the rudder blade tapers.

Special care is needed to ensure that the fibreglass rudder shell is tightly bonded to the stock and its plates. Though athwartships metal fastenings through the straps and the fibreglass shell have been used, this is not a recommended practice; too often high local loads occur round the fastenings and cracks round the ends of the fastenings soon appear. The common way of bonding the straps to the blade is with a resin dough. This must be copiously applied along the full length of all the straps and its hardening carefully controlled.

The heel fitting has to be secured with metal fastenings otherwise the rudder cannot be lowered without a 'surgical' operation on the boat.

and checking with a taut wire should show that the blade has no curve athwartships. Fore-and-aft curvature, while undesirable, is not critical provided all the pintles and gudgeons can be exactly lined up. In this connection, accuracy has to be to a boatbuilding standard which might be described, in this instance, as an error of less than 1/16 inch (1.6 mm) in about 6 feet (2 metres). Precision engineers will collapse on the floor, writhing with mirth by such standards. The rest of us, while admiring their meticulous workmanship, will remember that precision engineers make unhappy boatbuilders because they tend to take too long on the job.

To fit the rudder first secure the heel fitting or bottom gudgeon exactly on the centre-line on the boat. A heel fitting may need a little packing out one side, or the side plates may need grinding down, or even the gel coat may need filing slightly. The rudder is mounted with the bottom pin in the heel fitting or lowest gudgeon, and the other gudgeons are put on their pintles which are already on the rudder. The rudder is held exactly on the centre-line at the top, and pencil lines drawn round where the gudgeon plates lie on the transom. The rudder is taken off and the gudgeons are bolted to the transom. Anyone who is worried that his standard of workmanship is such that the gudgeons may move as they are being used as templates to drill the bolt holes should keep the rudder up, with the gudgeons in place on the pintles. This will call for teamwork; one person will hold the rudder blade exactly in place, another holds the gudgeon on the pintle, and a third drills through the gudgeon plate and on through the transom. On boats over 30 feet (9 metres) it may be necessary to have extra hands to help each of the people mentioned.

Where the pintles have arms which clasp each side of the rudder blade, and the work of fitting them has not been done by the moulder, the problem of alignment is doubled. First of all the pintles have to be in line, then the gudgeons. One way round this problem is to fit the gudgeons first; they are all put onto a long, solid rod having the same diameter as the pintles and held in place on the centre-line of the boat while their bolt holes are drilled. The rod must be perfectly straight. Once the gudgeons have been bolted to the boat the pintles are put approximately in place on the rudder which is then shipped. As the gudgeons are precisely in line, and the pintles are on the gudgeons, bolts are put through the pintle straps with confidence.

Massive doublers are needed inside the transom at each rudder hanging. Ply or a seasoned hardwood is used for these pads, which will have sides about $\frac{1}{30}$ the boat's length. That is, a 40 foot boat will have a 16×16 inch pad at each gudgeon. As a rough guide, the pad thicknesses should be about $\frac{1}{400}$ the boat's length. These reinforcing pieces which prevent the nuts biting into the fibre-glass when tightened are in addition to the normal transom reinforcing needed for the rudder. Such extra strength is supplied by a glassed-in ply or hardwood piece extending the full depth of the transom, or extra layers of glass, or both. The width of such stiffening is likely to be around one eighth the maximum beam of the boat.

When shipping the rudder some thick waterproof grease is applied to the heel fitting and each pintle. There must also be a device which will prevent the rudder floating off accidentally, but which can be removed fairly swiftly without major surgery. It can be a chock bolted through the transom just above the top pintle, or a substantial split pin through the bottom of each pintle under a washer.

21 *Tillers*

There is no part of a boat more important than the tiller. If it breaks, and surprisingly many do each year, all sorts of sudden and drastic events follow. If it is not elegant the first and every subsequent view of the boat is spoilt. All the time the boat is under way the tiller is held, so if its handle is rough, or too large or small or badly angled the helmsman is distracted and distressed.

A tiller can be made when other work is impossible. It can be cut and carved before the hull arrives, or made during evenings when the main hull is inaccessible, or while waiting for paint and fibreglass to dry. It is worth taking a lot of trouble to get the tiller exactly right because it is an expression of the builders personality, an advertisement of his skill, an important safety factor (if well made and strong) besides being a chance to decorate the boat and make her interesting.

Most tillers are of wood; it is usual to use the same timber as the rest of the deck trim partly so that all the woodwork matches, partly because the economical way to buy anything is in the largest possible quantity. Tropical hardwoods are the usual choice, with teak the leader. It weathers so well, it withstands blackening, rot and other troubles far better than other woods, so it is not surprising that other woods are always a poor second choice. However, teak is vastly expensive. Its price varies with the world's economic climate, with demand, current shipments, with fashion, and so on. Over the years it has often been four or six times as costly as other hardwoods. Also it is not the strongest of woods relative to its weight. In this connection it is worth remembering that a wood's strength is usually proportional to its density; a notable exception to this is spruce, which is sometimes used for racing boats' tillers because lightness combined with strength is essential.

If there is no wood trim on deck, or it is distant from the tiller so that matching is scarcely important, a common choice of wood for the tiller is mahogany. Sometimes a laminated tiller of alternate layers of spruce and mahogany are used to give strength, decoration and to help achieve bold curves. The layers are glued together with the dark wood on the outside.

A straight tiller is the cheapest to make. It takes little time, being fabricated from a piece of fault-free wood with the graining running straight and true. It must be tapered otherwise the result will be an insult to the boat and her builder. If the plans show no details of the tiller it may be tapered about 25 per cent in plan view and 45 per cent in elevation. However, the taper should begin quite 6 inches (150 mm) forward of the tiller end fitting arms, since this is where most breakages occur.

Most tiller grips are large enough for just one hand, though logically on boats over 35 feet (10 m) they should be long enough for two hands, and the paws of a hefty man too. For a single fist the length is 5 inches (125 mm) and double this for two. My own inclination is to be generous with the measurements, and go for a 6 inch (150 mm) length so that even a giant with a thick glove on is accommodated.

The maximum diameter of a hand grip is 1¼ inches (32 mm), this being in the middle. Each end tapers to 1 inch (25 mm) diameter, with the aft end sweeping out to the full width of the tiller in a gentle curve. Any abrupt change of shape here (or anywhere on a boat) invites a fracture and makes varnishing or revarnishing unnecessarily awkward.

Along the whole length of the tiller apart from by the arms of the aft end fitting the edges are planed away to a bevel which is about one eighth of the face of the wood. Before varnishing the tiller (painting being unthinkable) the edges are well rubbed over with sandpaper to give the varnish every chance to lie well and last.

If the tiller has a curvature of no more than 1 in 10 it can be cut from a solid piece of wood, selecting the sweep of the grain to give strength and appearance. For greater curvature it is usually best to laminate the tiller using strips of wood about ¼ inch (6 mm) thick. Either way, the tapering, bevelling and finishing are the same as for a straight tiller.

The aft end of the tiller will have a width to suit the rudder head fitting. If in doubt the depth will be the same as the width, but in practice it is often between 75 and 90 per cent of the width. Normally the length will be taken off the plans, but not everyone always has the opportunity to work to a full set of drawings, and some designers are careless about details like the precise location of the forward end of the tiller.

A long tiller gives a light easy feel to the helm, but when it has to be put hard over, the helmsman may have to gallop across the deck like a jockey unhorsed. Worse still, an over-long tiller will sweep the cockpit, bashing the crew about the kidneys while they wrestle with sheets and winches. A short tiller is a miserable thing, especially if the boat has a tendency to strong weather helm. If the pull of the tiller is fierce it takes the fun out of sailing, makes manoeuvring difficult, and can be dangerous.

Achieving a compromise is not easy without experimentation. If there is no chance to go sailing in a sister-ship and see how the helm feels, it is best to make the tiller too long, and after trials extending through periods of assorted weather, cut off as much as seems right. It is better to have to make two chops than to end with a tiller too short.

Generally, the tiller should not extend to the middle of the cockpit, because it will sweep too big an area. But if the rudder stock comes up ahead of the aft end of the 'pit, then the tiller almost certainly will sweep quite half the well length. In this case a hinged tiller is highly desirable, so that the helmsman can lift his wand as he puts it over, duck under it, and avoid fouling the crew while they handle sheets. A hinged end fitting is an asset in other circumstances. For instance, a party in the cockpit is more fun if there is space, and this is achieved by lifting the tiller and lashing it to the backstay. If the rudder head fitting is not the hinged type a hinge may be worked in halfway along the tiller with a pair of strong metal straps bolted either side of the tiller.

No one in their senses would suggest a standard length of tiller for a given size of boat, but as a rough general indication the following table may be useful:

BOAT LENGTH OVERALL		SUGGESTED MINIMUM TILLER LENGTH	
Feet	*Metres*	*Feet*	*Metres*
20	6	3	0·9
30	9	4	1·2
40	12	5·5	1·7

N.B. This is no more than a preliminary guide, a help when ordering timber (remembering that ample extra allowance should be made) and an indication of whether a proposed tiller is going to be drastically too short. It is not a design guide since tiller length is dependent on such factors as helm balance, space available, the distance from the rudder stock head to the cockpit, etc.

All the suggestions up to now have been on the basis that the tiller will be of wood, as most are. For anyone happier working metals, the choice lies between steel and aluminium alloy, because bronzes are so costly. But anyone who wants to make a boat more than slightly sensational might consider a polished bronze tube for a tiller. Knowledgeable viewers would gasp at such blatant but well-placed extravagance, and the rest of the world would be rightly impressed by the thrilling gleam of long sinuous polished metal – the hint of gold – always provided the crew were prepared to keep up the daily polishing.

A bronze tiller – and it is such a delicious thought I have trouble dragging myself away from it – would be made the same way as a steel or alloy tubular one. Fife favoured galvanised steel tubes and his were made like this: for a boat about 28 feet (9 m) overall galvanised pipe 1½ inches (40 mm) diameter was bent into a gentle S curve so that the handle lay at just the right height for the helmsman. The aft end was rivetted to a Y-piece like a misproportioned rowlock. The stem of the Y fitted inside the pipe and was held by three or five rivets; the arms of the Y snugly embraced the rudder stock and were held to it by a bolt about ¾ inch (20 mm) diameter, which acted as a pivot so that the tiller could be easily raised. The handle was formed by a piece of turned mahogany slipped into the forward end of the pipe and held by three screws. Naturally the turning was decorative, with a bold end knob and groovings – the possibilities here are endless. Because galvanised pipe looks commercial and out of keeping with a yacht, it was common practice to cover the pipe with heavy sail cloth stitched along the bottom so that the sewing was invisible. Each end of the covering was hidden by a Turks head, or double or triple Turks head knot. Or a Snaked whipping. Or a Rose lashing. Owners and crew have a chance to outshine rival boats here with a vengeance. Today the canvas might be replaced by leather-cloth, or the pipe epoxy painted after galvanising.

A form of tiller which is light yet strong is made up from two tubes or two pieces of wood in the form of a V with its base joined to make the handle and the aft ends located each side of the rudder stock (Fig. 41). This design particularly suits rudders hanging on transom sterns.

Modern boats, especially racing craft and light fast cruisers under about 35 feet (10 m) need tiller extensions. These can be bought from chandlers made up in the form of a universal joint, or double pivot, on the end of a tube about 3 feet (1 m) long, with some form of handgrip. The pivot is secured to the tiller just aft of the handle and further aft on top of the tiller a U-shaped spring clip is screwed down to take the extension when it is not in use. If this form of spring clip is not available a loop of shock-cord round the tiller serves well. It is fixed right round the tiller and kept in place by a screw under the tiller through the cord. This loop is located just forward of the point where the extension end comes when it is laid along the tiller top, so it is necessary to stretch the shock-cord over the extension and then release it, when it springs back and holds the extension till it is needed again.

An extension can be made from a piece of wood to match the tiller. In section it will be about 1¼×¾ inch (32×20 mm), with its inboard end secured to a standard universal joint. On the 'hand' end a cross-piece of wood about 2×¾×½ inch (50×20×12 mm) gives a convenient grip yet is not so obtrusive that it fouls oilskin pockets and safety lines.

Emergency tillers should be twice as strong as standard ones. After all, it is almost always in the worst weather than an emergency tiller is needed. This is no time for delicate equipment. The crew need reassurance and they will get this from a piece of spare gear which is massive.

All boats with wheel steering need an emergency tiller and all long range cruisers which are tiller steered should have a second to cope with a breakage. In shape and size the emergency tiller should be similar to a normal one, apart from extra girth which is particularly needed towards the aft end where virtually all breakages occur. The aft end fitting is designed to fit on the rudder stock and is kept copiously greased so that it goes on easily and cannot corrode.

Where there is wheel steering the rudder stock has to be topped with a length which is square in section. The emergency tiller has a square section tube or a length of solid rod drilled and machined with a square section hole which slips over the rudder stock top. It should be possible to ship the emergency tiller in a matter of seconds since there may be a lee shore close by, or the boat may be manoeuvring in a harbour mouth. One way to make the link-up quick and easy is to have the rudder stock emerge up through the deck at a ventilator. To ship the tiller the vent cowl is whipped off and there is the stock end, just above deck ready for the tiller.

A common arrangement is a flush plate in the deck. This is unscrewed using the same key which undoes the fuel and water deck filler caps. In severe conditions, with the boat throwing herself and crew all over the ocean, fiddling about with deck plates is slow and unfunny.

On a few craft the rudder stock is led up to deck level near an aft hatch. The main trouble with this is that the hatch has to be open all the time the emergency tiller is in use, and if there is a vast sea running a lot of water may come aboard via the hatch. A better scheme is to have the top of the stock just above the sole of a watertight cockpit, with a slip-on portable cover which is quickly lifted off.

Whatever arrangement is used, the compass must be visible from the emergency steering position, and the helmsman should ideally have a seat or nearby hand-rails or both. There should also be battens or a nearby seat edge, against which the feet can be jammed.

The tiller is so prominent on any boat that its fabrication and finish need more thought and trouble than other parts. A large scale factory turning out vast numbers of boats monthly used to boast about the tillers they put on their craft. In their full page multicolour advertisements they proclaimed to the world that there was no maintenance on their craft (balderdash – but that's another issue) apart from the annual revarnishing of the tiller. The inference was that all the time afloat is with tiller in hand, and this component alone is worth the trouble of rubbing down and recoating. For once unadulterated salesmanship was being sensible (apart from that rubbish about no maintenance).

Jeremy Lines, the development manager of Camper and Nicholsons, used to crew on a boat called 'Foxiana'. He carved a fox's head on the tiller end. It looked super and was a great success and everyone who saw the boat commented on it. In practice, though, there was a snag. The fox's upstanding ears caught on oilskins and generally made steering awkward, especially in very severe weather. Jeremy recarved the fox with its ears laid back so that they were no longer obtrusive and the end product was a total success. This is the essence of painstaking craftsmanship.

22 Finish

'Finish' might be described as the detail work during completion of a boat. It is the edge trimming, it is the way the decoration is completed, it is the way rough parts of the structure are hidden, it is the way joins in structure are made to look smart, or disguised. Above all finish is the art in the science of boatbuilding.

Finish is so important that it dominates the thoughts and actions of the best amateur and professional shipwrights. If an amateur cannot achieve a fine finish he will never get full 'pride of possession' from his craft. When the time comes to sell the price secured and the speed with which the boat finds a buyer are principally dependent on the standard of finish.

For the professional builder finish is everything. There are plenty of boats which are only moderately strong (and sometimes much weaker than this) and there are others which are slow, dreary to sail, impossible to maintain, bad value for money, and generally bad craft – but if the finish is superb they sell abundantly.

This may be depressing, it may be almost immoral to state out loud, it may be a poor reflection on the perspicacity of boatbuyers, it may suggest they are merely influenced by glossy advertisements, but it is a salient fact in the world of boats.

To get this all important good finish, it is only necessary to follow a few basic rules. Not everyone will agree with all these rules, nor with the order in which they are set down, but there is total agreement that the rules should be like the Ten Commandments – always in mind even if often broken.

1   Study other boatbuilders' products with a thoughtful eye. (This is what boat shows are for, contrary to the illusion that they are for selling boats!)
2   Keep up to date, but never despise sound traditional practice.
3   Keep everything simple. Two colours are ample inside and out. The inside pair can be different from those outside, but as the hatches and doorways are often open, it is a good idea to blend or work together the inside and outside colours.
4   One colour in different shades is often better than two colours. It may require more skill and more searching for matching materials and components, but it is often the cleverest.
5   All wood must be planed all over.
6   Very seldom should a ply edge be left uncovered.
7   Never leave any piece of wood untreated. If raw teak is used it should be treated with teak oil. Outside and inside, right up in the fo'c'sle where no one ever goes and away aft in the counter where only a skinny surveyor can penetrate, have every bit of wood painted or varnished or polished. In

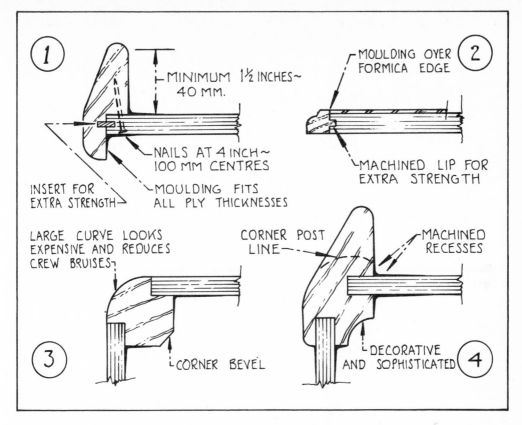

Fig. 42   Ply edge treatment

This section view shows ways for finishing off galley benches, lockers and all sorts of furniture.

Fig. 1 is the inboard edge of a galley bench or chart table. The wood section is designed to accept a wide variety of ply thicknesses; also making the fiddle extra deep gives it a rich professional appearance. The insert will seldom be used by amateurs and not often enough by professionals; it gives an extra area of gluing and added strength. If Formica is to go on the bench top it should be fitted before the fiddle. Notice how the fiddle is vertical on the bench side with only a small round of top edge, to make this efficient at keeping plates on the bench even when the boat heels.

Fig. 2 is a simpler finish, perhaps for a smart desk edge or on the shelf round a basin where a fiddle is not needed. Like the insert in Fig. 1 the lip is made by machining, as is the recess it goes into. Without this lip the moulding may get knocked off too easily by accident.

Fig. 3 can be used for vertical joins, perhaps at the end of a settee or berth, where the side and front have to be joined. This well rounded rebated post covers the end grain and makes for strength as well as reducing the incidence of crew damage. The ply may be glued without screwing here, though almost always the 'belt-and-braces' approach is better.

Fig. 4 is an amalgam of Figs. 1 and 3. The fiddle is large and looks expensive, with a deep section suggesting that masses of fine timber have been used. Two faces are machined to take ply edges and the bottom right corner is machined out to save weight and give a delightful finished appearance.

The builder may buy many feet of this section ready machined to shape and use it all over the boat, for corner posts, for cupboard edges, to join furniture to partial bulkheads and to make up pedestals for WCs. By cutting and planing to the dotted line this section serves as a simple, fully rebated corner post on a cupboard.

In different circumstances these various sections can be used running horizontally or vertically.

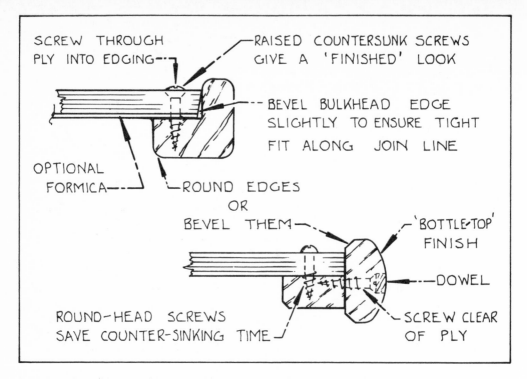

Fig. 43 Bulkhead edging

A ply bulkhead which has a raw, uncovered edge looks cheap and unfinished. It also tends to 'pant'. The different methods of fixing edge mouldings shown here are easy to apply and give the ply extra local thickness and strength.

The top section is made from a machined length of hardwood, screwed at about 6 inch (150 mm) intervals, always through the ply into the moulding. This style can be used when there is Formica on one or both edges of the bulkhead. The moulding, which has well-rounded corners, covers the Formica edges as well as the ply.

The lower section is made of two pieces. The first to be fitted has a bevelled corner as this is fashioned more quickly than a rounded edge. The outer piece has the traditional 'bottle-top' shape which looks terrific but takes a long time to plane to shape. It can be machined nearly to the right section first, then finished with a plane and glass-paper.

practice professionals do not paint or varnish the under sides of drawers and many do not even paint or varnish or otherwise protect the insides of drawers. Maybe they would sell more boats if they did.

8   The best edge trim, for a bulkhead, window edge, table rim and so on is often a hard wood. It usually looks better than plastic or metal. But a neat trim of plastic or metal is better than a crude one of wood.

9   To secure plastic edging bronze nails are used. They are spaced close enough to prevent the trim being knocked off even in tough conditions. The plastic should have no undulations. If in doubt a nail spacing of about 3 inches (75 mm) is about right.

10   Almost always the best way to treat screws is to sink them deeply and put dowels over. The wood of the dowels should be the same colour and tex-

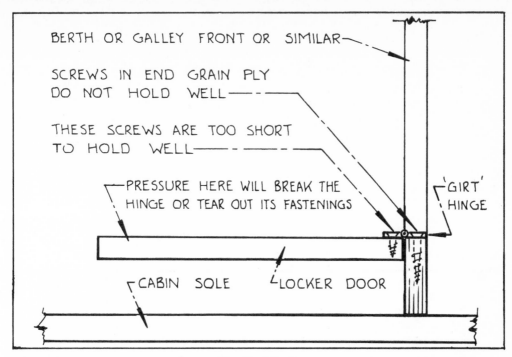

BERTH OR GALLEY FRONT OR SIMILAR

SCREWS IN END GRAIN PLY
DO NOT HOLD WELL

THESE SCREWS ARE TOO SHORT
TO HOLD WELL

PRESSURE HERE WILL BREAK THE
HINGE OR TEAR OUT ITS FASTENINGS

'GIRT'
HINGE

CABIN SOLE   LOCKER DOOR

Fig. 44   Mistakes

This section view through a galley front, or berth front, or similar piece of furniture is a warning.

The screws through the hinges will not last a single hard season. If a hinge has to be secured to a thin locker door there must be bolts right through with washers under the nuts. Screws into the edge grain of ply never hold well, so a piece of hardwood should be bolted or screwed to the ply, and the hinge fastened to that.

Worst of all, the door when open cannot fold right back so that its top edge is firmly down on the cabin sole. Any slight load on the door, forcing it downwards, will tear out one or both sets of screws. This condition, known as 'girting', has to be avoided on deck and below.

ture as the surrounding wood and the grain should align. Perfect dowels are virtually invisible.

11   If dowels cannot be used, decorative head screws are a good second best. They can be bought with a dark copper finish, or an intermediate or light coppery finish. Sometimes this attractive, artificial ageing effect is called 'BMA finish'. Naturally the screws are brass or bronze, never steel.

12   The slots in the screw heads should all be in line.

13   Coloured putty over countersunk screws is never acceptable when polished or varnished wood forms the background. Recessed screws in painted wood can be covered with putty carefully smoothed over, but this is an unreliable material and it is better to use a proprietary filling which stands up to sea conditions and remains unaffected by moisture, temperature changes and the slight movement aboard all craft.

14   It is a characteristic of good finish that it lasts. For example, nothing should be screwed or nailed into the edge grain of ply, not even thick ply, because it will not stay permanently in place.

15   Polish usually looks better than varnish but does not stand up to weathering so well.

16   Varnish usually looks better than paint, but is less weather resistant.

17   All edges and corners must be rounded or bevelled. This is partly to achieve a good appearance, but more important, it reduces crew injury in severe weather. It also helps paint, varnish and polish to stay on. Any sharp edge wears easily, and fluids like paint flow away from sharp edges when brushed or sprayed on. The sharp edge of a table which is varnished or painted often has a very thin covering which is doubly vulnerable. Bevelling is generally quicker than rounding but marginally less effective. A typical bevel is between ⅛ inch and ¼ inch (3 and 6 mm) wide.

18   Floorboards and sole boards edges should be bevelled about 10° to the vertical so that they do not jam easily even when wet. If they do jam they are easy to free if only the top edge is in contact with the next board or adjacent bulkhead. The bottom edges should be rounded to minimise the disadvantages of end grain and reduce the chances of chipping, also to help paint or varnish to stay on.

19   If the sole is teak faced ply with imitation seam lines, these should be positioned so that the lines on one piece meet the lines exactly on the next.

20   Alignment is important right through a boat; a cooker top should be at the same height as the neighbouring worktop, which should in turn line up with an engine casing or companionway step. Likewise, the bottom of the book-rack over the chart table should line up with the bottom of the nearby instruments such as the echo-sounder. Drawer and adjacent locker door handles should be in line, just as the top of the top drawer and the bottom of the bottom drawer of a set should align with the top and bottom of an adjacent locker door.

21   There are well established heights, widths and depths for every sort of furniture. By sticking to standard dimensions it is reasonably certain that components will line up closely, but to get everything exactly right it may be necessary to trim some items during fitting. Standard dimensions are listed in the *Boat Data Book*.

23 *Cabin doors and weather-boards*

At the entrance to the interior of any boat there must be either doors or weather-boards. The doors have to be strong enough to stand up to the worst sea conditions the vessel is likely to meet. Because it is not always easy or cheap to make suitable doors weather-boards are sometimes fitted. They consist of planks which drop into slots. These slots are either machined out of the solid wood or made up by assembling strips of wood into door-posts with deep grooves at each side of the entrance (see Fig. 45).

It is hard to lay down any specific differences between doors and weather-boards, but in general doors are marginally more convenient since they can be quickly swung open or closed. They tend to look a little more finished, and it is unthinkable that a large, elegant and sophisticated yacht designed to impress and intended to spend many hours basking in a sunny marina would have weather-boards.

In contrast, weather-boards suggest to the initiated a tough boat, one intended to thrash across raging oceans regardless of the hurricane's blast. Weather-boards tend to be cheaper but this is not always the case. As in so many different facets of boatbuilding bad doors look worse than moderate weather-boards; superb weather-boards can invoke as much envy as attractive doors, and once again we are back to the skill of the designer and builder.

Broadly speaking vessels over 50 feet will have doors: power boats have doors, boats biased towards living aboard rather than voyaging will have doors. In contrast deep sea boats tend to have weather-boards, cheap boats, small cruisers, certainly racing boats of almost every type have weather-boards.

In theory a racing boat has weather-boards because these items are lifted out of their slots and sent ashore before the race, or if the race is offshore the weather-boards are stowed low down in the bilge. However, it is possible to buy lift-off hinges so that the doors can be stored ashore or in the bilge almost as conveniently.

Weather-boards are usually made up in two, three, and occasionally four sections. This means that one or more can be dropped in according to the amount of spray flying about. The hatch can be kept shut but one or two boards are left out to ventilate the inside of the cabin and give extra light. Additional light inside a boat can also be achieved by having windows in either the doors or the weather-boards. Some builders make the whole of the doors or weather-boards out of Perspex (Luctite) or Polycarbonate and very smart they look, and they do not need annual varnishing or painting. Likewise ventilators can be cut

117

in doors or weather-boards, complete with baffles to deflect spray which comes in from aft.

If doors are used they should have hinges extending almost right across for extra strength, and of course the hinges are much better bolted on rather than merely screwed. Doors have to be designed either to swing back 180° so that they fold flat against cabin coamings or they have to lift off. A door which swings half open and will go no further will inevitably obstruct the cockpit or side deck and quite apart from the inconvenience it is likely to cause injury and get broken.

Whatever the choice is the access must be made as clear and as easy to use as possible. For instance, weather-boards are often locked by a hasp secured to the hatch. This hasp should be well offset to one side so that the tongue does not stick out in the middle of the hatch and hurt anybody hastening through the

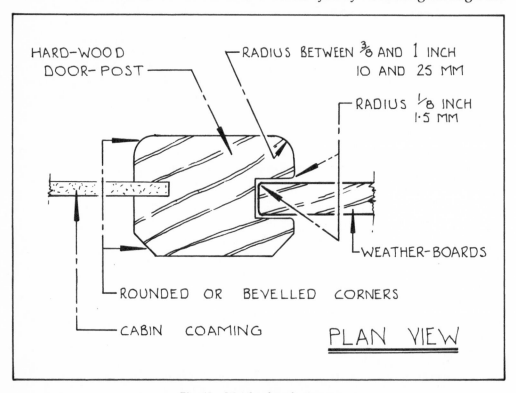

Fig. 45 Weather-board runners

If weather-boards are used to close the cabin doorway they drop into slots in door-posts. There must be just enough clearance between the weather-boards and the groove in the post to make it easy to fit the boards. About 1/16 inch (1.5 mm) is enough clearance provided the weather-boards are unwarped. If they have become curved through moisture change it is usually better to make a new set, though hard-wood vertical stiffening straps about two or three times the thickness of the weather-boards may be fitted. They will have their grain running at right angles to the grain in the weather-boards, and will need bolting or very strong screwing.

Where there are no facilities for grooving the door-posts the alternative is to make the posts up from pieces of wood glued and screwed or bolted together. It is usual to varnish door posts on all surfaces. Occasionally they are decorated with extra grooves like the 'ovolo' and 'cove' on beams.

118

companion doorway. In areas of bad vandalism it is good sense to have a hasp at each side.

Vandals need discouraging, and as they generally enter a boat through the main cabin doorway a good technique is to have all the fittings very obviously rugged and burglar proof. A thief likes to break in quickly and quietly so he will be put off if he sees massive metal defences. He will pass on to the next boat which is less of a challenge. In very bad areas it may be worth fitting an expanded metal grill of galvanised steel secured over the weather-boards or doors with padlocked hasps right across (see diagram on page 121).

Doors should open outwards even on boats used in sheltered waters. They are made of hardwood to match the rest of the deck trim on the boat and are

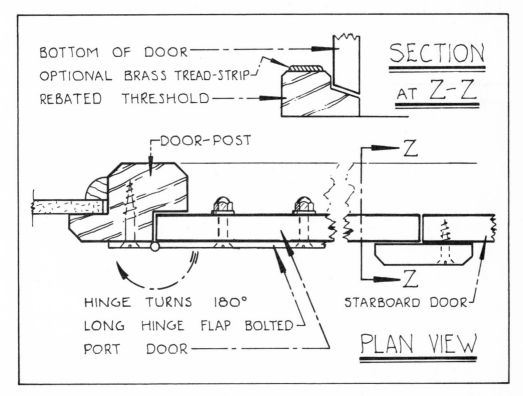

Fig. 46   Cabin entrance doors

A wave breaking on board will try to drive the cabin doors inboard. To prevent this the hinge edges and bottom edges of all external doors are made to lodge against strong structural parts. Door-posts are rebated to take the hinge edges and any water trying to get into the cabin has to work its way through a slit which has a right angle turn. For deep sea work a rubber seal may be fitted here.

The bottom of the door is sloped to discourage water from entering, and hasten drainage. A rubber seal may be fitted here, though this is rarely seen. If the door fits well the bottom will just jam on the threshold, so that water cannot find a way in.

To take the wear of feet treading on the threshold a brass or bronze strip is screwed along the top edge. Alternatively aluminium alloy or tuphnol may be used as cheaper alternatives.

To stop water entering where the port and starboard doors meet one door laps over so here again water has to get in by way of a slit with a right angle in it.

almost always varnished inside and out. The inside might be sheathed with Formica to cut down maintenance. However, the doors are often fully open so that the inside is displayed in the cockpit. The Formica will presumably be selected to match the decoration inside the cabin at the aft end by the cabin steps. When this Formica is swung out into the cockpit it is almost certainly going to look quite wrong and will spoil the general appearance of the boat for anyone in the cockpit.

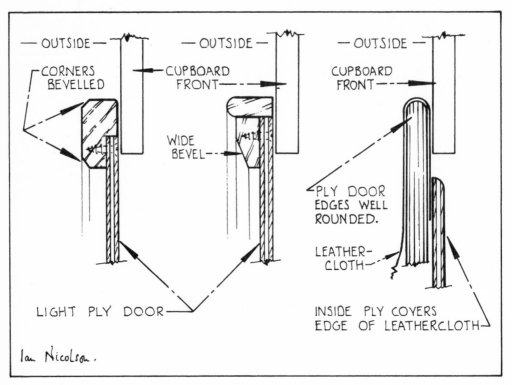

Fig. 47   Doors

Shown here are section views through the tops of three types of door. All are located on the outside of the cupboard or bulkhead, so that exact fitting is not needed. This speeds up and simplifies manufacture.

The one on the left is made from ply framed with a rebated moulding all round. Mitre joins at each corner and bevels on all the edges ensure a good appearance. The ply can be as light as 4 mm for cupboard doors in a racing boat and up to 25 mm for the cabin doors of a large craft. The moulding will normally be proportioned as shown and three or four times as thick as the ply.

In the centre is a similar section but made with no rebating. This is ideal for an amateur with no wood machining facilities. The joins of the inner part of the moulding may be halved and the outer parts mitred, but the appearance will be better if all parts are mitred. The extra wide bevel gives the appearance of professionalism and it looks good. All parts should be glued and screwed, but for minor cupboard doors screwing alone is adequate.

The right hand sketch shows a door made from ply covered with leathercloth. This eliminates varnishing and painting and it looks fine if the leathercloth matches the cushion covers. To get the leathercloth to lie smoothly the sort with a knitted, not woven backing should be used. Also the ply edges must be well rounded. A piece of leathercloth can be glued over the back to cover the rough edges of the front piece, but the inner, thin ply over the cloth edges is usually smarter. Also the inner ply stiffens and strengthens the door.

BOAT TYPES	DOOR OR WEATHER-BOARD THICKNESS	COMMENTS (With modified Beaufort scale)
Light racing boats, day boats, estuary craft, etc., under 30 ft – 9 m.	⅛ inch – 3 mm ply.	This thickness will only keep out rain and light spray. It is scarcely able to keep out a 7-year-old vandal.
Inexpensive production boats up to about 36 ft – 11 m use this size. Half-tonners, three-quarter-tonners, etc.	⅜ inch – 10 mm ply or 5⁄16 inch – 8 mm Perspex.	This will keep out heavy spray but not a serious breaking wave. Far from vandal-proof.
Offshore racing boats up to about 40 ft – 12 m. Cruisers up to about 33 ft – 10 m for passage-making.	½ inch – 12 mm solid wood or ply or ⅜ inch – 10 mm.	A widely used popular thickness. Will keep out a breaking sea inches deep on deck but not a really vicious one. Vandals start to get discouraged.
Large offshore racing boats, and coastal cruising craft where strength and sea-worthiness are more important than saving weight or money.	¾ inch – 20 mm solid wood or ply or ⅝ inch – 16 mm Perspex.	Recommended for seagoing boats as a good compromise, with ample strength for most emergencies without too much weight. Should resist most breaking seas and most vandals.
Long range deep sea craft.	1 inch – 25 mm solid wood or ply.	Recommended for offshore work in all weathers. Vandals need exceptional determination to get through this thickness.
For craft designed to stand up to hurricanes.	1¼ inch – 32 mm solid wood or ply. (Ply needs gluing up from 2 layers of ⅝ inch – 16 mm as this thickness of ply is not made commercially.)	Recommended for real peace of mind but rather heavy and inconvenient in between hurricanes. Needs metal mesh backing to be fully vandal-proof.

Fibreglass is not used for cabin doors because it is not a suitable material. The edges are very prone to chipping and the fastenings through the hinges are likely to give trouble.

The doorposts are rebated so that the whole vertical edge of the door lies in a recess. In the same way the door bottom lies in a recess along the threshold. When a sea breaks against the cabin doors the tendency is to press the doors against their rebates so that there is little chance that it will burst the doors inwards. It must be possible to close the doors and the main hatch from the inside, so suitable handles are needed. All the components like the locks, hinges, knobs and fastenings must be non-ferrous.

Weather-boards are made in such a way that water running down their outside face will not run in at the joins. This is achieved by rebating the bottom edge of the top board so that it recesses into and overlaps the top of the next board down. Alternatively the bottom of each board is bevelled with the outside edge lower than the inside, and water thus has to run uphill to get between two boards. Yet another technique, used especially with Perspex or Luctite or thin ply, is to have a thin batten secured and made watertight along the top inside of each board, overlapping on the board above. This works just like a bevel and has the advantage that it stiffens the board.

For boats going offshore boards should have a device which prevents them from falling out if the boat is rolled over by a rogue wave. A barrel bolt working horizontally over the top of the top board, with a handle inside the cabin and another outside is one favoured device. Another is a brass pin which can be inserted and removed from the cockpit or from below. Yet another arrangement is a normal door lock working athwartships, with a door handle inside and another outside; the trouble with this is that the tongue of the lock has to be held closed while the board is being slid down or up.

24 *Fitting a fore-hatch or a modern skylight*

Fore-hatches and skylights may be fitted at the same time as other deck fittings, on the principle that batches of similar jobs should be done together to save time, save wasting materials like bedding compounds, and because deck fittings tend to need the same tools and fastenings to secure them. However, deck fittings may be left till late in the construction sequence if the inside of the boat is warm and the outside weather is frigid, or if some deck fittings arrive late. It may pay, nevertheless, to fit the fore-hatch or skylight early to give better access into the boat, or for ventilation, or for passing through electric cables or even for getting gear into the cabins.

It is now universal practice to fit 'bought-in' fore-hatches. These factory-made hatches have transparent plastic tops and fibreglass or aluminium alloy frames. When it is closed the top part of the frame is pulled tight by clamps. This squeezes a rubber seal all round so that unless the rubber has perished or the hatch has been abused so that the frame has distorted there is no chance of a leak. Sometimes limited distortion can be taken up by the rubber seal.

Because they are so good these hatches are used as skylights. The traditional skylight was akin to the old fashioned type of hatch; being made of hardwood it dried out at the same time in hot weather, it sometimes cracked, often the corner joins opened, it always leaked after a short time unless it received more maintenance than a new-born baby.

One of the best makes of hatch is the Canpa type, made by Camper and Nicholsons and available worldwide through their agents. It has been developed so that it does not have protruding lugs or fastenings inside or out and is available in a variety of sizes and with clear or tinted plastic. The tinted version is always selected for siting over sleeping cabins or toilets or for hot climates.

Normally the moulded deck will have a flat area at the fore end of the cabin top for the fore-hatch. There may be a second amidships for another hatch which acts as a skylight over the saloon. Almost always hatches are set on the cabin top rather than lower on the fore-deck to minimise the chance of water getting below if the hatch is left open when a wave comes aboard.

If the design of the cabin top does not incorporate a flat or a very nearly flat area for the hatch, wood filler pieces are needed to take up the camber. A complete wood rectangle, something like a picture frame, is made up using well-seasoned hardwood. It is set on the cabin top and the shape of the camber pencilled in. The wood is cut away till the bottom face of the frame sits tight on the deck. The bolts which hold the hatch down also hold this frame down, and the same massive amount of bedding which is put under the hatch flanges is also put under the frame.

Over the centuries the world has been split by such acute questions as slavery, religious tolerance, free trade and nuclear disarmament. Now the really big division, which transcends country, creed and political allegiance is: 'Should fore-hatches open forwards or aft?' That is: should the hinge-line be across the front or the back? This is something upon which there is a vast disagreement. The arguments are approximately as follows:

If the hinge-line is aft the hatch acts as a better air scoop ventilator when moving, it is easier to get out of the hatch on most boats and it will swing up and lie open against the mast; whereas if the hinge-line is forward the hatch top may be opened too far forward, and the hinges broken off. It is claimed that with the hinges aft it is easier to get bagged sails up and down, the fore-deck is left more clear, and so on. The argument rages far into the night and through unlimited glasses of Scotch, Bourbon, beer, vodka, wine, pernod, chianti, etc. (This argument goes on in all countries all the time.) The opposition argue like this:

A hatch with the hinges forward provides better ventilation because the draft through a boat is from aft forward and the hatch which is half open with its hinges forward promotes this air flow; it is safer because if a sea comes aboard, the hatch top will divert a lot of water away from the yawning opening; it has always been done this way in the past and experience is everything in the tough environment of the sea; it can be left one quarter open even in quite severe conditions and spray (or worse) will not get below.

Summing up those points of view: the hinges should be forward because this is safer except:

1   On a racing boat where aft hinges may make for faster sail-handling and hence a faster boat.
2   On a boat used in *sheltered* conditions in hot places if the crew are sure this will make the inside of the boat cooler.
3   On boats where the designer has worked in some feature which makes it essential to have the hinges aft – the steps up through the hatch may be very awkward to use if the hinges are forward.

It is usual for the boat's plans to show the type and size of hatch to be fitted. The deck should be checked to make sure that the specified hatch will indeed fit, then the hatch ordered not just by catalogue number but also by size. Hatch makers and hull moulders both change their products so here as elsewhere when ordering equipment, a double check saves time and returned goods. Bolts to suit the hatch should be bought from the same source as the hatch to make sure they fit. It will be necessary to measure the length of the bolts through the deck and through any packing or levelling frame. This length is given to the chandler, with instructions to add this length to the hatch flange thickness, and nut size, so that the length of the bolt is correct.

Cutting overlong stainless steel bolts is tedious and sometimes hard work.

When the hatch arrives it is laid in place, carefully squared up fore-and-aft. Exactly in the middle a pilot hole which can be ¼ inch (6 mm) diameter is drilled. The shipwright now goes below into the cabin and marks out on the underside where the cut-out for the hatch will be. This is to ensure that nothing vital comes in the way. It may be that there is a stiffening beam or carline close by, so the hatch may have to be shifted a little to a new location. Usually fore-hatches are exactly on the centre-line of the ship, but other considerations may make it advisable to re-position the hatch to one side.

The hatch top is opened, with the hatch in its correct position and a pencil line drawn round the inside of the frame on the deck. Normally this is the line which the jig-saw follows when cutting out the deck opening. However, it may be necessary to cut back a little further for the deck-head lining which may be glued on the underside of the deck and folded up through the hole and under the hatch flange. If the deck is of sandwich construction the inner core of balsa or foam plastic should never be left exposed. First it is sealed with resin and afterwards either covered with a wood, metal or plastic edge moulding, or concealed with a soft lining folded over.

The bolts round the hatch should be tightened progressively, starting with the aft port one, then the forward starboard one, then the port forward one, then aft starboard, and so on. The nuts are first run up finger tight, then made fully tight in stages so that the bedding is squeezed evenly, and the hatch is pulled down onto the deck uniformly, without distortion.

25 *Engine bearers*

The best designers produce a separate drawing for an engine installation. They mark in the outline of the engine bearers but anybody building a standard boat is well advised to go and examine the whole engine installation of a sister ship even if this means making a journey of some considerable distance. A troublesome area in modern boats is the region round the engine, particularly at the bearer ends. Engine vibration causes cracking here in the hull and also breaks the bonding between the hull and the bearers.

To avoid this trouble it is important to have the bearers as long as possible and also to work in strong athwartships components. Bearer ends and floors athwartships should all taper away gradually to avoid 'hard spots'.

This tapering out is often difficult, particularly at the forward ends of the engine space in the sailing boat. Such craft have cabin steps right down the fore side of the engine. At the bottom of these steps the sole is put as low as possible down in the hull. This common arrangement leaves little room to extend the bearers forward of the engine. One cure is to have a floor right across the forward end of the bearers, this floor being carried well across the ship so that the width of the floor is of the order of half the beam of the boat. Even with this ample width the floor ends should be tapered away so that they are very flexible at the extremities. The middle of the floor between the bearers may be cut away at the top to give access below the engine. This forward floor prevents oily water flowing forward into the main part of the bilge and so it acts as a drip-tray.

There should be at least two athwartship floors or brackets even on small engine bearers. The bearers themselves should be made longer than the engine and its gear box. Even if it requires some cleverness and contriving the engine bearers should ideally be twice as long as the machinery; if the vessel is driven at over 15 knots then at least three times the engine length should be the aim. For fast planing boats the bearers should be extended half the boat's overall length.

If the engine bearer tops are made straight they tend to taper away to nothing quite soon aft of the gear box, while at the forward end there is a strong probability the engine bearers will be too high. So the clever thing to do is to have engine bearers which are straight and flat in way of the engine but curve gently up at the aft end and gently down at the forward end. In this way the bearers can be extended well fore-and-aft but at the same time kept to a sensible height.

Bearers may be made of foam filled fibreglass with a steel plate bonded in the top, as shown in the sketch. Sometimes wood is used, especially by amateurs who use plenty of wood and so have useful supplies but do not have a stock of foam plastic. Hardwood or marine ply should be used, all fully glassed in. If the bearers are to be made of metal no mild steel should be used because there is a risk that rusting may start. Even a little rust causes trouble; it pushes the glassing away from the steel which allows further corrosion to develop, so the glassing is progressively forced off the steel, and in times there is virtually no bond between the bearers and the hull.

One of the simplest, lightest and cheapest form of bearers is made from

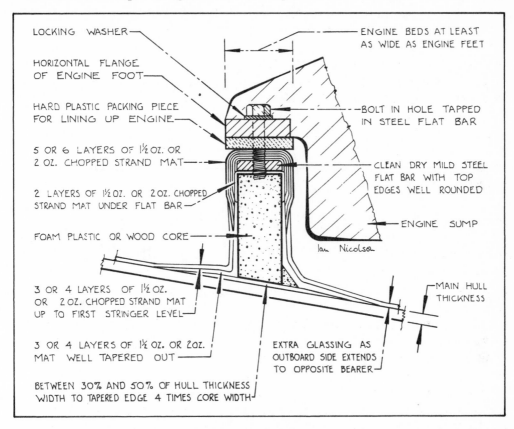

LOCKING WASHER

ENGINE BEDS AT LEAST AS WIDE AS ENGINE FEET

HORIZONTAL FLANGE OF ENGINE FOOT

HARD PLASTIC PACKING PIECE FOR LINING UP ENGINE

5 OR 6 LAYERS OF 1½ OZ. OR 2 OZ. CHOPPED STRAND MAT

2 LAYERS OF 1½ OZ. OR 2 OZ. CHOPPED STRAND MAT UNDER FLAT BAR

FOAM PLASTIC OR WOOD CORE

3 OR 4 LAYERS OF 1½ OZ. OR 2 OZ. CHOPPED STRAND MAT UP TO FIRST STRINGER LEVEL

3 OR 4 LAYERS OF 1½ OZ. OR 2 OZ. MAT WELL TAPERED OUT

BETWEEN 30% AND 50% OF HULL THICKNESS WIDTH TO TAPERED EDGE 4 TIMES CORE WIDTH

BOLT IN HOLE TAPPED IN STEEL FLAT BAR

CLEAN DRY MILD STEEL FLAT BAR WITH TOP EDGES WELL ROUNDED

ENGINE SUMP

Ian Nicolson

MAIN HULL THICKNESS

EXTRA GLASSING AS OUTBOARD SIDE EXTENDS TO OPPOSITE BEARER

Fig. 48   Engine bearers

Boats over about 45 feet (14 metres) often have this type of engine bearer, seen here in section. It is not hard to make and can be built up to suit the heaviest and most powerful engine. Its salient features are: a light, easily formed core set on a reinforced hull; a steel bar embedded on top, with copious fibreglass layers below and all round; careful tapering out of all fibreglass work; a flat top on which it is essential to have some packing before setting down the engine feet.

This type of bearer should be extended well fore-and-aft, and should have no sudden changes in area, or in the slope of the top. It should taper away at the ends which ideally will be one eighth of the boat's length beyond the engine.

The right bottom corner of the bearer is shown with a foam fillet piece. This results in the glassing over being turned through two 45° angles which is far better than the outboard bottom corner. Here the glassing is turned through 90° or indeed less, if there is much rise of floor. As a result the first layers of glass tend to leave a triangular hollow at the angle unless light glass (1½ oz chopped strand mat or less) is used and carefully worked in.

To secure the engine holes are bored through the feet smaller than the holding down bolts. These holes are right through the flat steel bar, and are threaded to take the engine holding down bolts which are tightened on spring washers.

127

marine ply with solid timber secured along the top edge. In section view this gives a bearer which looks like an inverted L. The horizontal leg is made as wide as the engine feet and about twice that depth. The holding down bolts go through the solid timber section, and there may be access holes (which also act as lightening holes) in the vertical ply section. The holes make it easy to put the nuts on the engine holding-down bolts.

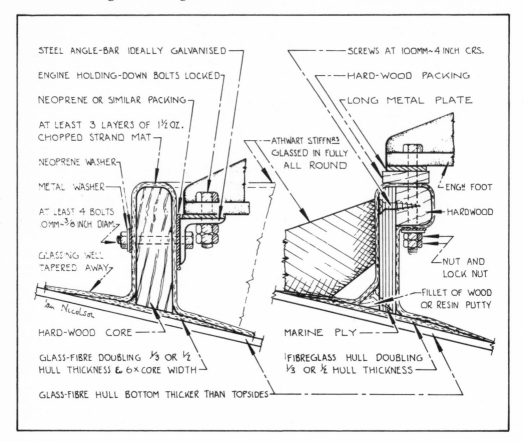

STEEL ANGLE-BAR IDEALLY GALVANISED
ENGINE HOLDING-DOWN BOLTS LOCKED
NEOPRENE OR SIMILAR PACKING
AT LEAST 3 LAYERS OF 1½ OZ. CHOPPED STRAND MAT
NEOPRENE WASHER
METAL WASHER
AT LEAST 4 BOLTS 10MM~⅜ INCH DIAM
GLASSING WELL TAPERED AWAY
Ian Nicolson
HARD-WOOD CORE
GLASS-FIBRE DOUBLING ⅓ OR ½ HULL THICKNESS & 6 × CORE WIDTH
GLASS-FIBRE HULL BOTTOM THICKER THAN TOPSIDES

SCREWS AT 100MM~4 INCH CRS.
HARD-WOOD PACKING
LONG METAL PLATE
ATHWART STIFFNᴿˢ GLASSED IN FULLY ALL ROUND
ENGᴺ FOOT
HARDWOOD
NUT AND LOCK NUT
FILLET OF WOOD OR RESIN PUTTY
MARINE PLY
FIBREGLASS HULL DOUBLING ⅓ OR ½ HULL THICKNESS

Fig. 49   Small engine bearers

These sketches show sections through typical engine bearers for boats up to about 35 feet (10 metres) overall length. Both have stiffening of several layers of chopped strand mat sometimes interspersed with woven roving, on the hull shell. The one on the left is made up of a single piece of hardwood which extends well forward-and-aft of the engine. For extra strength this type of bearer is made deep; unlike many designs of bearer the top does not have to be below the under side of the engine feet.

The steel angle bar is located at the right height to take the engine feet. Sometimes the engine is bolted to its angle bars, port and starboard, and lowered in place, then the steel bars are bolted to the glassed-in bearers. Where a steel bolt or bar lies against fibreglass neoprene washers or strip are used to cope with the unevenness of the surface of the glassing.

Under the engine feet there are metal plates or thin shims to give the correct alignment. All engine holding-down bolts are locked, so that they cannot come loose in spite of engine vibration. Locking nuts are usually used. The right hand drawing shows a light cheap type of bearer. It is supported athwartships by ply knees well glassed up the side of the hull. To let water drain away the knees have limber holes at the bottom.

Bearers should be fully glassed in all round. To make the join to the hull better it pays to have triangular fillet pieces along the bottom of each bearer, so that the glassing does not have to be worked into a sharp angle. If the bearers are joined together by athwartships components at each end they do not need any supporting while the glassing is setting, as the two bearers and the two ends form four sides of a box which has no top; the hull shell is in effect the bottom of the box. The bottom edges of the bearers will often need limber holes cut through otherwise bilge-water will lie along the outboard sides.

Before putting the bearers in, the hull thickness should be built up when an engine over about 15 h.p. is being installed. The construction plan should show the amount of thickening needed, but if in doubt it is usually right to increase the shell by about 20 per cent spread out over twice the engine width and over about 1½ times the bearer length.

The technique of glassing in a steel flat bar inside the top of the bearer, then drilling and tapping the engine holding down bolt holes suits professional builders, but it has a number of disadvantages. It is difficult to move the engine a short distance, it presupposes the builder has a suitable tap, the correct size of drills all fully sharpened; it hopefully assumes that access vertically above the bolt holes is clear, which is far from the case on plenty of standard engines, and so on.

A slightly different approach is to make glassed-in bearers and bolt steel angle-bars alongside, with a semi-hard packing strip between the steel and the bearer, with bolts at least three-quarters the diameter of the engine holding down bolts spaced about 5 inches (125 mm) apart in a staggered pattern. One tremendous advantage of this technique is that the bearers are outboard of the engine, and the top edges of the bearers need not follow the propeller shaft line. The builder can run his bearers away beyond the engine forward and aft, and the shape of the bearers in elevation need have no link with the engine shape and proportions. This is a boon for a professional builder as he can put different engines in a standard hull with standard bearers. It means that anyone can, within limitations, change the engine in a boat to a different model.

=26 *Engine installation*=

If the engine is heavy it may be good policy to have the hull moulder lift it in place onto the engine bearers. He will do this before putting on the deck. Where an engine is fitted after the deck it is important to make sure that the engine can go in through the available hatch. Sometimes an engine can be made narrower for this job by unbolting the engine feet, also perhaps the alternator and other protruding auxiliaries.

Where the hatches are too small a temporary hole is cut in the deck, or the cockpit well is cut out. After fitting the engine the cut-away part is reglassed in place. It will be virtually impossible to disguise the cutting lines on the outside so they are covered over with teak battens or Treadmaster or some similar overlay. Inside the cut lines will either be in places which do not matter or they will be covered by the usual lining.

Hoisting an engine inboard can be done by sheer manpower provided the engine weighs less than 200 lbs (100 kg) or maybe a bit more if the people concerned are tough and determined. Before lifting the engine the deck and cabin entrance should be well protected with planks, old carpets or sacking. Staging is fixed alongside as a platform onto which the engine is laid when it is picked up first, as the distance to the deck from the ground is too big for one lift. With one man at each engine foot, the machinery is moved in a series of small, slow, thoughtful stages.

It may pay to bolt the engine down onto a wooden stretcher, or have temporary fore-and-aft lifting handles bolted to the feet, so that more than four people can help with the lift. At no time does anyone stand under the engine, or leave a foot below it.

Another way to get the engine in is to use the same crane which lifts the boat off the lorry when the hull is delivered from the builder. Alternatively, there may be a strong beam over the building site, or a weak beam can be stiffened with extra supports and one or two additional crosspieces lashed alongside the beam to give it more strength. Lifting gear, possibly made from the yacht's running rigging, is suspended from this beam. Another approach is to hire some scaffolding and build up sheer-legs or a pair of bi-pods with a crossbeam.

A certain club which must be nameless uses a railway bridge over a canal. In the evening when the last train has run, the boat's engine is unobtrusively carried up on the bridge; the boat is floated along the canal till her hatch is just below the bridge, and there she is firmly moored so that she cannot drift away, even slightly. The engine is now lowered down through the boat's hatch and all the ropes, lifting tackle, planks for sliding the engine over the bridge edge are quickly hustled away. To see the operation efficiently carried out on a foggy winter night, with the minimum fuss and practically no give-away lights is to know the thrill of old-time smuggling. The rest of the engine installation work is done with the boat ashore.

The installation procedure can be divided into:

1   The lining up procedure.
2   The connecting of the piping, tanks, wiring and controls.

1   To get the correct alignment of the engine, propeller shaft, stern tube, and P-bracket, a taut wire is extended down the line where the centre-line of the shaft must be. This line is shown on the engine installation drawing. If it is not shown, the builder draws the line in on the print (see Fig. 50). Temporary structure is needed to hold each end of the wire. Sometimes a plank can be bolted to the transom, through holes which later serve for the permanent back-stay bolts. Another technique is to use scaffolding partly clamped to the hull, partly sunk into the ground. Inside the boat a bolt through a bulkhead, or temporary extension to the bulkhead, can be used. Another trick is to secure a plank with clamps across the settee fronts.

2   Where the wire will pass through the hull is marked and a hole is drilled. The wire is secured at just the right height at each end and pulled taut. It may well be that where the wire passes through the hull it touches the hull shell. Little by little the fibreglass is cut away just enough so that the wire can be pulled tight and it is clear of the fibreglass. To get the wire truly taut some boatbuilders use a rigging screw or a Spanish windlass.

If the engine bearers have not been put in, this work is done now. Generally the bearer tops run parallel with the taut wire, but 1 inch (25 mm) below it. Most engines have the centre-line of the crankshaft and the centre of the coupling and the base of the engine feet all on the same horizontal plane. This means that the engine bearer tops would logically run level with the crankshaft centre. But if they were at this height it would be impossible to lower the engine slightly during alignment, so the bearer tops are kept down about an inch and packing pieces put on top.

Packing pieces are made of hard-wood for engines up to about 15 horsepower with broad metal plates on top to prevent the engine feet biting into the wood. For larger engines a tough plastic may be used, or metal angle bar. If the engine feet are set on fibreglass they will damage it and the engine will get out of alignment.

The engine drawing needs studying because sometimes the reduction gear lowers the level of the propeller shaft. In such a case either extra packing is needed or the top line of the engine bearers must be higher. In practice thick packing pieces (more than 1 inch – 25 mm) are not good because they allow the engine to wobble.

Where a P-bracket is fitted, it too is aligned so that taut wire goes plumb through the middle of the bearing in the bracket. P-brackets, and A-brackets which are the same but with two legs or stems to give a better support for the propeller shaft, may be bolted to the hull or glassed in. If bolts are used there will be a flange at the top of the shank, this flange being at least as thick as the countersunk heads of the bolts through it so that the bolts do not protrude. Between the flange and the hull there should be a wood packing piece at least

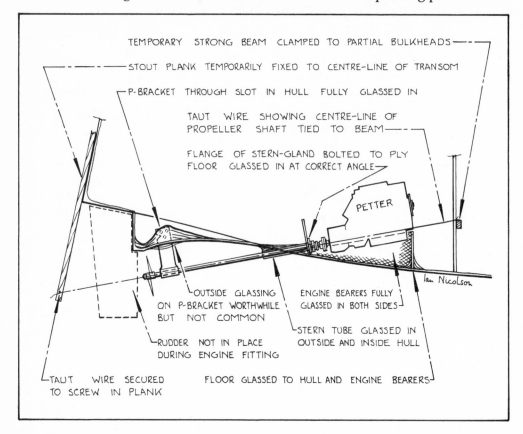

Fig. 50 Engine installation

To install an engine a taut wire is stretched along the line of the centre of the propeller shaft. Temporary structure is erected to take each end of this wire, and a hole is drilled in the hull for the wire to pass through. The tops of the engine bearers run parallel with the taut wire and usually 1 inch (25 mm) below it. This distance is chosen because the engine feet are usually in line with the centre of the crankshaft and hence the propeller shaft (a fact which should be checked on the engine drawing). Keeping the tops of the bearers 1 inch down allows for that much packing to be put in below the engine feet when aligning the engine exactly.

The hull is cut away where the wire passes through it just enough for the propeller shaft tube to fit. This tube has a gland on its inboard end with a flange which has two or four holes for bolts. These bolts are put through a strong floor (usually of marine ply) which is in turn glassed in place. The P-bracket is fitted on the shaft, with its stem up through a specially cut slot in the hull. The shaft is bolted by way of its coupling to the engine.

When all is aligned correctly the P-bracket and the stern tube as well as its floor are all glassed in. Once the boat is afloat the shaft coupling is 'broken' (i.e. unbolted) and the engine line-up checked with feeler gauges.

In this sketch the P-bracket is shown with holes and a large nick on the aft edge so that the glassing in can get a sure and firm grip.

¼ inch (6 mm) thick, but not more than 1 inch (25 mm). This wood pad is planed to the right thickness and bevel to get the right alignment. Inside the hull there will be another wood pad glassed in, also a further wood pad on top of the glassing. The wood inside the hull should be of the order of ¾ inch (20 mm) for every 20 foot (6.5 m) length of boat. There must be four bolts through each flange with locked nuts.

It is common practice to glass in the P-bracket. A slot is cut at the right fore-and-aft location (taken off the plan) and just wide enough to slip the stem of the P-bracket through. Some builders bolt a pair of short lengths of L-bar to the stem of the bracket inside the hull so that the glassing in can get a good grip.

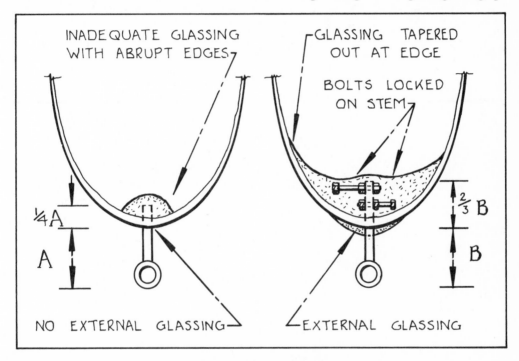

Fig. 51   Securing a P-bracket

The aft end of a propeller shaft is supported by an A-bracket, or sometimes as shown here, by a P-bracket. This has a single leg or stem which may have a flange bolted onto the outside of the hull. More usually, in order to keep the outside of the underbody of the hull smooth, and to save money, the P-bracket has no flange, but the stem extends through the hull where it is secured by being glassed over, as in these sketches.

On the left the glassing in is badly done. There is only a short length of the stem inside the boat so the glassing over cannot get a good grip. A sideways blow on the propeller shaft or P-bracket will loosen the stem where it passes through the shell. Leaking results and this will get worse as the engine is used, especially if sea conditions are bad, or the engine is run at full throttle.

On the right the stem is shown well inside the hull, with ample glassing inboard and a thin sealing layer outboard. All the glassing is tapered out to avoid high stress spots. For extra strength two or even four bolts are put athwartships through the stem after it has been pushed through the hull. These bolts are locked in place by tightening the nuts on each side of the stem. The bolts should be of the same material as the P-bracket and they have a subsidiary use: when the bracket is being glassed in place chocks or wedges under the bolts hold the bracket in exactly the right place.

Others go one stage further and bolt the athwartships flanges of the L-bar to a wood floor which is fully glassed-in. At least the stem of the P-bracket should have 1 inch (25 mm) diameter countersunk holes drilled in it so that the glassing in gets a good grip, and for good measure there should be a large nick cut in one edge. If these precautions are not taken the P-bracket may move when a rope gets caught round the propeller shaft.

When the time comes to glass in the P-bracket (or the stern tube for that matter) it is held exactly in position with wood wedges and possibly some putty or plasticine. Small pieces of fibreglass are applied to hold the fitting just where it has to stay and once these initial glassing in pieces are hard the wedges and putty are taken away so that full all-round glassing can be applied.

Resin will run out at the slot unless it is thickened with a thixotropic agent. Alternatively the slot may be sealed with multiple lengths of sellotape fixed across the underside of the hull. It may be worth using both techniques, especially in warm weather when the resin tends to be extra liquid.

Glassing in should be most generous. A failure here results in a leak which is often hard to find. If the propeller hits a piece of heavy driftwood the P-bracket or stern tube must be so rigidly secured that there is no risk that it will move, otherwise the resulting leak could be too fast to control.

The hole where the wire passes through the hull has to be enlarged just enough to take the stern tube. This can be done by cutting and trying, a little at a time. To speed up the job a little tool can be made up for marking the hole and this is a piece of piping with its ends blanked off. In the middle of each end there is a hole just the same diameter as the wire. On the outside of the tube a pencil is lashed. The distance from the point of the pencil to the centre-line through the tube is equal to the radius of the stern tube.

To work this gadget, release one end of the taut wire, pass it through the tube and resecure the wire tightly. Slide the tube up to the hull, then lock the wire close ahead and behind the tube so that the wire does not sag or shift sideways when the tube is pressed lightly against it. Rotate the tube so that the pencil marks the hull where the cut is to be.

To cut the slot in the hull a series of holes are drilled inside the marked line. These holes are joined up and the piece of hull removed. The rough edge is smoothed with Surform or file or electric grinder. On a thin hull a jig-saw can be used. When the stern tube can be put in place, with the shaft through it and the P-bracket in place, the coupling on the shaft is eased up to the engine. It should be possible to slide the coupling bolts through the flange of the coupling and the flange on the engine. In practice it will almost certainly be necessary to shift the engine a little, perhaps to one side, perhaps the aft end needs raising a little, perhaps all four engine feet need lifting. Thin metal shims are slid under the feet to get the engine just right. It may be necessary to cut away the hull a little in way of the stern tube or P-bracket so that the shaft can be bolted to the engine.

When the engine is secured to the shaft, which incidentally must lie inside the stern tube and P-bracket in such a way that it can be rotated easily, and be entirely free from side forces, the line-up is correct. This is the time to glass in the tube and P-bracket, also bolt down the engine. It is bad practice to use coach-screws to hold an engine down, but it may be unavoidable at the aft end in a small boat. It is unsafe to use more than two out of four coach-screws. Bolts need locking nuts, or nuts with nylon inserts which are self-locking nuts provided they are done up using a torque spanner.

The lining-up should be rechecked after the boat has been launched and left afloat for twenty-four hours. If this wait is unacceptable, then the lining-up should be checked before trials, and again after the boat has been afloat for two or three days. To check the line-up the coupling bolts are removed. They should

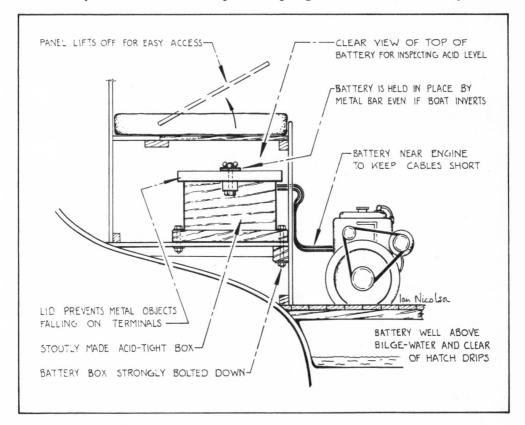

Fig. 52   Boat batteries

The first consideration, when fitting a battery, is to find a dry place near the engine, so that the cables are kept short. In general they should be under 6 feet (2 metres) and clipped up at about 8 inch (200 mm) centres. The battery box needs to be strong enough to take the heavy weight of the battery, and acid-proof inside to cope with spills when the boat heels or rolls.

Not only must the battery box be secured down, but the battery must be held in so that if the boat is capsized there is no risk that the battery will break adrift. The lid of the box is to prevent metal tools dropping across two terminals and causing the battery to spark and discharge.

Unless the battery is of the type which never needs topping up, there must be access above so that the level of fluid can be seen, and more liquid added when needed. Sometimes it is very hard to get a clear view into each cell in which case the crew may use a little mirror to give an indirect view, and a filler with a flexible plastic pipe for topping up.

slide out effortlessly. If they do not the engine needs moving just a little. It may well be that when the holding down bolts were tightened the engine was forced downwards slightly. Thin metal shims are slid under the feet to correct the alignment. A car jack or crowbar or both are used to lift and shift the engine.

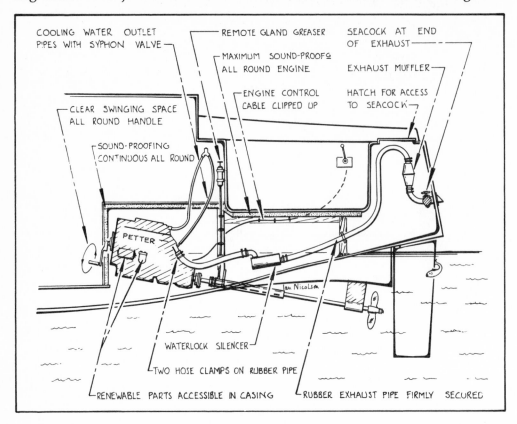

COOLING WATER OUTLET PIPES WITH SYPHON VALVE

REMOTE GLAND GREASER

SEACOCK AT END OF EXHAUST

MAXIMUM SOUND-PROOFG ALL ROUND ENGINE

EXHAUST MUFFLER

ENGINE CONTROL CABLE CLIPPED UP

HATCH FOR ACCESS TO SEACOCK

CLEAR SWINGING SPACE ALL ROUND HANDLE

SOUND-PROOFING CONTINUOUS ALL ROUND

PETTER

Ian Nicolson

WATERLOCK SILENCER

TWO HOSE CLAMPS ON RUBBER PIPE

RENEWABLE PARTS ACCESSIBLE IN CASING

RUBBER EXHAUST PIPE FIRMLY SECURED

Fig. 53   Engine piping and controls

If an engine is installed on or near the water-line precautions are needed to stop water flooding back up the exhaust pipe. Every exhaust should have an accessible sea-cock, but apart from this, there must be arrangements to stop water getting forward down the pipe. The first line of defence shown here is the exhaust muffler which has baffles inside its rubber body which act like valves. Then there is the high loop up to as near the deck-head as possible.

The water-lock silencer is located low down and to prevent syphoning back there is a valve in the cooling water outlet, before it discharges into the exhaust, which is made of rubber piping from the manifold aft.

Engine casings should be sound-proofed as fully as money, space and skill allow. To deaden noise all surfaces facing and adjacent to the engine should be covered with sound-proofing, with no gaps or slits or holes. Thick ply makes a good casing because noise is absorbed by wood, and thick timber is more effective than thin.

There are dozens of different ways of controlling the engine from the helm, but the most popular is by flexible cables. The Morse company provide a range, suitable for throttles and gear levers, for engine shut-offs and for shaft brakes. The cables should be carefully led with no very sharp bends, and clipped up to prevent the cables from dropping onto the whirling propeller shaft or hot exhaust.

If it is not easy to reach the stern gland greaser there should be a reservoir with pipe leading to the gland, and threaded plunger to force grease down the tube to the gland.

Engines are often fitted with flexible feet, sometimes with flexible stern glands and flexible couplings. Regardless of what is fitted, the line-up should be as accurate as possible, the flexible units should not be expected to compensate for the least alignment.

Once the engine has been bolted down, the piping, wiring and controls are fitted. To be sure that these all fit together it is good policy to buy as much as possible from the same source. Certainly the exhaust, silencer and sea-cock where the exhaust emerges should all be bought from the same supplier. Most engine makers supply the majority of the parts which go with an engine and they ensure that everything they sell mates together.

27 Plumbing

Seamless copper pipe is almost ideal for every purpose afloat but because it is expensive, plastic pipes are widely used. A pipe which has to carry hot water cannot be of plastic since the heat softens the material and the pipe sags between each support point. When a plastic pipe has to be forced onto a sea-cock which is slightly too large, the softening properties of heat are useful. The pipe is dipped into a bowl of boiling water, made very salty so as to raise the boiling point. After two or three minutes the pipe ends will be flexible and will stretch so as to fit onto the sea-cock.

A pipe which is under suction (such as a bilge pump suction line) cannot be of ordinary plastic because it may collapse, especially if the bottom end becomes partly blocked. For this situation the reinforced plastic pipe which is green in colour and has a white spiral stiffening is necessary. Perhaps the main reason for using plastic piping apart from its cheapness, is the ease with which it can be bent. However, it only bends quite slowly and where a sharp bend is essential a copper pipe elbow is inserted.

At each end of every plastic pipe there must be a hose clamp and ideally these should be of stainless steel. The galvanised type rusts in a few months, so if they have to be used they should be smeared with lanolin and covered with waterproof electrician's tape.

Pipes should be clipped up at intervals to prevent serious sagging. It is common practice to run pipes through the bilge or along the bottom of lockers under settees. No pipe, not even a copper one, should be run near a hot exhaust; between any exhaust and any plastic pipe there should be a gap of at least 8 inches (200 mm). On no account should a plastic pipe be run *above* a hot engine or exhaust because heat rises and it will soften the pipe which will then sag downwards, getting hotter and softer till it eventually melts. Where the combined convenience of plastic piping is required with the safety of copper, the trick is to run the metal pipes for most of the distance, and fit short lengths of plastic pipe at each end to take up vibration, make alignment and joining up easy and (if the plastic is clear) to enable the crew to detect waterflow by inspection.

Pipes have to fit onto sea-cocks, so the safe procedure is to buy both from the same source at the same time. Sea-cocks should be of bronze; the steel type rusts quickly and seizes, while to date the plastic version have not been tough enough to stand up to conditions afloat.

It used to be common practice to build in water tanks. Recently it has been found that the insides of such tanks get 'osmosis', the disease which takes the form of blisters on the fibreglass surface. This trouble is particularly common when fibreglass is in contact with fresh water. As a result drinking water tanks

138

are now no longer built in by sensible shipwrights. Apart from the deterioration of the fibreglass there is evidence that osmosis results in tainted water which tastes unpleasant and may cause illness.

There seems no reason why septic tanks, or sewage tanks should not be built in. They should be well painted inside with three or more coats of 2-pot polyurethane or epoxy paint to minimise the chance of osmosis occuring. In the tank top an inspection hatch is needed for every 3 feet (1 m) of tank length. Alternatively, the whole of the tank top is made semi-portable; it is held on by 3/16 inch (5 mm) diameter self-tapping, stainless steel screws or bolts driven through the tank top panel into a continuous external flange all round the tank. The fastenings are spaced about 2½ inch (65 mm) centres with a watertight sealing strip covering the full width of the flange.

The most popular form of fresh water tank is the flexible neoprene type because it is cheap, light and easy to install. The lighter versions have a reputation for developing leaks after about five years, sometimes sooner, often as a result of careless installation. These tanks are made in the form of a closed rubbery plastic bag, sometimes with a woven cloth outer protective cover. They are stowed under berths or below the cabin sole, or at the bottom of clothes lockers, or in any adequate space, preferably as low as possible. Being fully flexible the tank can be put in an odd-shaped space, or fitted through quite a small aperture into an almost inaccessible hide-away.

However, the fitting cannot be too carefree. The skin thickness of these tanks, especially the cheapest versions, is such that any sharp edge or pro-truding lump of fibreglass is likely to chafe through it. Careful shipwrights first line the tank space with thin marine ply, or ½ inch (12 mm) thick foam plastic cushioning or a similar material. Next they lay down a p.v.c. sheet which extends up the sides of the space, and finally the tank is put into this cosy nest, taking care to have no corner of the tank turned over or creased. As the boat rolls or pitches the tank will work, so there must be no chance that chafing can occur. This means the tank must be boxed in or lashed down so that it cannot shift.

A rigid cover is needed over a flexible tank to prevent heavy or sharp-edged equipment being dropped onto it, and to keep the tank in place if the boat is hove down 90°. One advantage of these tanks is that they need no breather or air pipes. As the contents are withdrawn the tank collapses downwards. The draw-off ought to be near, but not at the bottom so that sediment lies below it.

The filler pipe is joined to a deck filler. This pipe must be long enough to extend to the top of the tank even when the tank is almost empty and has collapsed, otherwise the weight of the tank will be carried by the filler pipe, which may then be pulled off the deck fitting or the coupling on the tank. It is best to arrange the filler pipe so that it runs vertically down from the deck, then turns at right angles and extends along the top of the tank to the filler inlet.

Some flexible tanks are supplied with all the connections loose. The boat-builder puts the filler, draw-off and other pipes just where he likes. The best tanks also have securing eyes at the corners for securing to bulkheads to reduce movement and wear.

The location of the fuel filler cap ought in theory to be on deck, so that spillage runs into the sea, and not into the bilge. A popular location is on the aft deck, which is easily washed if some fuel sploshes over the funnel edge. Various regulating bodies insist that the filler should be located on deck in such a way

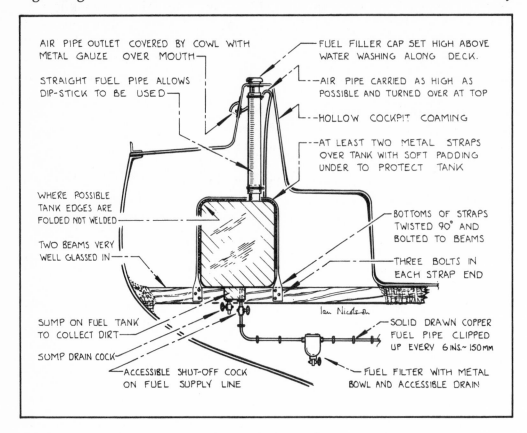

AIR PIPE OUTLET COVERED BY COWL WITH METAL GAUZE OVER MOUTH

STRAIGHT FUEL PIPE ALLOWS DIP-STICK TO BE USED

WHERE POSSIBLE TANK EDGES ARE FOLDED NOT WELDED

TWO BEAMS VERY WELL GLASSED IN

SUMP ON FUEL TANK TO COLLECT DIRT

SUMP DRAIN COCK

ACCESSIBLE SHUT-OFF COCK ON FUEL SUPPLY LINE

FUEL FILLER CAP SET HIGH ABOVE WATER WASHING ALONG DECK.

AIR PIPE CARRIED AS HIGH AS POSSIBLE AND TURNED OVER AT TOP

HOLLOW COCKPIT COAMING

AT LEAST TWO METAL STRAPS OVER TANK WITH SOFT PADDING UNDER TO PROTECT TANK

BOTTOMS OF STRAPS TWISTED 90° AND BOLTED TO BEAMS

THREE BOLTS IN EACH STRAP END

Ian Nicolson

SOLID DRAWN COPPER FUEL PIPE CLIPPED UP EVERY 6 INS.~ 150mm

FUEL FILTER WITH METAL BOWL AND ACCESSIBLE DRAIN

Fig. 54   Fitting a tank

Though this sketch shows how a fuel tank is installed, many of the details apply to water tanks. For instance, it is a great convenience if the contents can be gauged by using a dip-stick, but this is only possible if the filler pipe is straight and almost vertical. All tanks need strong supports to prevent even slight movement in any direction. Sometimes this is achieved by having straps welded to the tank, with pairs of bolts through each strap into adjacent bulkheads or beams overhead or below. Any tank, even in a small boat, should be so well secured that a man can tread heavily on the tank without moving it.

The supply pipe is sometimes taken from the top, with the pipe extending down to near the bottom of the tank, so that if there is a leak where the supply pipe comes out of the tank no fluid escapes except when the tank is full. However, this technique only works if the supply is taken from the tank by a suction pipe.

The sump is to collect dirt, and the supply pipe is shown extended up above the base of the sump. Sumps are usually made from short lengths of thick-wall pipe with thick bases since this is where the maximum corrosion occurs. The drain-pipe cock and supply cock must be accessible, or fitted with extensions on the handles. All pipes are run along bulkheads or battens or beams or sole bearers, so that they have continuous support.

that the filler is sealed onto the deck, otherwise driblets might find their way inside the hull. However, regulations have virtually always been made with a view to keeping boats safe from explosive petrol fumes. Now that there are few petrol engines, and diesel reigns supreme, there is a new approach. Roughly it is this: if the fuel filler cap is on deck water may get in, especially if refuelling is carried out offshore. When a boat has to carry extra fuel cans it is a safe bet that these will be used in exposed waters. Under conditions which arise offshore, it must be possible to pour the reserve fuel from portable cans into the main tank without getting great dollops of sea into the tank as well. The one time the reserve fuel is most needed is when a boat is in trouble, either because of torn

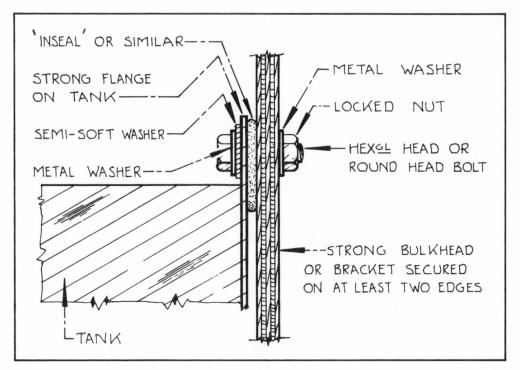

Fig. 55   Securing a tank

All tanks have to be so well secured that even if the boat turns upside down there is no movement. A quick and often cheap method of securing a tank is by way of three or better still four sets of bolts through flanges. The flanges must be well separated, since it is no good having the top and side flanges at one end of a tank secured, with no fastenings at the opposite end. There must be at least three bolts through each flange and these bolts should be spread the full length of the flange.

The sketch shows how soft bedding of 'Inseal' or 'Kwikseal' or a similar long life foam plastic extends well past the tank side, and is not made just the width of the flange. On boats subject to vibration the nuts must be 'Nylocs' or similar, so that they cannot shake free. To make installation easier the flanges should be drilled before the tank is put in place, unless the holes are drilled from the opposite side of the bulkhead.

When the tank is galvanised the holes in the flange must be drilled before galvanising. If there is any doubt about the strength of the bulkhead a doubler is fitted along each line of bolts. In practice most bulkheads less than ⅜ inch (10 mm) thick will require doublers quite 2×½ inch (50×12 mm).

sails or dismasting if she is a yacht and mainly sail-powered, or when bad weather has slowed the voyage in a fully powered craft.

When possible I design in a compromise like this: I locate the fuel filler cap on the aft deck in a sheltered space so that in anything but severe weather fuel can be put through it without water getting in. The filler pipe is located so that in really bad conditions it can be quickly taken off the filler cap below deck, and the reserve fuel funnelled in, working in shelter, inside a large cockpit locker or similar place.

Metal tanks have the virtues of strength, reliability and wide availability. For cheapness galvanised mild steel tanks are used, but stainless steel tanks are much to be preferred since they have an indefinite life, they look smart, they are hygienic and inert. Their principal disadvantage is their high price.

Securing a metal tank inside a g.r.p. hull is not straightforward. Tanks are often made with lugs or flanges to take bolts or screws. The problem is: what do these fastenings join? The hull shell cannot take them and it is bad practice to put such bolts through the deck. Sometimes the bolts which secure stanchions and pulpits can also support small tanks. The necessary stainless steel bolts are expensive, so they might as well be made to do two useful jobs. This calls for subtle design, as the tank flanges must either be so wide that a hand can be slipped between the outboard tank side and the hull, or the flange end must coincide with the underside of a stanchion with good access.

One end of the tank is often bolted to a well glassed-in bulkhead, but what about the other end? A useful idea is to design the tanks to extend almost from bulkhead to bulkhead. At one end a wood packing piece is put in so that both ends of the tank are now tight against bulkheads. Bolts or screws are driven through the end flanges, through the packing and into the bulkheads. This technique works best if the tanks are put in before the deck goes on, or if the tanks can be slewed into position after being passed down through the hatch. With all tanks as with furniture, the diagonal distance between opposite corners is greater than the distance along one side; this makes it impossible to fit a rectangular object into a space between two bulkheads if the distance between them is less than the diagonal length across the tank (see Fig. 56).

Another method of securing a tank is by straps round the belly. At least two straps are needed, and if the tank with its contents weighs more than 100 pounds (45 kg) there should be three straps. Flat bar is used for straps, each piece being able to carry four times the weight of the full tank. Between the bar and the tank a strip of felt or foam plastic is secured. One end of each strap is bolted to a strong point like a bulkhead or engine bearer, and the other end pulled up tight with two bolts to another strong point.

Instead of flat bar stainless steel flexible wire rope may be used. To prevent it chafing the tank plastic piping is slipped over the wire before the end splices are made. One end is shackled to an eye-plate bolted to a strong point and the other hauled tight with a rigging screw or lashing secured to another eye-plate.

Whatever technique is used to secure a tank, the result must be total rigidity.

If a tank can move just a little, after a few thousand miles it will move a lot, and finally break free. This happens in bad weather, when the crew has plenty of problems without itinerant tanks crashing about inside the hull. So if a tank is secured by wedges, these must be of well-seasoned hardwood, with a minimum of two screws or bolts through each wedge.

If an anchor locker is recessed in the fore-deck it needs drains, otherwise it will fill in bad weather and load the bow of the boat dangerously. The same applies

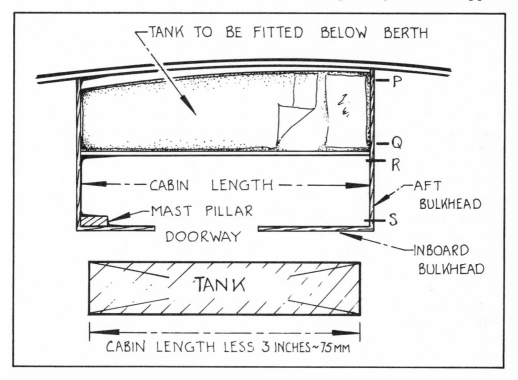

Fig. 56   Getting a tank in

Fitting tanks or any bulky part into a confined space calls for careful planning. A tank is required as large as possible, but is not made the exact distance between two bulkheads in case some minor projection makes it impossible to get the tank in place. Typically about 1½ inches (40 mm) is left each end, to give hand space. Wedges or chocks each end help to hold the tank in place.

First though, it has to be coaxed into position. In this plan view of a cabin it will be impossible to get the tank under the berth, unless the aft end of the inboard bulkhead can be taken down. If it has been glassed in, removing it will call for major surgery. The forward end of the inboard bulkhead is secured to a mast support pillar.

It is no good up-ending the tank, or putting it diagonally through the doorway. The problem here is that the diagonal length between opposite corners of the tank is greater than the distance between the fore-and-aft bulkheads. One solution is to cut a panel out of the aft bulkhead just large enough to slip the tank through. The hole must be big enough not just for the basic tank but also for any protruding pipe connections. If a panel cannot be cut out at the end of the berth, at P–Q, it is almost as good to take one out at R–S, then when the tank is in the cabin it is slid sideways under the berth.

Tanks can be made easy to fit by having two in the place of one, but this results in a slight loss of capacity and a very real increase in the total cost of the tanks and their installation.

to a sunken fore-deck. Drains are needed port and starb'd so that all the accumulated water can run away even if the boat is heeled.

This is one place where it is reasonable to omit sea-cocks; the outlets are high, often only half the way down from deck to water-line. Plastic pipes are used, and they should curve gradually to prevent mud from the anchor causing blockages. Muck is likely to bung up pipes less than ¾ inch (20 mm) internal diameter, and pipes smaller than this will result in slow drainage. Admittedly

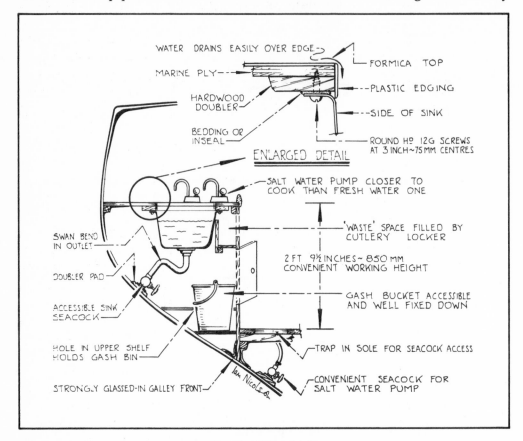

Fig. 57   Galley details

The sink is secured to the underside of the bench so that washing-up water drains effortlessly into it. A hardwood doubler is needed in way of the sink to give the sink screws sufficient depth of wood to bite into.

By putting the salt water pump nearest to the cook there is a good chance that it will be used most often, thus saving precious fresh water which is always in short supply aboard. Also for convenience the galley bench is made the standard height, and most of the side-boards, and other furniture with level top surfaces will be the same height.

Every time the boat is left sea-cocks should be turned off, so it is logical to make them easy to reach. Each day the 'gash bucket' has to be emptied, so it too has to be handy. However, it must be well secured otherwise in severe conditions its contents will be scattered through the boat. A pair of shock-cord lengths with clips each end will hold a bucket provided there is also a socket in a shelf at about half height to prevent sideways movement.

An interesting detail is the way the cabin sole is lodged on bearers resting on a fore-and-aft carline on the galley front which in turn is glassed to the inside of the hull.

144

plenty of production yachts have pipes only ½ inch (12 mm) diameter, but this is to save money; it results in anchor lockers staying half full of water in very bad conditions because the water cannot flow away completely before another wave comes aboard.

If a sink drain is led straight down to a sea-cock any small item dropped into the sink is likely to disappear overboard. To prevent this the drain-pipe is led down from the sink, then curved up, before winding down to the sea-cock. This forms a moderately effective trap.

A sink drain less than ¾ inch (20 mm) diameter is a great nuisance as even the smallest pieces of waste food will block it. If one of those cheap standard sinks which has a drain connection only ½ inch (12 mm) size is bought to save money, or because a bigger sink cannot be fitted in the available space, it is worth fitting the shortest possible length of pipe on the sink, then a connector for a ¾ inch inside diameter pipe, so that the main length of the drain is a sensible size. Even ¾ inch (20 mm) is cutting things fine, and for this location a full 1 inch (25 mm) bore is far better.

In the same way, for serious cruising two sinks are better than one. On a sailing yacht it is occasionally the practice to fit one sink with a drain on the outboard side, and another adjacent with the drain on the inboard side. The cook can use whichever sink has the drain on the downhill side, according to which tack the boat is on, so as to ensure the sink drains completely. If only one sink is fitted ideally it should have two drains, one for each tack. However, standard sinks are not available with this refinement, so the boatbuilder will have to buy a stock sink and fit the second drain himself.

Next to the sink is the fresh water pump or tap. The outlet may have to be raised so that a kettle or large pan can be slipped under. When a pump is fitted the 'flip-flop' type (with pivoting handle) should be bought in preference to the plunger type; at sea when the boat is jumping about the long plunger type is liable to have its handle bent if the cook holds on and gets thrown across the galley. Then the handle will not slide back and forth in its barrel and the pump is suddenly useless, as well as being virtually unrepairable. For a comparable reason, if a water pressure system is fitted giving a water supply from common taps, there should be a pump piped to the main tank in case the pressure system or the electrical supply fails.

On ocean cruising yachts it is general practice to fit a pump by the sink for salt water. This pump is well labelled, and is by tradition set nearer to the cook than the fresh water one, then there is every temptation to use salt water whenever possible. Sometimes the salt water pump is connected to the same sea-cock as one of the cockpit drains, as sea-cocks are expensive.

28 Bilge pumps

Any boat over 25 feet (7.5 metres) and smaller boats going far offshore need two bilge pumps. One is located near the helmsman, the other in the cabin where it can be worked long and hard without excessive discomfort. Both should suck from the lowest point in the bilge with strum boxes on the suctions. Both should discharge through the topsides or transom, at about ¾ freeboard height above the sea, with sea-cocks at the outlets. The suction and discharge pipes should have the fewest possible bends, all of which must be gentle.

All these and more precepts ought to be followed. In practice, concessions have to be made, especially on small craft or boats built with limited money. For instance, the second pump may double as a sink discharge pump, with a two-way full-through-flow cock to switch in an emergency from the sink outlet to the bilge suction. Alternatively, the second pump may be one of the toilet pumps, though it may be hard to test this pump both ways without some smelly consequences.

From the point of view of weight, adaptability, reliability and cost the diaphragm pump is best. Versions are made in several sizes by Munster Simms under the trade name 'Whale' and by Hendersons, sold under their own names worldwide and available through advertisements in yachting magazines.

It is possible to fit this type of pump under a cockpit seat or behind a bulkhead with a standard watertight seal over it. The socket for the pump handle is all that is visible and it is unobtrusive. It can be on a horizontal or vertical surface, as these pumps are wonderfully adaptable. They can be bolted in all sorts of positions to suit the available space.

No pump should be fitted so that a cockpit locker has to be opened to use it, otherwise water will flood into the locker in those severe conditions when the pump is most needed.

Because pumps are sometimes used in a great panic, they must be bolted, not screwed, in place. Ideally the nuts are locked on. The side of a typical fibreglass cockpit locker is of the order of ⅛ inch (3 mm) thick and this is unsuitable for supporting a pump without some backing up. Some hull moulders glass in a doubler piece of ½ inch (12 mm) marine ply where the pump is to go. If nothing like this is fitted some sort of doubling up of the structure is needed. To test if the structure is strong enough cut the hole for the pump handle seal and grasp the cut edge. If it is possible to move the fibreglass panel more than about ⅛ inch (3 mm) then reinforcing is essential. Put in doubling if there is the least doubt.

A ½ inch (12 mm) thick ply panel about 16 inches (400 mm) square is the minimum needed, but it is often better to have a pair of 4×1¼ inch

(100×32 mm) stiffeners extending well beyond the pump and bolted to a nearby structure.

Piping nowadays is almost always made of stiffened plastic. It must be properly stiffened on the bilge suction side otherwise it will collapse when suction is applied. Typical piping for this job is a characteristic, hideous green, well known to all yachtsmen, with a spiral of nylon reinforcing inside. This pipe is fairly hard, so it will not fit easily onto sea-cocks or pump pipes unless the size is exactly right.

Where a pipe goes near a hot engine or exhaust it is essential to use metal tubing. Copper is the usual choice here but galvanised steel is acceptable. The same applies to the strum box, which is a filter on the end of the suction. Boats are regularly sent to sea with no strum box but soon enough the suction pipe starts getting blocked with wood and fibreglass shavings. So, though a diaphragm pump will pass quite incredible lumps of rubbish, a strum box is essential. Is should be made portable so that it can be hauled out of the bilge and cleaned.

The essence of a strum box is that it has a large number of small holes, so that only the tiniest foreign matter can get into the suction pipe. Holes about ⅛ inch (3 mm) are usual. In total area there should be five times the cross-sectional area of the suction pipe to ensure there is no check to easy water flow.

In a sailing yacht with a wide flat bilge there must either be two bilge pumps, one for each tack, or there must be a forked suction each with its own strum box, one in the port bilge one to starboard, with a two-way cork at the fork junction. Without this sort of arrangement it is impossible to suck out accumulated water in the lee bilge when the boat is heeled.

The discharge pipe from the pump should go up under the deck, then down to the sea-cock which is useless if it is not accessible. The idea of carrying the pipe up as high as possible is to avoid syphoning back if someone uses the pump when the boat is well heeled, then forgets to shut off the sea-cock. The pump itself must be within reach without having to wriggle into tight tunnels because it needs servicing. The plastic valves get jammed with bits of rubbish and though the pump goes on working it is less than 100 per cent efficient. In time the jammed rubbish may cause a flap-valve to bend open permanently. Still the pump will work to a degree, but not as well as it should. On some of these pumps the flap-valve can be unscrewed, turned over and replaced. Anyway a new gland flap is cheap enough.

An electrical or mechanical bilge pump is no substitute for either of the main pumps. Power-operated pumps are a great convenience and have saved a few boats from sinking, but they are astonishingly unreliable, considering their function. Many of them suffer from an inability to run without constant water lubrication because they have neoprene impellers which wear away in seconds if not constantly wetted. One answer to this dilemma is to carry three or four spare impellers and learn how to fit them in adverse conditions. Another is to locate the switch so that anyone turning it on can stand and see the pump working; as soon as the water level gets low the pump is stopped and the rest of the water removed by hand.

Electric pumps tend to be made up in single compact units, with the pump on the same axle as the motor. They have their own grid round the base which is supposed to prevent rubbish getting near the fast rotating impeller, but so often a match or some unconsidered trifle jams against the impeller and the motor cannot stand the frustration. Another fault these pumps have is an inability to throw out much water, or up a useful height, without using a lot of electricity. So electric pumps have to be used with a careful eye on the state of the battery.

This is a major reason why engine driven pumps, though more expensive, are in many ways to be preferred. They are normally belt driven from the power take-off shaft of the engine, with a simple clutch to start the pump. Like electric pumps, a mechanical pump needs securing down with a minimum of three fastenings.

Mechanical pumps are so vulnerable to rubbish that it is worth surrounding their suctions with special large strum boxes made of fine wire mesh.

29 *The galley*

Like every compartment in a boat, this is built according to the naval architect's design. He should have drawn out the complex parts of the boat (usually the galley and toilet) in plan, elevation and section. If he has not, it is worth asking for sections at both ends of each of these compartments, since in all but the largest boats, every half inch matters.

Opinions about a particular set of plans vary widely. Often the original design is considered far too cramped by one person, and the next will swear it squanders the available space. If the standard design does not suit, the architect can be asked for another plan, drawn up to a specification written out for his guidance. If he is too busy there are in all yachting centres designers and draughtsmen who will take on this work for a fee.

Alternatively the arrangement can be worked out 'on site'. With coloured chalk the space is marked out and the chalk lines rubbed out and redrawn till everything is to the satisfaction of the owner and his wife. Women should be consulted in the design of a galley but it is not always easy to visualise in three dimensions what is drawn on a plan. Mock-ups are therefore needed. Cardboard pieces can be sellotaped in where the working top will go, where lockers will be fitted and so on. The sink, water-pump, matchbox holder and fire extinguishing blanket are all sketched on the cardboard. The fiddles, light switches, the stool, water-heater, even the ventilator should all be marked. When everything is in place the result has to be envisaged with the boat heeled horrendously and punching into a high, breaking sea. If the uncompleted hull could be tilted this would give everyone a far better chance to assess the proposed galley.

The basic dimensions needed for such items as the work-top, plate-stowage and cup-rack are available in *Boat Data Book*. Drawers or lockers are needed to fit large and standard sizes of tins, jars, bottles, loaves and other domestic commodities. When designing a galley or checking plans the following dimensions are a guide:

Drawers and lockers should not be made to these dimensions *exactly* because manufacturers change sizes slightly. Besides things stowed have to be taken out, so they should not be a 'jammed-tight fit'.

1 lb size jam jar	5½ inches (135 mm) high
	2¾ inches (70 mm) diameter
Big coffee jar	8 inches (200 mm) high
	3½ inches (90 mm) diameter
Big washing up liquid plastic dispenser	12 inches (305 mm) high
	3 inches (75 mm) diameter

1 lb size tins	4½ inches (115 mm) high
	3 inches (75 mm) diameter
Large tins	5 inches (130 mm) high
	4 inches (100 mm) diameter
Cutlery length varies but usually under	10 inches (255 mm) long
Cooking knives, spatulas, etc.	usually under 13 inches (330 mm) long
Large loaf (these dimensions apply to	Length about 13 inches (330 mm)
British and American bread; French	Width about 4½ inches (115 mm)
loaves appear in lengths up to 1 metre	Height about 8 inches (205 mm)
long and therefore defy all stowage plans)	

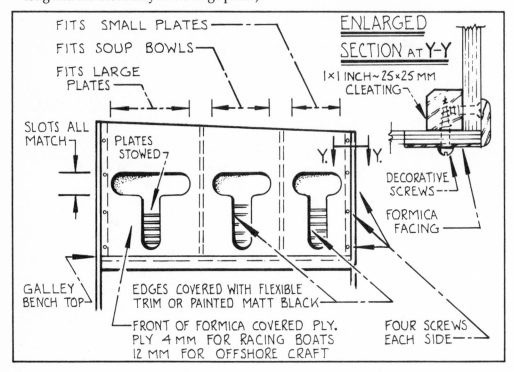

Fig. 58   Plate rack (View looking outboard)

One of the lightest, cheapest forms of plate rack is made by cutting these T-shaped slots in a Formica-covered ply panel. For a racing boat where the weight of Formica cannot be tolerated the ply is painted, varnished or polished. Behind the panel there are divisions keeping the piles of plates apart, and these simple separation boards can be of ply offcuts or solid wood, glassed or screwed in.

The galley work-bench is carried right out to the ship's side (though the fit against the topsides need not be accurate as plates will not slip down a small slot) and the racks made on top of the bench.

The top slots are made all the same size and height to give a smart appearance. Plates are dropped through these slots to stow them away. The edges of the slots are painted matt black to cover the edge grain of the ply, or a flexible wood (or plastic) edge trim is glued or nailed over the edge grain.

Perhaps the only disadvantage of this rack is the need to unscrew the front for thorough cleaning, though a hand can get through the slots for less efficient weekly cleaning.

The top edge of the front panel is shown right up to the underside of the deck, but a gap may be left to help ventilation, and save the trouble of precise fitting.

The central feature of the galley is the cooker. It is usually run on bottled gas, unless the boat is to be used for extended cruising in which case paraffin (kerosene in America) is favoured because for a given cost, weight and storage space more hours burning can be carried aboard. Also bottled gas is not available in remote areas.

It is best to have a small, tough cooker, though many production boats are sold with units which have four burners and an oven. In practice the oven is seldom used on a week-ender so it may be considered a great waste of space and money. It is also heavy and hard to maintain, given to rusting and fast depreciation. It is seldom wanted on a racing boat.

The cooker needs fiddles all round to keep pans in place in severe conditions, and even a power boat should have a gimballed cooker because these craft roll. Only if a boat is used inland can the gimbals be omitted, and fiddles must never be left off.

The space made available for the cooker must be the size of the cooker plus a space each side for the gimbals, which normally require about 1½ inches (38 mm) each side. This space also allows for the circulation of air and prevents scorching the surrounding furniture.

Inboard and outboard there must be enough space for the cooker to swing at least 60°; beyond that cooking is scarcely possible. To prevent the cooker coming adrift if the boat goes over 90° or more, the gimbals must not be open topped. Hose clamps round the tubes prevent the pivot bars from coming out of their rests.

The gimbals are bolted to the cooker and to the structure ahead and aft of the cooker, since gimballing is always athwartships. This structure has to withstand the weight of the cooker loaded with full pots, plus the weight of the cook who might fall against the cooker, plus a substantial allowance for shock loadings when the boat drops over the top of a wave with a jolt. In practice this means that each part of the gimbals should be secured with at least four ¼ inch (6 mm) bolts. The structure needs reinforcing if it is a typical fibreglass furniture moulding with something like a wood backing piece 8×¾ inches (200×20 mm) in section extended well beyond the load points and secured with a staggered pattern of eight fastenings, or fully glassed in.

Details of typical glass bottle sizes and piping specifications are given in *Boat Data Book.* The pipe attached to the cooker has to be flexible to allow for the swing of the stove. This length of pipe must be kept clear of the sharp flanges and edges found on stoves. The flexible pipe is secured to a seamless copper one which leads to the gas bottle. Sometimes this pipe is run along under the last one or two layers of glassing which secures the hull to the deck, sometimes the pipe has its own glassing to hold it in place and give it a measure of protection. At the gas bottle there is another length of flexible pipe with the regulator between this pipe and the bottle. Regulators are sold and maintained by chandlers who supply refilled bottles.

Gas bottles should be stored in lockers which drain overboard, or on deck with a casing over them. It is a good plan to have the spare bottle right alongside the one in use, so that the regulator can be taken off one and put onto the other without heaving heavy bottles about. All bottles, regardless of whether they are in use or stowed in a locker, should be so secured that nothing moves them even slightly. A typical arrangement consists of a chock cut to take the bottle

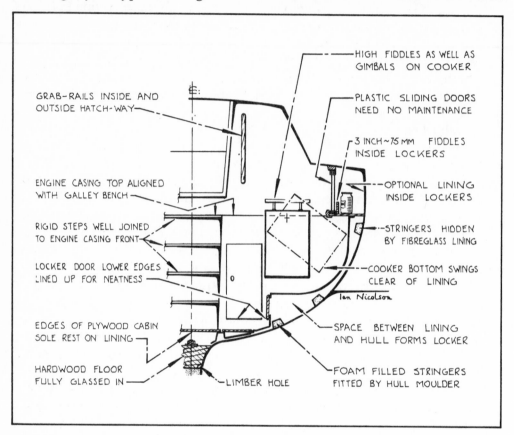

Fig. 59 Furniture techniques

In this section, looking at the aft end of the cabin of the 'Ruffian 8.5', 28 foot overall sloop, there are construction and furnishing ideas. The use of a fibreglass moulding as a lining and support for furniture shows up. The moulding extends below and outboard of the cooker, with a little locker worked in at the bottom, and a shelf resting on top. Unsightly stringers which are moulded in make the hull shell strong are neatly hidden by the lining, and the lower part of the lining is carried down to form a sole support. The sole overlaps the lining, hiding its rough bottom edge.

To stiffen that heavily loaded region where the main body of the hull meets the keel, there are hardwood floors sheathed all over in three or four layers of 1½ oz chopped strand mat. Each ballast keel bolt passes through one of these floors, so the wood has to be at least three times as thick as the bolt.

For rough weather it is important to have ample grab-rails including pairs inside and outside the entrance to the cabin. For the same conditions a cooker in a sailing yacht must be gimballed (near the top so that the centre of gravity even with heavy pans on top is well below the pivot) and have deep, strong fiddles.

To make the cabin look modern, tidy and uncluttered, locker top and bottom edges should be in line, shelves should extend into each other, or line up, and flat surfaces like the chart table should be level with the engine casing top.

base and a strap with strong buckle which goes over the top of the bottle. Another arrangement consists of a stowage locker with sides which firmly but not too tightly embrace the bottle, and a wood bar which goes over the top and is held by a ⅜ inch (10 mm) brass bolt with butterfly nut, or two such bolts for gruelling voyaging.

If besides the cooker there is a cabin heating stove or water heater or any other item which runs on bottled gas, it is best to have it run off its own bottle. This saves joins in the piping, reduces the chance of running out of gas at an awkward time, but above all it cuts down the chances of having a gas leak into the bilge. In time a spark will ignite the free gas and do much damage, or more usually destroy the boat. For this reason it is good practice to fit a gas detector in the bilge. These are sold by most chandlers and their installation instructions come with them.

Information about fitting a sink are in the chapter on Plumbing. Fridges are sold with installation instructions, but during the planning stage it has to be remembered that they need quite 1½ inches (40 mm) space all round for ventilation.

An icebox is easily made because it is nothing more than a well-insulated airtight container. Since heat rises, an icebox should have its opening on top. This is convenient because it can be located outboard, in a space where a locker with front access would be hard to fit, or too deep to reach inside.

It is usual to make the icebox of fibreglass with about 4 inches (100 mm) of insulation all round. The bottom has a drain which usually leads to the bilge, though sometimes it is piped to a special tank, possibly with its own discharge pump which has a changeover cock for use as an extra bilge pump. The top is made in the form of a flanged drop-in board which may double as a chopping board. It must be as thick as the sides and a good fit, so a lifting ring or handle is essential. An icebox is kept cold by putting in, before the food, one or more special packs which are kept in a deep freeze for a day or two before they are required. To get these packs from the deep freeze to the icebox they are wrapped in ½ inch (12 mm) thick layers of newspaper, or put in portable cool boxes. Some owners supplement these cold packs (sold by chandlers and suppliers of camping equipment) with blocks of ice from a deep freeze.

There are never enough lockers round a galley so all available crannies should be made into stowage for cutlery, jam jars and dried foods. One locker is often set aside for 'ready-use' foods, and the main stores stowed in the saloon, not too far from the galley.

If lockers are in short supply 'put-down' space is far worse. It is usual to arrange something like the engine casing top to supplement the galley working top, or some lockers may have doors which fold down horizontally for use as temporary shelves. Sometimes the partial bulkhead between the galley and the saloon has a top section which folds down level, with fiddles all round. For use at sea, where only half the cooker burners are needed most of the time, a metal tray may be clipped over one end of the cooker. This tray has high fiddles all round, and is large enough to take a mug for each member of the crew. So when soup or a stew or porridge is being served, it is ladled straight out of the pan into the mugs which stay level because of the cooker gimbals.

Finally, a galley strap is needed to keep the cook close to the work bench especially when the boat heels or rolls wildly. The strap extends horizontally along the galley, either from one end of the bench to the other, or diagonally across the angle of a galley which is built in an L-shape. If no strap is shown on the plan this is one of those items of gear which are often best planned at sea. During trials the boat is put first on one tack and then on the other. The cook will soon see what length and location of galley strap would be best. In a power boat a few minutes in rough waters will show how the cook is going to be flung about and where a strap is needed. On larger craft a pair of straps may be necessary especially if the galley occupies a length of more than 7 feet (2 m).

Galley straps are not stocked in chandlers and have to be specially ordered from a local sail maker. Three or four thicknesses of terylene cloth about 10 oz weight are sewn together into a tough tape about 3 inches (75 mm) wide. Some cooks like a much wider tape, perhaps 8 inches (200 mm) wide in the middle tapering to narrow ends, as they find this more restful and less likely to cut into the back when cooking for a long period. Tanned terylene is best as it does not show the dirt.

Each end of the strap has a 'worked eye', that is a sewn ring-and-turnover or its modern equivalent which is a hydraulically pressed in eye, about ⅝ inch (16 mm) internal diameter. Ordinary hammered in eyelets are not strong enough. Anyone who is making his own galley strap and does not have the facility for fitting worked eyes can turn the end of the strap over into a loop strongly sewn.

Each end loop or eye has a lashing of four turns of 5 mm terylene line which is used to adjust the length of the strap. Small people will need the strap tighter than giants. One lashing goes through the eye-plate, the other holds a snap shackle which engages another eye-plate. Both plates are bolted to bulkheads or the galley front or some other strong point.

—30 *Toilet compartments*—

There used to be an airline flight across the Atlantic which took off in the evening and landed after dawn. Part of the airliner's cabin was arranged with bunks in tiny cabins, so that some of the passengers had a good night's rest during the flight. The cabins had curtains instead of doors, allowing anyone passing down the central aisle to see in when the curtains were ajar. One night an air hostess glanced into one of the cabins, gasped, gulped, turned round and hastened to the flight deck where she burst out:

'There's a madman in cabin 5!'

'How do you know?' asked the captain, reaching for his cap, and climbing out of his seat to go and investigate.

'He's got a tape measure, and he's measuring the bunk,' wailed the hostess.

So the captain went to cabin 5 and politely knocked on the bulkhead before squeezing in.

'Anything wrong, sir?' he asked the passenger, who held a notebook in one hand and a tape measure in the other.

'No. On the contrary,' said the passenger. 'You see I'm having a new yacht built, and this berth is the smallest possible one, yet it is entirely comfortable. So I'm taking its dimensions and I'll get the boatbuilder to reproduce my boat berths exactly like it.'

The amount of space needed in a toilet compartment is hard to determine. If a boat is being built to plans, the designer will have made the decision and with luck anyone following on can go aboard a sister ship and see if the space is going to be adequate. First a decision has to be made as to what standard of comfort is required. For racing it is common to put the WC in the fo'c'sle with sail stowage all round, and very little privacy. Most cruising yachts over about 26 feet (8 m) have a separate compartment because designers feel that this is what boat-buyers want. Bearing in mind the few minutes per day that his cabin is used, a good case can be made for not having a special compartment, but fashion and feminine influences work the other way.

A sole space of 13½×13½ inches (340×340 mm) is enough, but shoulder space about 20×20 inches (510×510 mm) is needed to turn round, and this is very cramped for dressing or washing. If no plans are available, or they are being changed, it is best to go aboard other yachts with notebook and rule and follow the example of the 'madman' on the airliner. Measure everything possible in plan and elevation and note where the designer has been too hopeful and not allowed enough inches.

Toilet compartments are sometimes used for elaborate washing, and this needs elbow room. But when using the WC offshore space is a disadvantage

155

and it is better if the bulkheads are close so that there is no chance of being flung about like a dice in a shaker. One way round this dilemma is to make the compartment just large enough for basic use, but capable of enlargement by opening the door. If this door can be so swung that it shuts off the saloon but makes the toilet into part of the forward cabin this makes for comfort and convenience. To achieve this it may be necessary to have two doors, or a curtain, or a door and a curtain.

One of the principal advantages of a curtain is that it cannot swing about in severe conditions and bash knuckles. However, it gives little privacy and may not, therefore, be acceptable. This is a pity because curtains are light and cheap, quick to fit and slow to give trouble. They can be made up of double thicknesses of spinnaker cloth, or of towelling. Each weekend the curtain-cum-towel is taken home for washing and it can even have pockets sewn into it for stowing toothbrushes.

Once someone is inside the compartment there is no room for the door to swing inwards, unless the space is palatial, as it may be on a vessel bigger than about 45 feet (14 m). As the door swings outwards it needs a strong lock to take the thump when someone, hauling on his trousers, falls and crashes against the door. The standard barrel bolt is no good because it is only available in non-rusting materials up to 3 inches (75 mm) long – a mere toy. A sliding bar of wood 1 inch (25 mm) square in section works well and costs little, also it never needs oiling, as other door furniture does.

The entire toilet compartment has to be easy to clean, from deckhead to sole. If it is lined with Formica or one of the other glossy, hard, plastic finish boards a wipe with a cloth is all that is needed. However, these modern decorative plastic boards are expensive and being so hard they are slow to work and quick to chip. So some people prefer painted or varnished finishes which are cheaper in material costs. In a boat-yard Formica is preferred because it is relatively cheap in labour, compared with painting which needs successive coats. It is heavy, though, which rules it out for racing craft.

To make any compartment easier to clean fillet pieces are run along the angles between sole and bulkheads, and along the joins between the bulkheads and the deck-head. This cuts out right angle joins and makes them 45° interior angles. To make life even easier and more sanitary rounded fillets are put in which entirely eliminate angles.

Another way to make cleaning easy is to have the minimum changes of shape and extra parts. This gives an added bonus in that the finished appearance looks modern and tidy. For example, if there is a basin which needs a shelf to support it this is incorporated in a box for the toilet paper, lockers for toothbrushes and the end is formed into a grab-rail. Or if there are separate cave lockers where each member of the crew is to keep his washing gear, all these lockers can be worked into one panel which fits tightly between the bulkheads. Here, as elsewhere in the boat, horizontal and vertical lines look best if kept continuous. Thus the top of a basin should line up with a hand-rail which in turn is at the same level as a stowage locker, and this extends across in the form of a towel-rail.

To get hand-rails just right it is best to mark the plan 'Site at ship' and locate them where they are most convenient. Metal hand-rails tend to be sharp-ended which causes bruising; wooden ones should have well-rounded ends. If a hand-rail is carried vertically down to the sole it makes a good wedging corner for a foot, and can double as a towel-rail provided it has a series of holes scalloped out down its full length. It may also serve to stiffen a flimsy bulkhead.

On cruising boats over about 35 feet (10.5 m) an electric extractor vent over the WC is fairly common. Alternatively, a simple cowl or mushroom vent is fitted. There must be an inlet for the air, otherwise the outlet cannot be expected to work – air must flow which demands an inlet larger than the outlet. A grill in

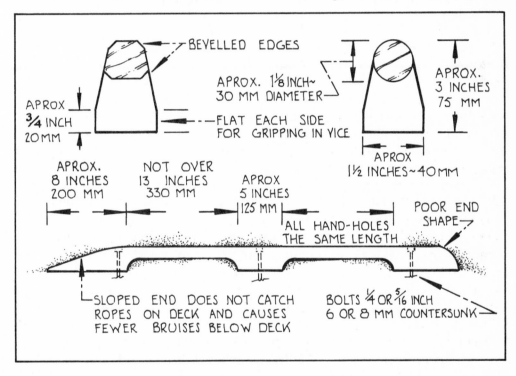

Fig. 60 Hand-rails

At the top are alternative sections through hand-rails. The one on the left is made more quickly and some people claim it gives a better grip, but the one on the right holds varnish better.

These hand-rails are fitted on deck and below, wherever the crew need something to grab to avoid being flung about. Hardwood which matches the rest of the trim is used, and at least three coats of varnish is put on all new wood.

The ends are snaped away to avoid accidents. On well-built boats the end bolt will be helped by a strong screw put in through the cabin top (or whatever the hand-rail is on) up into the base of the hand-rail.

If the scalloped-out parts of the hand-rail are made much longer than 13 inches (330 mm) they are liable to be too weak to stand hard usage. Before making a hand-rail its final length is drawn out full size, then the spacing and length of the cut-aways planned. A row of short cut-outs looks odd, and the solid section by each bolt must not be too short or it may split.

the door makes a good inlet, but grill holes are small and do not promote airflow in sluggish conditions. As a result the grill must be about five times the ventilator area, and grills this size are not easy to obtain. Builders nowadays tend to leave bold slots along the top or bottom or both when making a toilet door. This reduces the level of privacy and raises the level of ventilation. It also makes fitting the door much quicker and cheaper – a typical boatbuilding compromise.

If an electric vent is fitted it may be left on by accident. To avoid this either fit a time-switch or put a red light in series with the fan, locating the light in the saloon or wherever it will be seen most often. My enthusiasm for electric extractor vents is at a low ebb because like so many other components which depend on electricity they have a poor record of reliability and repairs are costly.

Whatever type of vent is fitted in the deck-head, sooner or later it will let in drips. To minimise the discomfort the vent is sited clear of the WC and basin, also away from the toilet paper holder. The WC operating instructions and clothes' lockers also dislike drips from above. Siting a vent is like trying to find a location for a sewage works – nowhere is right.

Damp and soggy toilet paper is no ones idea of fun, so a waterproof container is needed. This can be a large envelope made by the local sail maker from the same p.v.c. he uses for sail covers. Three screws through a batten hold the envelope to the bulkhead and the flap over diverts drips. Alternatively, one of the multiple lockers for the crews' wash gear can have the toilet paper in it. Whatever stowage is used, polythene bags are needed, a separate one for the roll in use and another for the spare.

This discussion about keeping the loo-paper dry may seem a trifle obsessive, but it is becoming increasingly common to fit a shower in the toilet space. As a result the whole compartment becomes drenched, though there is normally a plastic curtain which is intended to divert the flow of water into the shower tray. This tray is below a grating in the sole and is usually of fibreglass. Sometimes the inside of the hull forms the tray.

A depth of around 4 inches (100 mm) is needed for the tray, though less can be tolerated because showering only occurs in harbour or very settled weather at sea. At the lowest point in the tray there is a drain hole to an electric pump which discharges well above the water-line. Arrangements are needed to avoid leaving this pump on a second after the last of the water has been sucked away because most of these pumps have neoprene impellers which quickly burn out if run dry.

Showers are bought as complete units from chandlers. The best type has a portable rose so that the spray can be directed where needed, and there is less chance of soaking the whole cabin. If the rose has very tiny holes it will still give a good wash but use very little water. Some boats have arrangements for taking first a salt water shower, then finishing off with just the minimum of fresh to clean off the salt left behind.

Ideally the shower should have a proper teak grating, but it takes a long time and either a lot of skill or full wood-working machinery to produce. Admittedly there is nothing like a grating to make a boat attractive. Put gratings in the cockpit, toilet, and maybe below the cabin steps, and a middle class boat suddenly becomes an aristocrat, a peer among the plebs.

A halfway house in the grating world is a well-made set of teak duck-boards. Instead of carrying the slots the full length either they are stopped about

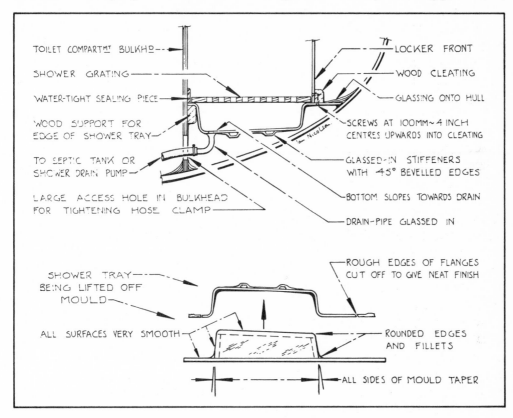

Fig. 61 Shower tray

When a toilet compartment has a shower in it, below the grating there is a tray or sump. This catches the shower water, which must not be allowed to go into the bilge, and channels it overboard by way of an electric pump, or into a septic tank.

This section through the shower tray shows how it is made and fitted so as to be watertight all round. The tray itself is a simple fibreglass moulding, stiffened enough to stand a man's weight. It has its smooth surface uppermost so that it looks smart and is easy to clean. The drain-pipe is glassed in before the tray is fitted, and is made with a right angle elbow so that the flexible plastic pipe does not have to go round a sharp bend in the restricted space under the tray.

On the right of the upper sketch the tray flange is shown glassed onto the inside of the hull. This type of glassing is unlikely to look neat, so it is hidden by the locker front. To hold the bottom of the locker front there is a stout wooden cleat which is screwed onto the outboard flange of the shower tray before the tray is fixed down.

The mould is shown as a crude box with sides angled so that the tray eases off without effort once the fibreglass has cured. An extra large base is needed for most moulds and the object is made slightly too large all round, then trimmed back to the right size.

3 inches (75 mm) in, or a surrounding frame is fitted. This looks much more attractive than the normal type of duck-board (see Fig. 62). Teak is by far the best material for a duck-board or grating, but if it is too expensive a hardwood like afrormosia might be used. Softwoods are no good here. A quick cheap grating is made by drilling a pattern of holes in a piece of marine ply. After all the edges are well rounded the whole affair is well varnished and made non-slip (see Fig. 63).

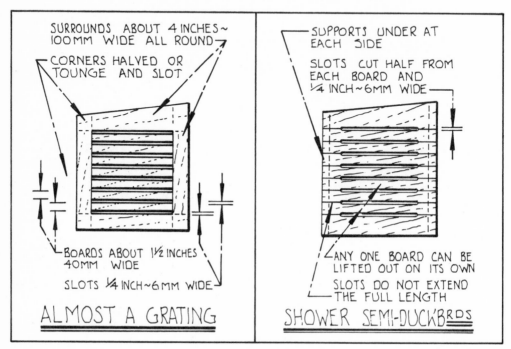

Fig. 62   Gratings (plan views)

There is nothing so much enhances a boat as a teak grating. But for anyone without the time or skill or machinery for making gratings this form of slatted floorboard (on the left) is almost as good, especially if well made of teak. Thickness depends on the distance to be spanned but will generally be the same as the sole. If in doubt use 1 inch (25 mm) wood to finish about ⅞ inch (22 mm) thick.

On the right is an even simpler type of grating substitute. Each board can be lifted separately which is a great asset if something drops through a slot, or for cleaning beneath. The margin is made much wider than the individual boards which might be about 2 inches (50 mm) wide.

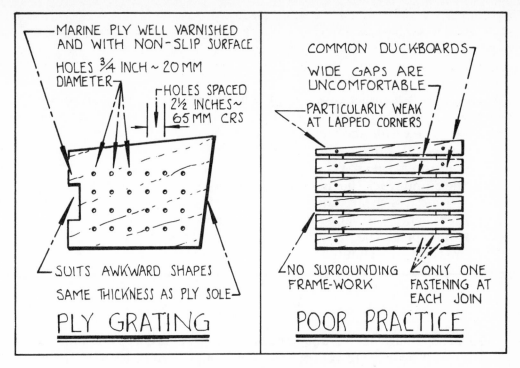

MARINE PLY WELL VARNISHED
AND WITH NON-SLIP SURFACE

HOLES ¾ INCH ~ 20MM
DIAMETER

HOLES SPACED
2½ INCHES~
65 MM CRS

SUITS AWKWARD SHAPES

SAME THICKNESS AS PLY SOLE

PLY GRATING

COMMON DUCKBOARDS

WIDE GAPS ARE
UNCOMFORTABLE

PARTICULARLY WEAK
AT LAPPED CORNERS

NO SURROUNDING
FRAME-WORK

ONLY ONE
FASTENING AT
EACH JOIN

POOR PRACTICE

Fig. 63   Gratings (plan views)

The cheapest grating, and the one which is quickest made is cut from a single piece of marine ply as in the left sketch. A pattern of holes is drilled, using the drill from both sides to avoid splitting. A margin round the edge may be painted, or stained darker than the main central part.

To avoid sharp edges the top of each hole is either well sand-papered, or just slightly countersunk. The outer edges are slightly bevelled or chamfered too.

On the right is a normal ugly duck-board which seldom improves the appearance of a boat, quite apart from its structural disadvantages.

31 WCs

A famous yacht chandler gave me this simple formula: 'You can always tell a gentleman's yacht, a *real* gentleman's yacht – it has heated toilet seats.' I only know two such yachts and one of them is the rather vast 'Norge' owned by the King of Norway, so maybe the chandler was exaggerating.

There are three types of WC, the basic bucket, the chemical type and the most usual, the pump type. The first is nothing more than a common bucket with a seat over, and it is cheap. The second comes in various versions and is often sold by suppliers of caravan equipment; it has the virtue that it is cheap to install and has no piping. The third type is made especially for yachts and is like a miniature version of a house WC but with pump(s) instead of a cistern.

Bucket type

The great advantage of an ordinary bucket is that it is so cheap and universally available. Half an inch (12 mm) of sea water is put into the bucket before use to make it easy to clean, and after use the bucket is emptied overboard. This can be a bit of a nuisance in a very public harbour, or far offshore in a raging gale, which is why the bucket is not universally popular.

The need to empty it easily suggests that the bucket should have its permanent home near the main hatch, or in a compartment close by a fore-hatch which is easy to climb through, with full bucket in hand.

A location near the main hatch has much to recommend it in a very small boat, around 23 feet (7 m) long overall, because this size of boat can hardly have a separate toilet cabin which is only used for a few minutes each day. If the bucket is in a box which slides on runners underneath the cockpit when not in use, little space is taken up by the WC. In use the main hatch is open, so smells easily escape upwards, and for dressing the headroom provided by the main hatch is a great asset. Even if there is an engine under the cockpit, provided it is far enough aft, the WC bucket in its 'drawer' can be forward of the machinery. The top of the WC box may form one of the steps up through the main hatch.

Another location is under one of the berths, either in a box which slides out like a drawer, or with access by lifting a cushion and then a cover. The drawer idea is better in that someone sleeping in the berth does not have to be disturbed if the WC is required during the night. But then one of the advantages of a bucket WC is that it can be put out (in toto) in the cockpit after dark when on moorings.

If the bucket is mounted in a box which is slid out from some recess when needed, ordinary sail track can be used as runners, or the box may slide on wood runners, just like a drawer. A barrel bolt is needed to secure the box in the stowed and 'in use' positions.

The best style of bucket to use is not the familiar cheap kitchen version because it is too flimsy. If a rope is knotted or spliced round the handle and it is thrown overboard when the boat is going fast the chances are the handle will break or tear off. So the heavier industrial plastic bucket is better. It is available from firms which supply industrial equipment and farmers' goods; often it is coloured black, and it has a thicker wall, stronger handle and general feeling of ruggedness not found in cheap plastic buckets.

The bucket needs holding firmly so that it does not tip over when the boat heels. A box with a double bottom works well. The lower bottom supports the weight of the bucket, and the upper bottom has a hole cut out which exactly fits the bucket. This holds the bottom part of the bucket and the upper edge is supported by a pair of wood chocks or another piece of ply with a suitable hole cut out to take the top diameter.

Over the bucket a seat is needed. This seat has a hole cut out of it having a diameter about 1 inch (25 mm) less than the internal diameter of the bucket top. So that the bucket can be lifted out for emptying overboard the seat is hinged, and there is a cover over the top which is also hinged. Both seat and cover need self-locking clips to hold them up when the bucket is being taken out. The seat needs to be strong enough to support a heavy man, so it can be modelled on seats from standard toilets. Alternatively it can be made from 18 mm ply with the hole edges well rounded and smoothed.

On a meticulously finished boat there may be a temptation to have a rather special toilet seat fully upholstered. I have it on (almost) the highest authority that the dark purple velvet seat over the principal WC on the old Royal yacht 'Victoria and Albert' was not a continuous success, since it became smelly after prolonged usage. A simple wood seat is easier to keep clean and smell-free.

Chemical type

Halfway (technically speaking) between the plain bucket and the pump type, is the chemical toilet. It is also halfway in price, in complications, but not much heavier than a bucket. For a racing boat the absence of skin fittings and their slight drag is an attractive feature. Ocean cruising owners do not like sea-cocks because they are not 100 per cent reliable. If they give trouble a cure can be hard if not impossible at sea, and a simple sea-cock defect has in the past been the cause of a boat's total loss. Any hole through the hull below the water-line is anathema to dedicated deep sea sailors.

Chemical toilets are sold complete with seats and lids, but the whole unit needs the same sort of securing down as a bucket. A hole may be cut in the sole into which the toilet fits exactly, with two 1 inch (25 mm) square section bearers below the sole to take the weight of the toilet and occupant. These bearers will be about 1 or 2 inches (25 or 50 mm) below the sole. Some form of stabiliser near the top rim is needed to prevent the toilet from tipping over, especially when loaded. A piece of hardwood with a recess cut out will restrain it provided there is some lashing to keep the toilet tight in the recess. A length of flexible steel wire rope secured at one end with a pelican hook (as used on life-lines round the deck) at the other works well. The wire needs a length of soft plastic tube slipped over it so that it does not damage the toilet. When the toilet has to be taken out for emptying the pelican hook is quickly released. If this type of hook is not available other forms of snap shackle can be used, but they do not pull the wire up tight, so a 6 inch (150 mm) length of trebled ¼ inch (6 mm) shock cord on the end of the wire gives the necessary elasticity. The eye-plates at each end of the wire are bolted to the bulkheads.

Another way to hold down the toilet is to bolt it to a 12 mm ply base, and have four barrel bolts to locate the base on the toilet compartment sole. Only two barrel bolts are needed if one edge of the ply is slipped under a wood lip which holds it vertically and laterally. In theory a single barrel bolt or even a turn button would do, but for such a vital fastening as this duplication is a commonsense precaution. No one likes to be unseated violently in the middle of a gale at sea.

Prominently displayed above the WC are the operating instructions. These notes are best typed on waterproof paper and mounted behind a perspex panel, because if they are lost or become saturated, then disintegrate, life aboard may become smelly.

A principal advantage of the chemical toilet is that it can be used in those areas where an overboard discharge is forbidden. The whole toilet can be humped ashore for emptying into either a normal domestic toilet (in a house near the harbour) or into special disposal points, which are normally found at marinas.

This type of toilet scores over the common 'piped-in' type because the first cost is far less, installation costs should be less than half, the weight is less, and if anything goes wrong after a few years the best plan is usually to throw the lot away and buy a new unit. The cost of a new chemical toilet will often be far less than a factory overhaul of a pump type.

Chemical toilets get their name because the excreta is broken down by a small quantity of a chemical fluid which is put into the toilet before use. One 'shot' of the chemical, which is sold at chandlers, will last a weekend.

Pump type WCs

Most small boats are fitted with this type of WC because:

1   There is some prejudice against more primitive 'machinery'.
2   There is no carting ashore or emptying overboard.
3   The discharge is prompt and is either overboard or into a holding tank in the

bilge. This means that sources of smell and disaster cannot accidentally slop into the boat's bilge to lie around and cause all sorts of distress.

4   Water from an adjacent hand-basin can be poured into the WC to be pumped overboard. This avoids the need to have a special pump to empty the basin.

5   In an emergency some types of WC can be used or adapted to work as a bilge pump. However, apart from the Lavac, few have adequate pumps for this sort of emergency.

6   For anyone who is prepared to pay three or more times the usual price an automatic WC is available. At the press of a button flushing and refilling occur, always provided the electric motors and their pumps are still in good fettle. On boats under 50 feet (15 m) electricity is seldom reliable season after season, especially if the craft goes far offshore in all weathers.

All these advantages are offset by problems which get little airing, perhaps because few people like to discuss such basic toubles. Among the snags are:

1   Quite small objects such as a rolled up toothpaste tube will clog the outlet pump. The cure involves dismantling, which probably has to be carried out with some excreta still in the system. It is an understatement to say that this is a distasteful job. As a blockage can occur at the beginning of a fortnight's holiday, and far from boat-yard facilities, the crew has to do the repairs.

2   Leaks occur and they can transfer smells.

3   Two carefully located sea-cocks are needed, one to take in clean water, one to take away the foul contents of the WC. These sea-cocks are a recurring source of trouble because they corrode unseen and have been known to fall off, resulting in a sudden substantial leak. In any hundred boats surveyed there will be at least forty seized sea-cocks and in some areas the average will be nearer eighty.

4   Maintenance can be difficult because parts corrode together, the job is unpleasant and spares are not widely available. If a boat-yard does the job it is likely to be costly. A major overhaul often costs almost as much as a new toilet, so the clever owner sells his old toilet to a pauper building or refitting a yacht and buys a new WC. One problem is that repairs are carried out by mechanics who are relatively highly paid, and the spare parts are not cheap. So compared with, say, sail repairs, the cost of toilet repairs tends to be sensational.

5   Many versions have china bowls which crack if bumped hard. If a razor is dropped into the bowl a leaking crack may appear. Nothing on a small boat should be even slightly vulnerable and no one has china crockery – so a china bowl in the WC is illogical. The reason it is favoured is that the alternatives do not last. Nylon coated metal bowls peel after a few seasons, plastic bowls are seldom strong enough. There is a dilemma here with no entirely satisfactory solution in sight.

165

In spite of the disadvantages the majority of boats have the pump type WC because of its convenience (no pun intended). Knowing the annoying features makes it possible to minimise them when doing an installation. For instance, the shelf by the wash-basin must not be above the bowl so that razors fall off into it. The shelf should have a sensible 3 inch (75 mm) fiddle along the edge. Sea-cocks should be located where they can be seen daily, and serviced yearly without difficulty. For a long trip one or two sets of spares should be bought with the toilet. When the toilet is new it may be worthwhile stripping it down and reassembling it with additional grease on all bolt and pipe threads.

Installation ought to go something like this:

1   Two people lift the toilet aboard because it is too heavy and awkward for one to do the job without chipping woodwork and stumbling.
2   It is sighted where the plans indicate and someone sits on it to ensure that the best, precise location has been chosen. He is asked if the grab-rails can be reached, do his feet find corners they can jam into when the boat heels and has he shoulder room. If the first 'test pilot' is large and long-legged a small person now ascends the throne and makes similar tests, so that the WC suits all sizes of crew.
3   Pencil marks are then made round the base flange and in the bolt holes, on the sole or plinth. The WC is lifted off the sole and taken out of the way. Holes are drilled for the bolts, and if there is no access under the sole, a 6 inch (150 mm) diameter hole is cut nearby so that a hand can be put through it to put the nuts on the WC holding-down bolts.
4   The sea-cocks are fitted and the piping put onto them.
5   The piping (which is plastic) is led to near where the WC will be and the stainless steel hose clamps put on tightly at the sea-cocks, loosely on the other ends which are not yet on the WC. There must be no sharp bends in the pipes because plastic pipes kink if asked to go round tight corners. It is sometimes necessary to introduce a metal pipe bend to avoid kinking the plastic. Ideally non-ferrous pipe should be used, but if this is not available, a mild steel swept bend (not a sharp right angle) should be bought and sent for hot dip galvanising. Ordinary galvanised swept bends are seldom satisfactory as they have threads cut each end after the galvanising so the threaded parts soon rust.

The inlet pipe is led directly from the sea-cock to the inlet on the WC by a convenient short route, avoiding locations where crews' feet will tread. The outlet pipe must sweep up from the sea-cock to a height 3 feet (1 m) above the normal water-line or better still to the deckhead and turn round and down to the outlet point on the WC. This high loop is to prevent the toilet flooding back if the sea-cock is not turned off or is defective. It is a safety precaution but not a very satisfactory one because syphoning can still occur. To avoid the risk of syphoning a few of the best builders used to fit little cocks at the top of the pipe's travel, and provided these taps were left open when the boat was not in use, syphoning could not occur. Of course this assumes the cocks are kept clean and free from corrosion. Nowadays modern builders do not fit this sort of safety valve and so boats occasionally sink for this reason.

It is not easy to buy a metal 180° slow swept bend, and the plastic pipe may not be coaxed round 180° in a confined space without kinking. This problem is overcome by using a 90° metal pipe bend and taking the plastic pipe round 45° each side of the metal elbow, in slow careful curves.

The discharge pipe can in theory be any plastic pipe having a wall thickness of more than 1/16 inch (1.5 mm), but in practice chandlers sell a green plastic with nylon spiral reinforcing. The wall thickness is about 1/8 inch (3 mm) and the internal diameter must be selected to fit the WC, also the seacocks must have the same pipe connection sizes as the WC.

The inlet pipe is under suction so it must be of reinforced material which does not collapse inwards easily. Again the green plastic pipe with the nylon continuous insert is sold by chandlers for this work.

6   When the pipes are in place the WC is lifted back and bolted down using stainless steel or bronze bolts.

7   The pipes are connected to the WC and tests should ideally be carried out right away. This is seldom practical because a water supply cannot be connected without disconnecting the inlet cock. Tests should be made to look for weeps (boat-builders' slang for slow leaks). If they occur the hose clamps are tightened, or doubled up. If weeps occur anywhere in the WC it must go back to the supplier.

So much for the theory. In practice two sources of frustration are often present and obtrusive: lack of space and lack of local strength. Toilet compartments are almost always the smallest cabin in the boat, so there is seldom enough room to reach round under and over the WC. To make life doubly difficult modern boats do not have all that thick woodwork or steel structure which used to be so common, so it is not a simple matter of dumping the loo in place and fixing it down. Reinforcing is needed.

To make the access easier, the WC may be offset to one side. It is usual to put the bowl close to a bulkhead to give extra room on the pump side. However, the bowl cannot be placed right up against the bulkhead; something like 5 inches (125 mm) is needed between the outside rim of the toilet seat and the bulkhead to allow shoulder room for a big man swathed in sweaters and oilskins. This dimension is about the minimum.

On the pump side knuckle room is needed to work the handle. This assumes a traditional type of WC is being installed such as the Baby Blake, which is recommended. It is 1 ft 8 in. ×1 ft 6½ in. ×1 ft 5¼ in. (510×470×440 mm) and it stands up better than most to usage, corrosion and hard sailing, not least because it has pump glands which can be repacked and greased. It is heavy in spite of its name, so it may not suit lightweight racing machines.

For anyone who wants a more compact, lighter or cheaper toilet there is the Lavac. It is 1 ft 3½ in. ×1 ft 2½ in. ×9¼ in. As the pump is entirely separate the installation is much easier, but there is a temptation to install the bowl in a very tiny space. Something like 2 ft 2 in. (660 mm) is about the minimum though in special circumstances one might shave this a little. (Here and elsewhere, if critical dimensions are needed, Chapter 6 of *Boat Data Book* gives a lot of critical dimensions based on the size of the human frame.)

All toilets have smaller base flanges than top areas. The rule of thumb which has been passed down through the generations is that a base area of 1 ft 6 in. (460 mm) across and 1 ft 4 in. (410 mm) from back of the WC to the front is needed. This is a handy guide, but far from accurate and if the space is very limited the builder has the choice of shopping around to see which machine will fit, or how much the space must be increased.

It is usual to set WCs on ½ inch (12 mm) ply soles but some local stiffening should be fitted. If the seat is rather low the sole doubler is put on top. A rot resisting hardwood is needed, at least ½ inch (12 mm) thick extending quite 2 inches (50 mm) clear all round the base flange. Whether the sole doubler is on top or underneath, it should be well bedded in place because there is always dampness hereabouts.

If the space is very cramped it may be hard to get all four bolts into the base flange, so some builders take the easy way out and only fit two. This results in various accidents which are only hilarious for people not intimately concerned. If it is impossible to get bolts with nuts on the underside it is permissible to use four bronze coach-screws of the full diameter to fill the bolt holes in the flange base. Ordinary screws are not tough enough for this job.

Another technique is to have four bolts fixed upwards in the sole, so that the WC is lowered onto them and the nuts put on top. To achieve this the sole is made to fit but not secured down. Next the WC is positioned and the base flange holes marked, then drilled. The doubler is fitted, and made at least ⅜ inch (10 mm) extra thick and 50 per cent bigger in area. The bolts are put in from below and held in place by half nuts. These nuts have to be recessed well, which explains why the doubler has to be larger. To make life easier the ends of the bolts may be pointed so that fitting the WC is even easier. With the bolts standing up, the sole is put in place and screwed or glassed (or both) to keep it safely in place. It is easy to lower the WC on and put the nuts in place from above.

There are variations on this technique. For instance, if the boat arrives with the sole fixed, a large doubler may be made and the WC fixed to it. The doubler is slid into position and held down by screws at about 3 inches (75 mm) all round. Naturally, the bolts in this case have to be upwards through the WC feet and must have counter-sunk heads, so that there is nothing protruding on the bottom of the doubler.

If coach-screws are used it will probably be necessary to get hold of a stubby screwdriver, or one of those screwdrivers with the 'sharp end' bent over at right angles. On one occasion I had installation troubles and ended up recessing the nuts on the underside of the sole, securing them with Araldite. I cut slots in the bronze bolts and turned them in with a screwdriver as the available spanners would not fit in the tiny corners.

In some areas such as marinas it is forbidden to discharge a WC overboard. Instead a septic tank (also called a holding or sewage tank) is fitted in the bilge. Waste from the WC goes into this tank, which in time becomes full so that it has to be emptied by a suction pipe into a special shore establishment. The suction from the shore connects to a standard fitting on the side deck. Piping to the septic tank is made with only the gentlest of bends to minimise the risk of a blockage. To avoid noisome repair jobs the tank should be semi-portable, but secured down well enough to withstand the worst the sea can do. This means at least eight $5/16$ inch (8 mm) bolts through lugs spaced round the tank. The air pipe from the septic tank needs very careful thought. It has to be sited so that smells from it do not obtrude. If the tank overfills, the WC discharge pump will force liquid up the air pipe till it overflows. So this consequence must be remembered when deciding on the location for the air pipe.

A convenient way of avoiding some of the unpleasant events which may occur with a septic tank is to use a flexible one. No air pipe is needed; the tank is flat and 'collapsed' when empty. As it is filled the top is pushed up and the sides outwards and it is easy to see when the tank is getting full. If there is any trouble with this kind of tank it can be thrown away and it is not too expensive to buy a new one. Installation consists of pushing it into place and connecting up the pipes but if the boat is going offshore she may be rolled over, so there must be some restraining structure to keep the tank in place when the boat is inverted.

There is one final refinement which should be considered by anyone going offshore in a sailing vessel. This is the 'tackable toilet'. Briefly the problem is this: when a boat heels it is not comfortable or convenient to use a toilet which is angled. Going hard to windward, the boat may lie over at 40° and the toilet takes up precisely the same tilt. To overcome this, on a few select craft, the toilet is mounted on a base which can be tilted to port or starboard. The inlet and discharge pipes must have enough slack in them to allow for this tilting, and the mechanism which holds the toilet at the new angle must be rugged enough to withstand the weight of a heavy man. As the boat may be pounding hard allowance has to be made for shock loading. This is not the place to skimp the safety factors.

32 *Anchor winch and chain* ═══════*locker*═══════

An anchor winch should be bought from the same source as the anchor chain to make absolutely sure that the chain fits the gipsy. A chain which is too small may jam in the gipsy and be almost impossible to pry out. If the accident is not spotted promptly the winch may go on winding round causing a serious snarl-up. A chain which is too big for the gipsy may slip and run out, roaring away out of control.

When buying a winch it is best to avoid the very smallest unless weight and cost are critical. This applies whether the winch is hand-operated or mechanical. Hydraulic powered winches are tough, reliable, difficult to abuse, and generally long lasting. Their principal disadvantage is that they are costly. Electric winches are cheaper to buy and install but they tend to resent overloading. Their weaknesses are usually in the switching gear and in the override devices. One way to avoid trouble with an electric anchor winch is to have the auxiliary hand lever kept stowed permanently on deck so that the crew can help the winch when it begins to labour. And of course with all anchor winches it makes more than average good sense to steam up so that the anchor chain hangs down vertically, otherwise the winch is pulling the boat up against wind and tide as well as dragging the chain inboard; this double load of work is the cause of many winch failures.

The gipsy must be very carefully lined up with the stemhead roller. If the chain is not to jam and is to ride safely onto the gipsy the chain must come in over the stemhead roller and straight back to the gipsy which must have its axle parallel to the stemhead roller axle. The centre-line of the stemhead roller must lead straight back to the centre-line of the gipsy. This often means that the anchor winch is not bolted down on the centre-line of the boat. To make sure everything is correctly aligned a short length of chain or piece of rope is brought up over the stemhead roller and put round the gipsy before the winch is bolted down. This rope must run over the stemhead roller and over the gipsy in such a way that there are no kinks in the rope when seen from above.

If the winch has a warping drum on the opposite side of the gipsy and this drum is intended to pull in ropes running over a second stemhead roller, it will almost certainly be necessary to fit up some sort of lead block on deck.

An anchor winch has to be bolted down with a wood pad between it and the deck, and a second equally large pad under the deck. These pads must be of hardwood and should be about ⅝ inch (16 mm) for every 20 ft (7 m) of a boat's overall length.

It is good practice to have the pads carried well beyond the winch base in every direction so that extra bolts can join the two pads through the deck. If the pads are made extra big in area then there can be more than the four bolts through the winch feet, so that there may be eight or even twelve bolts to spread the load. If the on-deck pad extends forward it will prevent the anchor chain from chafing the deck, and nothing grinds away the gel coat quicker than an anchor chain. With careful planning the large pad on deck can also double as one or even two of the anchor chocks.

The bolts through the winch base should be of stainless steel or bronze because galvanised ones are almost bound to rust within three or four years. It is good practice to put on locking nuts but this precaution is only seen on one boat in forty. There should be ample bedding under both pads and under the winch. The bolts are not tightened up one at a time, but progressively and diagonally. That is, all the nuts are tightened by hand first. Then the aft starb'd bolt is done up fairly tight with a spanner, followed by the forward port one; next the aft port one is tightened and then the forward starb'd one. This is the same procedure that is used when tightening any machinery down, and the aim here is to avoid unfair stresses on the winch feet and bottom flanges.

The winch should not be used as a mooring post, and a few winch makers mention this important limitation in their literature. Every time there is a really severe gale one or two winches collapse under the unusual strain and boats are driven ashore. Close by the winch, and ideally just ahead of it, there must be a really stout mooring cleat or samson post.

On boats over 50 feet (15 m) or so, there should be an arrangement for holding the chain temporarily while it is transferred from the winch to the mooring strong point. Alternatively, the mooring strong point may have on it an arrangement such as a cable clamp and tensioning screw so that the load can be permanently taken off the winch. On a vessel of this size a chain brake is a great asset. This is nothing more or less than a channel through which the chain runs in and out with a cam over the top. The cam has a groove so that the chain runs through it easily; there is a long handle on this cam which can be pulled back to pinch the chain between the cam and the channel.

The chain locker should be vertically below the winch. If this is not possible the winch must be at least near the chain locker so that the chain drops at no more than 40° off the vertical line.

Between the winch on deck and the chain locker there may be a pipe or an open top trough. The pipe will be made from a length of plastic tube or drain-pipe for boats under about 40 feet (12 m) and above this size they will be either steel or aluminium pipe. The great advantage of a pipe is that it keeps water and mud confined so they drip down into the anchor locker. On the other hand a trough, usually made of hardwood, is much less likely to allow the chain to jam when it is running in or out. Perhaps the best compromise is a trough with a hinged lid so that muck cannot spread about the cabin but if the chain has a tendency to jam it can be easily seen and cleared.

Some owners like an anchor locker to retain all the mud and muck, since in theory they clean out this space three or four times each year when the anchor and all the chain are down on the sea bed. Other owners recognise that this cleaning out process seldom takes place and they fit a large limber hole with a grid over it to prevent the chain catching in the hole.

The whole locker must be designed with no ledges or obstructions otherwise the chain will find some subtle way of jamming and refuse to run out.

Near the top of the chain locker there must be a strong eye-plate for tying on a length of rope made fast to the bitter end of the chain. This lashing must be clearly accessible regardless of whether the chain is all in the locker, partly in, or completely out. The eye-plate holding the lashing must be strong enough to stand up to accidents like a runaway chain thundering out, and the lashing too must match the strength of the chain and the eye.

33 *Life-lines*

Round the full perimeter of the deck of any cruiser, sail or power, it is usual to have wire life-lines. Just occasionally on power boats and some very heavy sailing craft, galvanised steel tubular stanchions with matching steel tube life-lines are fitted because they are stronger, last a long time and give an additional feeling of security. Common pipe is used for these heavy life-lines with standard threaded connections and base flanges, or the horizontal rails may be passed through standard pipe holding rings on the top, and at the middle of each stanchion.

By far the commonest type of life-line is made from stainless or galvanised wire with a plastic sheath. This type of wire is sold just for life-lines by chandlers and rigging makers. Since the plastic skin is vulnerable and chafes through at stanchions, where sheets pass over and anywhere subject to abrasion, it is probably best to go for the stainless wire core. However, frequent testing by violent tugging is essential, as the wire in the course of about five seasons fatigues where it flexes against stanchions. This is one reason why the galvanised wire is favoured; it rusts and warns any reasonably observant ship's husband that the time has come to renew. Also the galvanised wire is cheaper.

The two standard sizes of life-line wire are 4 and 5 mm. As always, with wire, these dimensions refer to the maximum outside diameter, but this is of the *wire*. The plastic sheathing puts up the overall diameter by roughly 1/16 inch (1.5 mm), but all standard stanchions have holes which will take either size of wire.

For racing machines, inshore craft and boats under about 23 feet (7 m) overall it is usual to use the 4 mm diameter size. In all other cases the larger size is best. For extending cruising, commercial craft and such like a bigger diameter wire, often the biggest standard unsheathed material which will fit through the stanchion holes, will be used.

It is usual to have two life-lines right round the boat, but when the 4 mm size is used, a single wire may be the choice – and it may not go right round. There may be a pulpit at the bow, but none aft, or no pulpit, just three stanchions each side. Often on small craft and racing machines (where the racing rules permit) there will be low stanchions, typically 18 inches (500 mm) high. These low life-lines and reduced length ones are only selected to keep down weight and windage. They result in a much lower standard of safety, and are not acceptable for serious offshore work unless the crew are keen, fit and prepared to accept the extra danger.

When there are to be children aboard, or the voyage is a long ocean cruise, three wires are sometimes fitted. They need special stanchions which take some finding. There have been instances of men being washed overboard between or under normal double life-lines. I once had a seasick crew member, swathed in sweaters (it was a bitter December day) with oilskins on top, slither between standard life-lines. This happened even though his girth was vast due to the multiple layers of clothing he was wearing.

For extended cruising, or if the children aboard are under ten, it is better to have two stout life-lines all round and netting extending from the top wire to the deck, where it is secured continuously to the toe-rail. Nylon or terylene netting with a mesh size of about 3 inches (75 mm) works well. It needs a quick release arrangement such as a row of snap shackles at the bow to allow the anchor to go overboard. Another arrangement is a hardwood bar about 1½×1½ inches (40×40 mm) in section lashed along the bottom of the netting, with a quick release lashing to the toe-rail. To get the anchor over, the bar is freed and the netting swings clear.

Life-lines are a great nuisance, forever in the way of sheets, headsails, and when the dinghy has to be launched they seem designed to create an obstacle course. This inconvenience is widely accepted as part of the price of safety. Headsails have their flow spoiled by the stanchions and wires and sheets chafe – we all accept this, though, with reluctance. A few owners take trouble to minimise the disadvantages; for extended cruising the headsails may be cut high, so as to clear the wires. An allowance of 3 feet (915 mm) is enough here and it gives a subsidiary advantage because the crew have vision forward to leeward, so they less often crash into other craft.

Plastic tubing slipped over the life-lines, between the stanchions cuts down chafe and makes it easier to launch and recover the dinghy. Racing boats will not have this safety feature because it means there is a tiny bit of extra weight and windage well above the water-line.

Life-lines are made up like the standing rigging. Each end has an eye which is shackled to the pulpit forward and 'pushpit' (slang for aft pulpit!). Where there is no pulpit the ends are shackled to eyeplates or to the toe-rail. Incidentally, eye-bolts are virtually never used on well-built boats because their single rod through the deck allows them to twist and pull forwards or sideways. Eye-plates, with their two or four bolts, are so very much more reliable, and unlike eye-bolts, very seldom cause deck leaks.

At the end of each life-line there is a rigging screw which should be tightened up till the wire is taut, but the stanchions are not visibly strained inboard. If the sag is taken out of the wire and then an extra 100 lb. pull added that will be adequate. Thereafter the rigging screw is wired up, and taped over so that neither fingers nor clothes are gashed by outstanding split pins or wire or other sharp projections.

At one end of each wire there must be a break in the metallic contact, otherwise the radio direction-finder will suffer from interference. Plastic toggles are sold (by the suppliers of the life-lines and end terminals) for this precaution, which is only needed if an R D/F. set is aboard.

There is a trick, much seen aboard boats whose owners are trying to save expenditure, which cuts out the need for plastic toggles. Terylene line about

⅛ inch (3 mm) diameter or less is used as end lashings on each wire. Six or more complete turns of this thin rope is needed. Using line here has the advantage that the life-lines can be released fairly easily, perhaps to lift aboard a heavy dinghy.

It is normal practice for the crew to climb over, or if arthritic through the life-lines, when coming aboard. This is not convenient, but the majority of boats are built as cheaply as possible and the absence of a break in the life-lines is widely considered to be a reasonable economy. If proper access through the life-lines is needed there must be stanchions with supporting diagonal legs (extending fore-and-aft) each side of the 'gateway'. The life-lines are led up to these stanchions and ended there, with portable sections or wire across the opening. The closure of the gap may be by short lengths of wire held tight by pelican hooks, or by a light chain with a snap shackle on the end.

Access through the life-lines is normally where the dinghy is most conveniently brought alongside. This will be by the cockpit, or on a power boat by the wheel-house door. Occasionally there are steps up the transom, so the break in the life-lines will be opposite them. Not every boat has access port and starboard, the latter being the traditional side. One access only is an economy and a safety precaution because any break in the safety ring is a weakness and a danger area; it is surprising how often the closure is forgotten at sea, or a snap shackle fails or the adjacent stanchions become slack where they are bolted to the deck, or they get bent.

Once the wires have been threaded through the stanchions, and the end terminals fitted, it is not easy to take the life-lines out. When the boat is laid up for the winter the stanchions can be lifted out of their sockets, but they must all be kept together because the wires cannot be withdrawn. In the boat's store the wires are so often kinked and this weakens them. Some stanchions cannot be lifted out of their sockets, so the wires cannot be removed and suffer from weathering and general damage during the winter period.

If the wires are bought from a rigging supplier or a chandler with rigging facilities an inexperienced builder will have one end terminal fitted onto each wire. The other end is threaded through the stanchions, but then the problem is: how is the second end to be made into an eye for the rigging screw or lashing? The simple and inexpensive answer is: bend the wire round a thimble, and seize it back along itself. Four *very* tight seizings each ½ inch (12 mm) long are used, then the surplus wire is cut off.

The seizings must be so tight that they bite into the plastic sheathing and so gain extra grip. The end lashing or rigging screw is hauled up tight and the seizings watched. If they move they are not tight enough. The line used for these seizings is terylene or nylon, and less than 1/16 inch (1.5 mm) thick so that it has no difficulty in biting tenaciously into the plastic of the life-line. A great advantage of this technique is that the life-lines are quickly stripped off the boat at laying up time. Wire clamps are sometimes seen on the life-line ends, but they make a boat look like an unkempt dredger and they are not totally reliable.

175

34 Spars

Masts and booms, spinnaker booms and staysail booms, motor-boats' signal masts, bearing out poles and every sort of spar is made of aluminium alloy tubing. Virtually all spars are bought from specialist mast-makers whose addresses are found in the advertisements in yacht magazines. Because it is always a good idea to support local industry it is worth working through the small advertisements in the magazines to discover if one of the spar-making companies has a branch near the boat-yard. Buying locally brings four advantages: it reduces the high price of transport, it means that the details of the spars can be discussed with the local manager so that the precise and best specification can be obtained without correspondence or delay, the work can be monitored so that late deliveries should be avoided, and if a breakage occurs the local branch of the spar-makers should have a special interest and sympathy in completing a prompt replacement or good repair.

To get quotations or to order a set of spars the sail plan (or above-water profile plan of a power boat) is sent to the spar maker. With this and a list of the owner's needs he will be able to work out the detailed specification which will include such fittings as: cross-trees, slots for internal halliards, spinnaker pole track, cross-tree and masthead lights, reefing gear, kicking strap attachments, climbing rungs (for ocean cruisers), eye-plates for spinnaker boom lifts, cleats, halliard winches, burgee halliard eyes and so on.

When getting quotations it is important to remember that each spar-maker will try to minimise his price to try to win the order. He will specify the minimum number and the smallest size of cleats, for example. This often results in a mast which is skimped and inconvenient, occasionally even dangerous. I prefer to follow a plan which I use repeatedly when specifying any part of any vessel: I imagine the worst situation the boat will encounter, and I assume this occurs during trials when I am aboard, when the boat is not tuned or 'worked up'. I pre-suppose that everyone aboard is tired, hungry, seasick and frightened. This is a good way to write a safe specification, which includes one cleat for each rope on the mast plus at least one spare. Little cleats have little fastenings, which have little strength. To be safe have 6 inch (150 mm) cleats on a 20 foot (6 m) boat, 9 inch (230 mm) cleats on a 40 footer (12 m) and 12 inch (300 mm) cleats on a 60 footer (18 m) – and bigger for long range cruising.

Mast-makers are good at giving specialised advice. If an existing design is to be changed from four lower shrouds to two lowers and an inner forestay, the first person to consult is the designer but at the same time contact the mast-maker. If the designer is not available or cannot help, the mast-maker will supply technical advice and possibly a drawing. In the same way when building a racing boat it is important to approach the spar-maker early on in the development so that they can set aside production time, and if the boat is important, designing time. They have vast experience: it is significant that few builders or designers are responsible for more than dozens or occasionally hundreds of boats each year whereas mast-makers turn out thousands of spars annually. For a specialised craft they will offer the latest ideas in an advancing technology. For a cruising boat they will suggest a standard spar because this is the cheapest and most reliable. There are dozens of standard classes of boat and anyone involved in the designing or building of a boat is advised to select a stock class mast where possible. If the boat is not to fit some racing rule there is little point in specifying a mast say 35 feet 2 inches long, when a stock mast is available 35 feet 4 inches long. Apart from the saving in design and draughting costs, spares and replacements are more conveniently available to replace breakages.

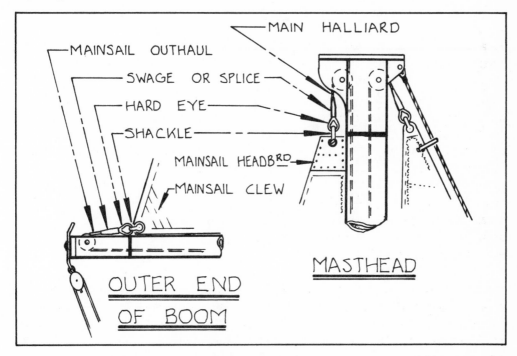

Fig. 64   Spar details

When ordering spars or sails or making alterations to drawings it has to be remembered that the corners of sails do not normally reach to the ends of spars. For instance, the top of the headboard of a mainsail must be well below the centre of the main halliard sheave. Just how far depends on the size of the main halliard shackle, eye, and end splice or swage. Where possible these should be measured, alternatively an allowance of about 2½ per cent of the overall length of the boat should be taken. The shackle or the swage should not end right on the sheave otherwise the halliard wire may fatigue and in time break at the ends of the swage or splice.

The same applies to headsails although here it is usual to allow a much bigger gap to prevent the wind being 'choked' between the head of the sail and the mast.

Similar considerations apply at the outer end of a boom. However, the outhaul wire with its swage or splice, eye and shackle tend to be smaller than the halliard. If the individual parts cannot be measured allow 2 per cent of the boat's length here.

Alloy spars are sold protected by an anodised coating which may be gold or silver or black. The colour chosen should match the rest of the boat's colour scheme. It is a false economy to buy spars which are not protectively coated by anodising.

As much equipment as possible should always be bought from one source, partly to avoid dealing with a host of suppliers, partly to save money but most of all to make sure that mating parts fit together. From the mast-maker it is

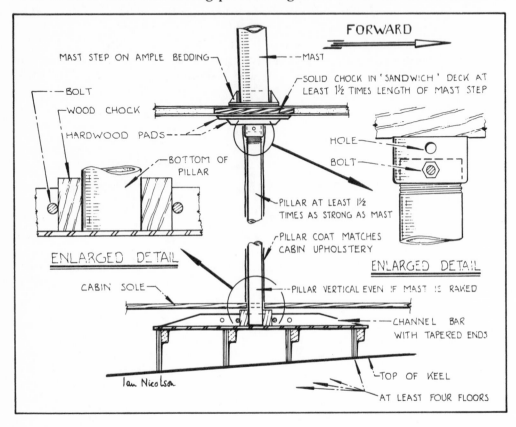

Fig. 65   Mast support pillar

The mast, particularly on a sailing yacht with a big sail area, needs ample support. A tubular pillar made from a steel pipe is economic and easy to fit. The heel of the pillar lies in a metal channel, which has been pre-drilled with holes athwartships. To spread the load the channel lies on at least four floors which are well glassed in and rest on top of the keel. So that the floors do not distort under load they are stiffened across the top by hardwood doublers, or the floors may be of flanged fibreglass. To avoid problems associated with precise fitting the pillar can lodge anywhere in the middle of the channel. Once it is in place bolts are put in athwartships ahead and behind it, with hardwood chocks taking up the space between the bolts and the pillar.

The top of the pillar is threaded, with a sleeve screwed on. The length of the pillar should be such that when it is in place the sleeve is rotated till it lodges tight under the deck-head. Holes in the top of the sleeve take bars used to force the sleeve up firmly, but not so tight that the deck is pushed up. Next a bolt or two is put in to lock the sleeve so that it cannot unwind and loosen the pillar.

Between the top of the pillar and the mast step there must be hardwood or ply wood pads. The one immediately above the pillar will be bit into slightly by the sleeve.

178

logical to buy the mast step, the standing and running rigging and (on racing craft) the hydraulic gear for adjusting the rigging. At the same time obtain drawings of the terminals of the standing rigging to make sure they will fit the chain-plates. It is bad practice to fit shackles between the chain-plates and rigging ends because it adds one more link to each 'chain' and so increases the risk of failure. It also puts up the cost, quite apart from the fact that shackles seldom have a good engineering fit in rigging screws or chain-plates. Some mast steps are extra long, and have a selection of holes for the mast location bolts. As a result the heel of the mast can be moved forward or aft, to adjust for weather helm and performance. This is an asset on an untried or changed design. Other mast steps have pivot bolts through the mast heel which helps when raising or lowering the mast by hand without a crane. This convenience is only of use on boats under about 30 feet (9 m). The types widely available are intended for infrequent raising and lowering of the mast. If the main spar is to be lifted and lowered more often than at the beginning and end of the season a proper tabernacle is needed. It has a high strong metal casing enveloping the lower part of the mast almost up to the boom height. There are strong bolts through the mast; one acts as the pivot, and they all help the shrouds hold the mast up.

Wood spars are nowadays only fitted by amateur builders who wish to save every penny, or builders cut off from the supply of boat equipment. Spar making in wood takes a lot of time, but it is not difficult for a competent wood-worker. Spruce is the best wood but it is expensive and not available in some areas. Oregon pine is a cheaper heavier substitute which is easier to get, but it must be specially selected, free from all but the tiniest knots and blemishes.

An amateur builder energetically trying to save money might compromise by using an aluminium mast but make up his own wood boom. This may be solid or hollow (in the form of a long narrow box), and it may have roller or slab reefing. Before beginning fabrication it is important to get the goose-neck or a drawing of this fitting. The forward end of the boom is made to fit the standard goose-neck. It is likely that special metal joining arms will be needed to mate the wood boom to the goose-neck, because the latter will have been designed to slot into a standard alloy tubular boom and held only by a dozen small rivets.

35 Buying sails

The cost of a boat's sails is often a tenth of the total value, and may be as much as a fifth. Also whereas discounts on other gear are not always available, by timing the purchase of sails correctly it is nearly always possible to get a special price.

The sail-maker's year follows a pattern. There is always the hectic rush in the spring and a very quiet spell in the autumn. The year goes something like this (the months in the southern hemisphere have to be reversed since the spring there is during the northern autumn): January is when yachtsmen emerge from hibernation, so it is already too late to get the lowest price. February is busy and deliveries are often measured in months not weeks. March is frantic and the sail-maker is beginning to look haggard. April is worse – sail-makers have no time for eating, sleeping or breathing. By mid-May the very worst is over and sail-makers start to enjoy three meals almost every day, apart from Thursdays and Fridays because of the approaching weekend when sails are wanted. June is almost fun. The worst of the rush is over and the sail-maker manages to go sailing one weekend in two. By July the sail-loft is peaceful and this is a good time to talk about ordering sails. Place the order in August or September at the latest; these are the famine months and sail-makers are looking haggard again but due to lack of work this time. By October a few boats are laid up so repairs and new sail orders are trickling in. November sees a firm trickle of repairs as the majority of boats are laid up and new boats have been ordered for the coming summer. By December sail-makers are ordering drink for Christmas and wondering whether to take two or three days off over the holidays. This is no bad time to corner a sail-maker at the yacht club bar and get his advice about new sails. Deliveries are measured in days and in Britain that sudden burst of activity occasioned by the London Boat Show has yet to occur.

The ideal time to order sails is during a week day. There is no sense in talking to a sail-maker on Saturday when the rest of the sailing world is clamouring for his attention – Sunday is seldom much better. If he cannot be visited, write a letter detailing the type of boat, the kind of sailing planned and the level of spending possible. Sails are costed on their area and type. The cost of the material forms nearly half the final cost of the sail, so light displacement boats, which have small sails, are cheaper to 'dress' than heavy ones.

Racing boat sails are limited in size and number by rules, so the sail-maker's advice is needed to get the fastest combination. A cruising wardrobe depends on the type of voyaging planned. For general week-ending and the occasional club race a mainsail (and mizzen on a two-master), a fairly light no. 1 genoa, a no. 2 genoa which reefs to no. 3, possibly a working jib and a storm jib covers all wind speeds. A spinnaker may be left till the second season if building the boat has left the owner nearly broke, because in addition to the actual sail there are the sheets, halliard, boom with its uphaul and downhaul and extra winches to buy. A spinnaker is an expensive sail when grouped with all its equipment.

There is a widespread tendency to omit the storm jib from the initial list to save money. This sail may be used only once in every second or third season but when it is needed it is as vital as an anchor or a box of flares. It should be classified with the safety gear rather than the sails. It is the cheapest of all the sails and there is little sense in taking the risk of doing without it.

For long range cruising order triple stitching, extra doubling at the corners, extra large corner eyes, hand-worked or hydraulically pressed eyes for slides and hanks, also extra large hanks with 30 per cent closer spacing than usual, and double slides at each end of luff and foot. At the same time make sure the sail-maker puts offcuts of cloth with each completed sail for repairs.

Ask for different colour sail bags so that there is no confusion in a hurried crisis. I work on the principle that 'the darker the skies the worse the weather', so my sail bags range from white for the ghoster to dark blue for the storm jib.

When asking for quotations the sail-maker needs to know only the name of each sail and its area, plus the number of reefs and any special requirements such as triple stitching. He normally charges extra for a sail number, at so much per digit (which explains the joke about everyone in the Clyde Cruising Club wanting the number 1C!).

For making the sails the sail-maker needs a sail plan and it is best when possible to send it to him even for quoting. The designer may not show the sizes of the mainsail luff and foot slides. Occasionally these two sets of slides are a different size or pattern. Sometimes the luff has slides and the foot slips into a groove, sometimes it is the other way round. The sail-maker needs to know. The same applies to a mizzen. He also needs the 'knock' or 'knock-back' which is the distance from the back of the mast to the foreward side of the pin holding the mainsail tack eye, and likewise with the mizzen. For headsails the size of the forestay dictates the size of the headsail hanks. If a luff groove unit is fitted on the forestay its type and size are required so that matching luff tapes can be sewn on.

When an order is placed the sail-maker requires a deposit which is 40 or 50 per cent of the price, the balance being paid when the sail is ready. By going to a local sail-maker transport costs are saved and if the sail needs altering or if it has an accident, the ideal man for putting it right is close-by.

A careful sail-maker can save an owner money. He can point out that on some boats two deep reefs are virtually as good as three medium ones. And it may be cheaper still to go for roller reefing. There is the cost of the roller boom gear but this has to be compared with slab reefing gear plus the cost of each slab reef in the sail. For extended cruising a single very deep slab reef is put in mainsails and mizzens which have roller reefing gear in case this gadget breaks down or seizes up.

When ordering sails a cover for the mainsail should be bought. Sunlight is the great destroyer of sails, so a substantial cover is an economy. Very cheap sails are seldom worth buying. They are usually made of cloth one or two weights below the recommended level so they stretch and wear out quickly. They are made with undersize corner eyes insufficiently reinforced. This results in corners which distort and sometimes tear right out – and this sort of accident happens in a rising wind.

36 Standing rigging

Those wires which support the mast(s) on a sailing yacht or power boat are called the standing rigging. They are made of wire which may be of stainless steel or galvanised mild steel. The latter is cheaper by a factor of about five, but it does not last so long. However, galvanised wire, when it is approaching the end of its useful life, turns red with rust, which is fair warning given in ample time. Stainless rigging fails with little warning, sometimes apparently with none. A strand or two may break, usually near the closure of the end eye, or at the end of a swagged fitting. Fatigue is often the cause of stainless wire failure, and it sometimes gives insufficient or no hint of trouble.

However, stainless steel wire is widely available in the yachting industry because it has become the popular material, almost universally used. So anyone who wishes to save money by selecting galvanised rigging must first be sure it is available in the correct size. *Boat Data Book* should be consulted for standing and running rigging sizes. The money saved by going for galvanised rigging is not so very great if the builder cannot do the end splices himself, and has to pay someone to splice or otherwise make the ends using one of the patent terminals available from firms which advertise in yachting magazines. These special end fittings are in the form of eyes or forks which attach to the mast or chain-plates, and they are relatively expensive. However, they normally have a long life, and some versions can be used again and again each time the rigging wire is renewed. They do tend to be made to fine tolerances, so it is best to order the wire and the fittings from the same source to ensure they mate together safely and easily.

Anyone rigging a boat for the first time is advised to get expert help. A small mistake can result in the loss of a mast and injury, in contrast to many other parts of the boat where a mistake is seldom so frightening. Even when help is available (and certainly when it is not) a close inspection of a similar boat is a good first move. Ideally look over a sister-ship professionally rigged and take photos or make sketches. Designers will in some cases help a builder who is having difficulties, or a local yacht surveyor can be called in to help. The easiest approach of all is to buy the complete gang of rigging (i.e. a collection of shrouds, forestay, backstay, etc., is called a gang of rigging) from the hull moulder, when this is possible. It is not an infallible solution; some hull moulders do not supply rigging, or there may be a delay before a gang is available, or the boat may in some way be just sufficiently non-standard to require special rigging. And there is one firm which supplies one set in ten with at least one item the wrong length; no one, least of all the people who work in the firm, knows why!

To make up rigging, the lengths of each item is needed. Though there are

183

other conventions, it is usual to give the length of a piece of rigging from the bottom of the hole in the tang on the mast to the top of the hole in the chain-plate. This distance will be the length of the wire with its rigging screw and toggle. If the wire passes over the end of a cross tree, then the distance via the end of the cross tree is given. Relatively few designers show these lengths on the rigging plan, though Billy Brown of Weatherly Yachts does. He gives co-ordinates, one vertical and one horizontal, for each rigging termination. This means that the rigger can make up each piece just from a slip of paper, he does not even need a drawing.

When making up the wire, its length is taken with the rigging screw and toggle on. Just occasionally it is possible to leave off a toggle without risk, notably on a forestay and backstay where there is no danger that the rigging screw threaded bar may be bent sideways. The rigging screw length is taken with the ends opened out to about ⅞ the maximum span. This is because when set up, slight kinks and all slackness is taken out of the wire, so it is much more likely that the rigging screw will be tightened up, when it is fitted on the boat. Besides, if the wire is accidentally made too long by a small amount the rigging screw will take this discrepancy out. If far too much length is put into the wire the end can be chopped off and refitted. When the wire is made slightly too short, the rigging screw will still be able to open out and cope with a small error. A larger mistake can be cured by the addition of an extra toggle. Putting shackles in the rigging to lengthen it is a mistake, though one often seen. If the wire is just a little too long or short, small variations in length can be achieved by unwinding, or winding up the twisted lay of the wire. This is not advised, it is the sort of professional trick which should be used with caution and never on a boat rigged to a low factor of safety.

Much better than any description, the sketch shows how to get the rigging lengths if no drawing is available. Once the mast has been dressed with all its rigging the cross tree ends are padded to protect the sails. Camper and Nicholsons supply standard plastic cross tree end pads, or a winding of a soft cloth held in place by a light lashing can be used. The aim is to avoid any contact between the sail and the metal end of the cross tree which is usually sharp, being a Y-fork and bolt to hold the shroud end in place.

The inner end of each cross tree is held by a bolt with its head at the top and a shake-proof nut (the sort which has a nylon insert) at the bottom. A stock of these nuts is needed because their nylon strips become compressed and less effective with use, so this type of nut is thrown away (in theory!) after it has been used once and taken off.

Once all the rigging has been set up and the boat in commission, the rigging will stretch. After a gentle sail in settled conditions the rigging is tuned, as detailed in any of the standard books on racing, then finally secured. This is done by twice passing a piece of soft stainless or galvanised wire first through the top end, then the barrel, and finally the bottom end of the rigging screw. The wire ends are twisted together and the rigging screw cannot come undone accidentally even when there is a lot of tension on it, and the rigging is vibrating. This wiring up is extremely important, and should be done even if there are locking nuts on the rigging screw. At sea locking nuts, especially stainless steel ones on stainless rigging screws, have proved unreliable. Some

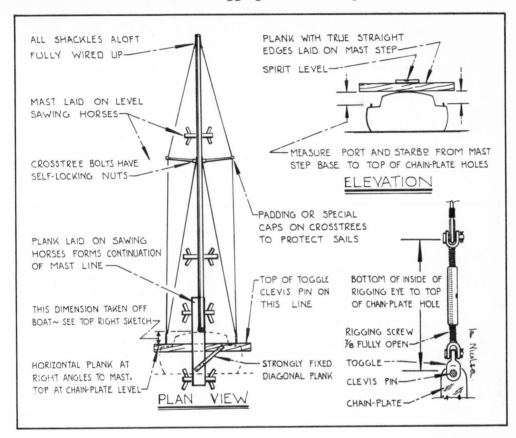

Fig. 66   Standing rigging

To make standing rigging the correct length a plank is laid on edge across the boat exactly level as shown top right. This plank's lower edge is resting on the mast step where the bottom of the mast will lie. Measurements are taken port and starboard of the distance from the plank bottom edge to the top of the holes in the chain-plates. The measurements port and starboard should be close, but may not be identical. A mean of these measurements is calculated by adding them together and dividing by two. If the mast goes through the cabin top down to the keel the plank edge is laid on the cabin top at the mast hole.

Next the mast is laid level on sawing horses or similar, with the rigging wires secured at the masthead and cross trees, each piece of standing rigging being cut too long. If the mast does not go through the deck it is extended by a plank lashed to it. The plank used to get the distances from mast heel to chain-plates is secured at right angles, as shown at the bottom of the 'Plan View'. A diagonal plank is fixed to hold the cross plank steady and at right angles. The rigging end bottom fittings are put on so that the top of the lower eyes of the toggles line up with the plank edge. The distance from the top of this plank to the heel of the mast (or if the mast goes through the deck, to the line on the mast where it passes through the deck) is made exactly as the mean of the distances measured at the beginning of the operation.

This technique can be used for main or mizzen, and it works whether there is a normal amount of rake on the mast or if the mast is upright.

rigging screws have split pins which go through the ends of the threaded bars, and these can be trusted provided new pins are used each year.

Over the top of the wire or split pins electricians tape is wound, to protect the crew from scratches, and the sails from rents. Some owners also tape over the clevis pins too on the correct principle that no one ever took too many precautions on any vessel.

37 *Running rigging*

Man-made fibres have taken over from natural ones for rigging. Terylene (which is called Dacron in America) is used for sheets and the hauling parts of halliards. Sisal and hemp are cheaper to buy but they last such a short time that no one uses them now on small craft.

It is cheaper to use white rope throughout but for racing or for a beginner colour coded ropes make sense. There is less risk of mistakes being made and sail handling is speeded up. The accepted standard is:

Main halliard and general use	WHITE
Genoa sheets and halliards	BLUE
Other headsail sheets and halliards	GOLD (orange-yellow)
Spinnaker sheets and halliards	RED
Topping lifts do not have a designated colour but	GREEN suggested.

Some rope-makers supply two-colour line. For example, there are white ropes with one or two strands of black or red interwoven. This is handy for extending the code. The spinnaker boom lift might logically be a white rope with red fleck on it, since the spinny halliard itself will be red. Anyone who likes this code but wants to save money might use the cheaper all white rope but make the end whippings the correct colour. At present amateur dyeing of terylene rope is not recommended; one reason why coloured rope costs more is because it is so hard to dye.

All ropes should have two sail-makers' whippings spaced 6 inches (152 mm) apart each end to stop fraying. Chandlers burn the ends of ropes with hot-knives to seal them, but in gale conditions a rope thrashing about will unravel after a time unless whipped. As a further precaution and to prevent the rope running out through its block or lead, a figure-of-eight knot is put in the bitter end of each rope, or it is knotted to its cleat. Halliard ends are sometimes passed through a hole in the middle of the cleat, then given a figure-of-eight knot, to make sure they never get lost aloft.

Rigging sizes are detailed in *Boat Data Book* complete with the correct sizes of block. To see how each item is rove-off the ideal approach is to look at a sister-ship or similar craft. With photos or sketches it is easy to copy the layout. Alternatively, the halliards can be ordered already on the mast. Normally masts are supplied with internal sheaves for each halliard, but sometimes the spinnaker has a block which shackles onto an eye well forward of the spar. Mast-makers do not normally supply this block or its shackle. When putting any shackle aloft it should be tightened with a pair of pliers then the pin wired up so that there is no risk that it will come undone accidentally. Masts vibrate in violent winds, and this rattles loose anything which is not super-safe.

A mast arrives from the factory with thin coloured lines threaded over the sheaves and tied end to end, if the halliards are to run inside the mast. It is tempting to cut these coloured lines and tie the end of each to its halliard and pull the halliard through. This is a bad idea, because if anything goes wrong such as the lead line coming adrift from the halliard it takes a lot of sweat and swearing to get the halliard rove-off. Instead seize the hauling end of the halliard to the lead line at the top, then go to the bottom and pull the lead line through. Being a continous line it rotates through the upper and lower exits on the mast, pulling the halliard with it.

If a lead line is lost, or one has been forgotten, another can be used to pull an extra lead line through. If all else fails, the end casting of the mast is removed by unscrewing the stainless steel screws through the bottom of the alloy tube. Tight-fitting castings may not come out easily, so a sharp-pointed screwdriver is inserted between the alloy tube end and the heel block, to lever the two apart. The tube is now open its full length except for the mast cap though there may be horizontal bolts across (by cross trees) which form internal obstructions. Also the inside of the tube may be lined with sound-proofing which also helps to make the next job more difficult. A long light wooden pole with a nail driven across the top is pushed up the full length of the mast till the nail is visible at the top by the sheave. A light line, such as heavy sail-makers' twine or flag halliard cord or similar is tied in a loop at the end, and this loop slipped over the nail. Back at the bottom of the mast the wood is pulled out and with it the light line emerges. This is used to pull a halliard down the mast.

Before putting the mast heel back:

1   Thread all the other halliards through. If another lead line breakage occurs one does not want to have to waste time taking the heel casting off again.
2   Drill a ½ inch (12 mm) drain hole in the casting if there is none.
3   Annoint the inside and mating surfaces with a thick layer of lanoline partly to ease the refitting, partly to minimise future corrosion.

When the heel is back on, the casting and bottom of the mast tube should be painted with a corrosion inhibiter, because this is the region where most trouble occurs; alloy masts have few ills apart from corrosion. The name should also be painted on the mast at top and bottom if the boat is ever to be laid up in a boat-yard so that the right mast goes back on the yacht in the spring. The boom and spinnaker boom also need the boats name painted on twice each.

Halliards may be made entirely of terylene, or half of terylene and half of wire, or all wire. The latter needs a reel type winch. To hoist the sail the winch handle is wound and the halliard is coiled on the drum of the winch. To make it possible to coil the whole of the down-haul part of the halliard onto the winch the drum must have sufficient width and there must be adequate depth of side flange. If these two dimensions are inadequate, before the sail is fully hoisted the wire will clog up the drum and it will not be possible to get the sail right aloft. So before buying a reel winch the diameter of the halliard must be known, plus the length of the luff of the sail. Reel winches are sold in sizes which are stated as 'capable of taking 40 feet of 6 mm wire' or some such specification. It is essential to get a winch which has a 10 per cent factor of safety. This is in case the halliard wire winds on irregularly, with crossovers and other zigzags of the wire which result in less than the potential maximum length going onto the drum.

There was a time when the reel type winch was popular but it is losing favour, in my view rightly. This type of winch tends to have a drum brake instead of a ratchet. Such a brake in theory grips the reel whenever the handle is released whereas a ratchet often lets the drum run back a little, maybe a twentieth part of a full turn, before gripping. The ratchet, however, is the only reliable style of brake. Letting a band brake go is frightening if there is a very high tension on the wire. Sometimes, in spite of precautions, the drum unwinds too fast and the wire snarls. Some models of winch have brakes which always maintain a modest pressure on the drum so that overrunning is in theory impossible. In theory!

Before winding up the last turn or two on this type of winch a soft leather patch is slipped under the wire, to prevent the final turns bedding into the previous turns and making it impossible to get the sail down.

The attraction of reel winches is that it coils the halliard as the sail goes up. There is no risk that the down-haul part of the halliard will come loose and slip overboard, and it is a tidy arrangement. But if the halliard jams as the yacht comes hurtling up a constricted channel, and the sail refuses to come down when urgently needed then one is in deep trouble!

Halliards made entirely of terylene have the advantage of simplicity. An eye is sliced round a nylon or metal thimble for the halliard shackle, and the halliard rove-off. Three-strand 'pre-stretched' terylene is used, but it does not live up to its name, and in use there is noticeable stretching. In heavy weather, when stretching halliards are least wanted, most stretch occurs. For a motor-sailer, or limited local cruising this defect may be acceptable, but for serious work it is more than just a nuisance.

For racing boats and serious cruising halliards are made of flexible wire rope from the head of the sail up over the sheave and down to just above the winch. Joined with either a wire-to-rope splice, or mating eye splices the wire links with terylene which leads onto the winch. Multiplait terylene is normally used by professionals but amateurs with less skill find three-strand easier to work. End splicing wire to rope is not difficult though it needs a little practice to make a truly neat job which renders effortlessly over the sheaves at a mast exit point. Making an eye splice in the end of the wire, and splicing the terylene through this is soon learned and quick to do. When the wire rusts or starts to fail by individual strands breaking it is easy to replace. If the terylene chafes or becomes hardened by weathering, it can be renewed without wasting good wire.

The length of the wire is best measured on the mast. Allowing for the shackle which engages in the eye at the top of the headsail, the wire should reach down to about 3 inches (75 mm) from the winch, if there is an eye-splice to eye-splice join. If the terylene is joined by an end splice, the end of the wire in the splice comes the same distance from the winch barrel. The length of the terylene must be enough to reach to the top of the mast when the sail is lowered, plus enough slack to reach to the securing cleat.

The number of halliards will be shown on the sail plan or rigging schedule. Some boats have more than the basic main and headsail halliards, so if one is out of action by being broken, jammed or lost aloft, there is another which can be used. On a cheap cruising boat there may be only two halliards, in which case the topping lift should be arranged so that it can be used either as a headsail or main halliard in a crisis. If a cheek block on the side of the mast is used and the whole topping lift is of terylene, either end can be the hauling part. Sometimes the topping lift is made of nylon because it is more stretchy, this being an advantage for supporting the boom end. It is a disadvantage for a halliard, but tolerable in an emergency.

To join the sails to the halliards it is logical to use snap shackles, though hard-up owners will have ordinary galvanised shackles. Common stainless steel shackles are a risk because they come undone by accident unless tightened with a pair of pliers, which is a nuisance; if the shackle has to be undone in a hurry and the pliers or shackle-opener are not handy, there may be a panic period.

Snap shackles should be chosen with caution and cynicism. The type sometimes called 'Swedish Snap Hook' is not strong enough for serious hard cruising. The bronze version which is not tested and also stamped with the maximum load is risky. Some stainless steel versions are sold with reliable safe working loads listed in the catalogue. This is the type to use, selecting a size which has a working load equal to half the wires' breaking load. The resulting size of snap shackle will disconcert the inexperienced buyer, being very large and correspondingly expensive.

A cheaper alternative is the 'Key pin shackle' which is made in two versions: standard and extra long. The latter are often needed for engaging in the mainsail head-board. This type of shackle has a pin which cannot be lost, but the whole shackle can slip out of the thimble. To prevent this sail-maker's twine or similar thread is lashed across the shackle after it has been put through the thimble.

Where there are several halliards for headsails there should be some form of identification at both ends. Colour coding using plastic tape is fine during the day, less effective at night. A number code combined with colour is probably the best compromise. One halliard will have blue tape, in the form of a single binding, the next red, with two separate bindings which can be easily felt as distinct in the dark, the next three yellow, and so on.

Whenever possible rope is bought by the coil because this is markedly cheaper. Having a whole coil also helps when measuring off the sheets, because the right length can be rolled off the reel, cut and whipped, but only yacht yards can have whole coils of each colour. This is why colour coding is expensive, quite apart from the extra cost of coloured ropes as compared with white.

Headsail sheets have to extend from the clew of the biggest genoa, forward round the mast and ahead of the inner forestay if one is fitted, then back down the other side to the main winch. In addition there has to be enough length to lead twice round the winch and give a tail of about 5 feet (1.5 m) beyond.

Each sheet is better made separate, with a bowline through the clew eye. There are other techniques, including (a) the use of snap shackles onto the sail, (b) port and starboard sheets made up as one, (c) sheets with hard eye ends and so on. Taking all the advantages, simple sheets knotted with bowlines are cheapest, cause less damage when the sail is flogging and so this technique is recommended. The less there is in the way of metal at a sail's clew, the lighter and safer it is. Besides in extreme conditions a thrashing sail can undo all manner of shackles.

Sheets have to lead clear to the winches, without touching cabin sides or cockpit coamings. A tight rope being hauled in on a winch acts like a file on fibreglass. In the course of a day's intermittent tacking it can cut a groove right through a thin coaming. The usual precaution is a 'turning block' which is bolted to the deck, aft of the winch and about in the middle of the side-deck. Turning blocks have to be aligned with the winch and the sheet lead block on the genoa lead track. If there are these lead blocks (and in a few ships it is essential to have *two* each side to get a fair run for the sheet) the measurement of each sheet has to include the journey through these blocks.

Chafe is a universal enemy of everyone who goes afloat, and it is mostly found near sheets and halliards. Precautions can be taken during building and fitting out, but it is during trials that the actual rubbing points are discovered. This is one reason why the first days of trials should be in settled weather, with no 'passengers' aboard.

Inspecting a sister-ship which has done a substantial mileage will show up the chafe points and maybe ways to cure the trouble. Plastic tubing on the lower parts of the shrouds and on the life-lines forms good protection.

Where main and mizzen sheets pass over the top life-line is a notorious spot, and a chafe guard here is needed if the horse is set low. To see how the lead is, rig the boom squared right off and tie a line between the traveller on the horse and the sheet lead block on the boom. Where the line touches the life-lines will be a chafe area, but the boom must be gradually brought in, as the region which needs protection will extend aft. While the boom is right off measure the length of the line and multiply this by the number of sheaves on the horse block and boom end block, to get the total length of sheet needed. Add extra footage for the distance from the traveller on the horse to the cleat as well as the usual reserve on the end of say 6 feet (2 m).

Sheets are normally made of plaited line which is matt finished for a good grip even when wet. As an economy some owners buy large coils of rope and have the same size (and type) of line for genoa and spinnaker sheets, if necessary sharing the coil with a friend so as to buy to advantage.

For light weather work keen owners have special sheets between 50 and 70 per cent the diameter of the normal ones to reduce the chafe on the 'everyday' sheets, and to ensure the sails set better.

During the commissioning of a boat pieces of line are needed for lashing the boat-hook, tying down the emergency tiller, flag halliards, lee-board lashings, securing pipes clear of the engine until a permanent clipping-up operation can be carried through, securing coiled-up warps, and so on. For this sort of work it is usual to buy hanks of 2, 3 and 4 mm diameter lines. For boats over about 40 feet (12 m) a small reel of 5 mm rope soon gets well used.

For the mainsail out-haul and reefing lines ropes about the same size as the topping lift will be required. The exact length of these minor items can be measured off the sail plan, but in practice it is better to reeve off each line once the sails are set.

Appendix

Chandlers

Local chandlers supply virtually everything needed for boat construction except basic materials. They tend to stock a range of fittings and what they have not got in stock they can obtain. Ranged behind them are the wholesale chandlers who produce catalogues which have to be bought, but the latter more than save the purchase price because with careful planning and research an economic programme can be worked out. For example, most local chandlers will give a discount if a large number of fittings are ordered together. A good plan is to make out a full list of fittings needed and split it in two. The primary list includes all the items needed for the early stages of construction; the second one has all the later items plus anything forgotten during the initial planning. Fastenings for each fitting, plus bedding materials are included in each list. This technique results in two substantial lists, on both of which there is a good chance of getting a discount because each list amounts to a substantial purchase.

Publications

For buying materials, services and gear the yachting magazines are a great help. They run critical articles and have copious advertisements covering every aspect of building. In alphabetical order they are:

Australia
Australian Seacraft: Power and Sail, Murray Publishers, 142 Clarence Street, Sydney, N.S.W.

Britain
Motor Boat and Yachting, Quadrant House, The Quadrant, Sutton, Surrey.
Yachting Monthly, I.P.C. Publications, Kings Reach Tower, Stamford Street, London SE1 9LS.
Yachting World, Dorset House, Stamford Street, London SE1 9LS.
Yachts and Yachting, 196 Eastern Esplanade, Southend-on-Sea, Essex.

France
Les Cahiers du Yachting, 43 Boulevard Barbes, 75018 Paris.

Netherlands
Watersport, Bouwerij 81, Amsterdam.

New Zealand
Sea Spray, Box 793, Auckland.

South Africa
South African Yachting, Van der Stel Building, 58 Burg Street, P.O. Box 3473, Cape Town.

United States
Sail, 38 Commercial Wharf, Boston, Massachusetts 02110.
Cruising World, Cruising World Publications Inc., 524 Thames Street, Newport, Rhode Island 02840.
Yachting, One Park Avenue, New York 10016.
Wooden Boat, P.O. Box 78, Brooklin, Maine 04616.